Gone to Croatan

Origins of North American Dropout Culture

"GONE TO CROATAN"

The first "drop–outs" from English colonization in North America left the "Lost Colony" of Roancke and went to join the natives at Croatan (also spelled Croatoan).

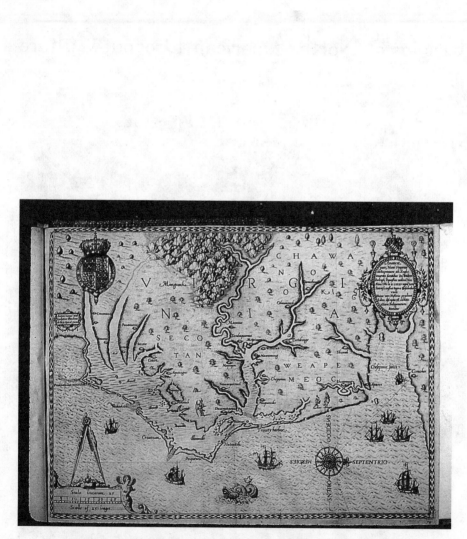

MAP OF 1590 INDICATING LOCATION OF "CROATAN"
(From J. Hariot, "Brief and True Report...")

Josiah Warren and Lysander Spooner—but Harris had expounded all the central ideas of "Individual Sovereignty" in the mid-17th century, on the basis of radical Antinomian speculation. Hutchinson died before she could fully develop all these ideas, so the title of first American anarchist seems to belong to Harris.

* * * * *

THE BIG DIFFERENCE BETWEEN QUAKERISM AND OTHER Antinomian sects lay in the Quaker adoption of pacifism and non-resistance, as opposed to the open revolutionism of the Levellers or Ranters. But in most respects the early Quakers were scarcely distinguishable from other extremists. When the Quaker prophet James Naylor rode into Bristol (England) on an ass in 1655, Cromwell responded to this messianic display with violent persecution—Naylor's tongue was bored. Cromwell took it all quite seriously, and launched a general persecution of the mystical "left." The Quakers reacted by distancing themselves from politics and preaching against Ranterism, and this relatively conservative policy undoubtedly preserved Quakerism as an institution in the long run—and in fact made it respectable enough to be granted its own American utopia in Pennsylvania.

The Ranters also came to the New World—but as refugees or transported criminals rather than as decent (if nonconformist) colonists. "Perrot, the bearded ranter who refused to doff his hat to the Almighty, ended up in Barbadoes,"[14] as did Joseph Salmon. The latter, a drop-out from the New Model Army, began as a Seeker but moved toward more extreme positions in the mid-1600s. One authority reported his "wicked Swearing, and uncleaness, which he justified and others of his way, *That it was God which did swear in them, and that it was their liberty to keep company with Women, for their lust.*"[15] As Salmon put it, "The Lord grant we may know the worth of hell, that we may forever scorn heaven: For my own part I am ascended far above all heavens, yet I fill all things, and laugh in my sleeve to think what's coming..."[16] Salmon was arrested in 1649 and "was able to attract a considerable audience by preaching through the gates of the prison on Sundays."[17] After his release he seems to have emigrated voluntarily to Barbados, either "in a Zen-like search for 'nothing',"[18] or else to cause "trouble (by) organizing separatist meetings."[19]

Perrot and Salmon were intellectuals and their names at least are remembered—but rank-and-file Ranters also emigrated or were deported; a Quaker lady "found herself troubled by the Ranters at general meetings in Oysterbay and Rhode Island" as late as 1680.[20] It seems logical to assume that when Boston Puritans accused people of being Ranters, Familists, Libertines, etc., they were not necessarily just mud-slinging. Some of their victims really did belong to these sects, and had doubtless ended up in Massachusetts as deported "rogues" (especially after the mid-1650s). Similar suppositions may be made about Rhode Island and Pennsylvania. The Carolinas were called "the refuge of the sectaries" in 1683,[21] and Georgia may also have served this function. Would it then appear unreasonable to suspect the influence of these "sectaries" in various Colonial-era uprisings such as Bacon's Rebellion or the Regulator movement? "Rogue" Quakers were implicated in the latter event, at least.

As for the Quakers of Pennsylvania, although they lacked some of the flair for self-martyrdom exhibited earlier in both Old and New England, nevertheless they took the idea of the "Holy Experiment" quite seriously—in fact, a good deal more seriously than William Penn himself. As a wealthy Protestant grandee, Penn envisioned Pennsylvania as his own feudal fiefdom, complete with quitrents and monopolies. True, he preached religious toleration and peace with the Indians—but compared to Roger Williams he was a rightwing reactionary. Luckily for the holy experimenters, however, he was an *absentee* landlord—and they simply decided to ignore him. Spurred on first by the Lloyd family (Thomas and David), and later by the offshoot "Keithean" radicals, the colonists ceased all governmental activity, refused to vote taxes, and ceded all real power to the consensus rule of the Friends' Meeting. According to Murray Rothbard's analysis,[22] Philadelphia enjoyed four years of total *de facto* anarchy from 1684 to 1688, and thereafter struggled to retain it till at least 1696. At that point the first tax bill was finally passed—and of course denounced by the radicals as an attack on "our ancient rights, liberties and freedom." As one of Penn's unsuccessful agents had complained in horror, these Quakers "have not the principles of government amongst them, nor will they be informed." And when the conservative party condemned George Keith (who preached that Friends should not engage in government any more than in war) they quite properly pointed out that his pamphlets showed "a tendency to sedition, and disturbance of the peace, as also to the subversion of the present government."[23] Keithean doctrines are said to have interested Ben Franklin and Thomas Paine.

* * * * *

DEISM, WHICH IS USUALLY DEPICTED AS A STAGE ON THE way to cool agnostic rationality, also had a hot and mystical side to it. After all, it was but a short step from the Antinomian God of inner light to the Deist God of the inner light of "Reason" (a word which then meant something more like "mind" than mere "rationality"). The Ranters (who sometimes spoke of God as "Reason") were accused of "atheism," which in the 17–18th centuries meant denial of religious authority rather than materialism (as in the 19-20th centuries). Deists were also "atheists" in this sense, and like the extremist sects they had their mystics and visionaries. Their mysticism however tended away from the pole of contemplation toward that of action. As free thinkers and as heirs to much libertarian Protestant thought, their imaginations worked in utopian and revolutionary ways. Nor can all Deists be described as middleclass intellectuals. Paine was a workingclass Deist (and very nearly an anarchist), and so were many soldiers who later came to swell the ranks of the Revolutionary Army in 1776.

One brand of mystical Deism cystallized as Freemasonry, an occult order with radical revolutionary aims. The first American Masons appeared a few years before the official establishment of the London Grand Lodge in 1717, and by 1730 Franklin provided the first reference to organized lodges in the New World. (The Masons themselves claim that Raleigh and Dee were Masons and Virginia a Masonic experiment). In their recent (and surprisingly unsensationalistic) book on Masonry, *The Temple and the Lodge*, Baigent and Leigh document the fascinating double nature of New World Masonry.[24] On the one hand more bourgeois colonists tended to belong to lodges chartered by the "official" London Grand Lodge; on the other hand many soldiers of lowerclass origin joined "military" lodges which were not chartered by London but by the Grand Lodge of Ireland. These Irish charters, which were considered spurious by London, gave rise to a kind of underground masonry (the so-called "Scald Miserable Masons"), which was never successfully reintegrated into mainstream masonry. George Washington and his cronies of course belonged to the "official" branch—but clearly both branches found common cause in the vision of American independence. As everyone knows, Washington won. Somewhat less clearly remembered however is his private inauguration ritual in full Masonic regalia. Baigent and Leigh make a very convincing argument for the Constitution as a Masonic manifesto and America as a Masonic Republic. It would be interesting however to know more about the politics of the Irish or Scald Masons. Were they among the extreme democrats who felt betrayed by the oligarchic counter-Revolution of 1789? Were they among the Revolutionary veterans who fought against Washington and his cronies in Shays Rebellion and a handful of lesser uprisings in the 1790s? A futile inquiry perhaps—but in any case, clearly Masonry cannot be excluded from the roll of revolutionary mystical sects of Colonial America.

* * * * *

THE DEISTS, LIKE ALL ANTINOMIANS, WERE ATTRACTED BY the image of the Wild Man and of the Wild Man as Noble Savage. It's no accident that the conspirators in both the Boston and the New Jersey "Tea Parties" dressed up as Indians, nor that rebel backwoods farmers declared their region—the Berkshires—reverted to the "State of Nature." For both revolutionary intellectuals and the revolutionary "Mob" felt a certain kinship with Native American spirituality. The "Five Nations" Treaty of Confederation exercized powerful influence on the Articles of Confederation (a radical democratic document) and even on the Declaration of Independence. This unlikely line between native shamanism and Deism emerges with poignant clarity in the mysterious case of Christian Priber of Georgia.[25]

Priber (probably originally German) arrived in the New World in the 1730s as an accomplished *philosophe*, conversant in English, Dutch (German?), French and Latin, with one all-consuming obsession: the founding of a utopian socialist/libertarian community amongst the natives of South Carolina and Georgia. At his trial in 1743 (coincidentally the same year American colonists first rioted against impressment, marked by some historians as the beginning of the Revolutionary movement), it was said that Priber had schemed to set up "a Town at the Foot of the Mountains among the Cherokees, which was to be a City of Refuge for all Criminals, Debtors, and Slaves, who would fly thither from Justice or their Masters." Moreover,

> "There was a Book found upon him of his own Writing
> ready for the Press, which he owns and glories in...; it
> demonstrates the Manner in which the Fugitives are

to be subsisted, and lays down the Rules of
Government which the town is to be governed by; to
which he gives the Title of Paradise; He enumerates
many whimsical Privileges and natural Rights, as he
calls them, which his Citizens are to be entitled to,
particularly dissolving Marriages and allowing
Community of Women, and all kinds of
Licenciousness; the Book is drawn up very methodi-
cally, and full of learned Quotations; it is extreamly
wicked, yet has several Flights full of Invention; and
it is a Pity so much Wit is applied to so bad
Purposes."

During the previous years Priber had sold all his possessions and
disappeared into Cherokee country, learned the language (and wrote
the first dictionary of it, which was later lost along with his "Book"),
and went native to such an extent that he "ate, drank, slept, danced,
dressed and painted himself, with the Indians," and whites could no
longer "distinguish him from the natives." According to one of Priber's
enemies, "he proposed to them a new System or plan of Government,
that all things should be in common amongst them, that even their
Wives should be so and that Children should be looked upon as the
Children of the public and be taken care of as such & not by their natural parents....And that they should admit into their society Creeks &
Catawbaws, French & English, all Colours and complexions, in short
all who were of These principles, which were truly such as had no
principles at all"!

Priber was no authoritarian utopian in the Plato/More tradition;
he stressed "liberty" along with community of property, and in his
"Kingdom of Paradise" the only law was to be the law of Nature.
"Moreover," as his biographer notes, "the liberty which was allowed to
men should be shared equally by women; in sign of which no marriages should be contracted. The children of the temporary unions
were to be reared by the state, and instructed in everything which
they were capable of learning."

Apparently Priber won the hearts of the Cherokee, though he may
have ended by learning more from them than they from him. In any
case, they protested angrily when the colonial authorities (under
Oglethorpe of Georgia) arrested and imprisoned him. Priber languished in gaol a few years, then died. His books vanished. He was
another "failure," another bit of lost American history condemned to
insignificance by his victorious enemies.

Or was he? The Cherokee later became famous, after all, for developing the first Native American system of writing. They were also known for their hospitality toward Maroons (runaway slaves) and white indentured servants. Certain sub-tribes of the Cherokee, such as the Lumbee, are classified as "tri-racial." Perhaps some of them are actually descended from Priber, that obscure savant and gentleman who played out again the story of Roanoake, but this time in full consciousness of its utopian implications. Priber came to America in order to "go to Croatan," to seek redemption in wild(er)ness. Like Morton of Merry Mount, Anne Hutchinson and the radicals of "Rogue Island", his spirituality was bound up with that of the vast wilderness and its natives; a strain of American spirituality summed up by Thoreau muttering on his death-bed: "...forests...Indians...". But Priber also encompassed the European radical tradition, which in turn was rooted in libertarian heresy and Antinomianism. In fact he synthesizes all the main currents of the tradition this essay has investigated, and we may well nominate him for one of our saints.

* * * * *

THE AMERICAN REVOLUTION IS GENERALLY INTERPRETED as a bourgeois liberal movement. But recently some radical American historians[26] have begun to pay closer attention to the role of the "Mob," to proletarian and extremist elements in the struggle, and to their antecedents and influences. Just as official Puritan Protestantism has been considered in some ways a foreshadowing of official American republicanism, so one may argue that *non*-official radical Protestantism (and its attendant "Indianism") served as the matrix for extreme revolutionary tendencies within the general dissidence and the anti-Imperialist movement. The nameless Antinomians of low estate who followed Anne Hutchinson into exile were the spiritual ancestors of the rioters, farmers, sailors, soldiers, freed slaves, Irish laborers and debtors who pushed "leaders" like Sam Adams and Thomas Paine ever farther to the "left." "Spiritual anarchy" is America's oldest heritage, and its most secret and submerged tradition.

And although we've limited ourselves here to the Colonial period, we cannot end without asserting that our invisible "Church" outlasted not only the Revolution but also the Federalist counter-Revolution.

> Nathan Barlow, the New England mystic, led the squatters of Kennebec country in Maine during the 1790s against the sheriffs and land agents of the out-of-state proprietors in small bands of armed "white Indians." He wrote "every man to his right and priviledges and liberty, the same as our indian nation injoys." They burned barns, rescued prisoners, upset courts, and destroyed writs into "attoms." [27]

Here, trembling on the verge of the 19th century, we'll close our story—confidant that the reader will be able to trace the trajectory of our tradition into this more "modern" age—and indeed, even into the 20th century and our own days. Caliban's Masque is not yet played out, nor can spiritual anarchy be consigned to the catalogue of dead things.

Midsummer, 1991
Long Pond

REFERENCES

[1] Quoted in A. L. Rowse, *The Elizabethans and America* (NY, Harper Colophon, 1959), p. 204.

[2] As Gonzalo puts it in *The Tempest*,

> I' the commonwealth I would by contraries
> Execute all things: for no kind of traffic
> Would I admit; no name of magistrate:
> Letters should not be known; riches, poverty,
> And use of service, none: contract, succession,
> Bourn, bound of land, tilth, vineyard, none;
> No use of metal, corn, or wine or oil;
> No occupation: all men idle, all;
> And women too, but innocent and pure—
>
> ...All things in common nature should produce
> Without sweat or endeavor: treason, felony,
> Sword, pike, knife, gun, or need of any engine,
> Would I not have; but nature should bring forth,
> Of its own kind, all foison, all abundance,
> To feed my innocent people.

3 For Raleigh and Roanoake, see Rowse, *op. cit.*; also C.M. Andrews, *Our Earliest Colonial Settlements* (Ithaca, Cornell Univ. Press, 1959); and Robert Lacey, *Sir Walter Ralegh* (NY, Atheneum, 1973).

4 The Great Dismal Swamp made an excellent hide-out for Maroons and other escapees from civilization. According to the historian H. Leaming-Bey, the Swamp was home to black conjure-men and women even in Colonial times, and eventually became headquarters for the "hidden masters" of HooDoo, the so-called "Seven-Finger-High Glister", a council of elders who directed magical operations, rebellions and escapes among the slaves of the South, and survived until at least the Civil War. See Leaming-Bey, *Hidden Americans: Maroons of Virginia and the Carolinas* (microfiche, 1979), Chaps. VIII, XIV, and XIV. For evidence on the "Indianization" of the Roanoake settlers, see David Stick, Roanoke Island: The Beginnings of English America (Chapel Hill, NC, Univ. of North Carolina Press, 1983), chaps. 17–20.

5 Bradford, *History of Plymouth Plantation* 1620–47, ed. W.C. Ford, 2 vols. (Boston, Houghton Mifflin, 1912), pp. 54-58.

6 Nathaniel Hawthorne, "The Maypole of Merry Mount", in *Works, Vol.I: Twice-Told Tales* (Boston & NY, Houghton Mifflin, 1882). For some reason he substitutes John Endicott for Standish, and instead of naming Morton he calls the pagan leader Blackstone, perhaps confusing Morton with William Blackstone, a Cambridge graduate who came to America to escape the Anglican Bishops, but couldn't bear the Puritans either and ended up a hermit alone on Beacon Hill. (See Rowse, *op. cit.*, p.111.)

7 For Morton and Merry Mount, see Morton's *New English Canaan, or New Canaan*, Amsterdam, 1637 (facs. ed., Amsterdam, Theatrum Orbis Terrarum Ltd., NY, Da Capo Press, 1969); Donald F. Connors, *Thomas Morton* (NY, Twayne Publ., 1969); Richard Slotkin, *Regeneration Through Violence: The Mythology of the American Frontier, 1600-1860* (Middletown, CT, Wesleyan University Press, 1973), Chap. 3; and Devyn, "Of Mine Host of Ma-re Mount", in *Green Egg*, no. 88, 1990, pp.14-16.

8 See Kai T. Erikson, *Wayward Puritans: A Study in the Sociology of Deviance* (NY, John Wiley & Sons, 1966); and Selma R. Williams, *Divine Rebel: The Life of Anne Marbury Hutchinson* (NY, Holt, Rinehart & Winston, 1981).

9 S.R. Williams, *op. cit.*, p. 193.

10 One of her associates, John Underhill, had first been a successful Indian fighter. Accused of Antinomianism (and adultery) he was persecuted rather than rewarded for his bravery, and like Morton fled to England in 1637 to write an apologia, his *Newes from America*. Later he returned and started an experimental commune in Dover, New Hampshire. Eventually he was excommunicated and exiled to Rhode Island, where he ended as a Quaker (like Mary Dyer and other Hutchinsonians). See Slotkin, *op. cit.*, pp. 69-71.

11 Murray Rothbard, "Individualist Anarchism in the U.S.: Origins", in *Libertarian Analysis* (I/1, Winter, 1970), pp. 14-28.

12 James Ernst, *Roger Williams: New England Firebrand* (NY, Macmillan, 1932), p. 368.

13 *Ibid.*, pp. 368-69.

14 Peter Linebaugh, "All The Atlantic Mountains Shook", in *Labour/Le Travailleur*, #10, Autumn 1982, p. 103. See also A.E. Smith, *Colonists in Bondage: White Servitude and Convict Labor in America 1607-1776* (NY, Norton, 1971).

15 Quoted in Nigel Smith, ed., *A Collection of Ranter Writings from the 17th Century* (London, Junction Books, 1983), in the foreword by J. Carey, p. 13. For more 17th century radical Protestant tracts, see the catalogue of various reprints and studies from Aporia Press, c/o Counter Productions, Box 556, London SE5 ORL, U.K.

16 Joseph Salmon, "Letter from Salmon to Thomas Webbe", in Smith, ed., *op. cit.*, pp. 201-2.

17 *Ibid.*, p. 13.

18 Linebaugh, *loc. cit.* Salmon wrote, "I appeared to myself as one confounded into the abyst of eternitie, nonentitized into the being of beings." (*Heights in Depths & Depths in Heights*, in Smith, ed., *op. cit.*, p. 212.)

19 *Ibid.*, p. 17.

20 Linebaugh, *op. cit.*, p. 105.

21 *Ibid.*, p. 104.

22 Rothbard, *op. cit.*, p. 21. See also Frederick B. Tolles, *Meeting House and Counting House: The Quaker Merchants of Philadelphia 1682-1763* (NY, W.W. Norton, 1948), esp. Chap. 4.

23 Rothbard, *op. cit.*, p. 25.

24 Michael Baigent & Richard Leigh, *The Temple and the Lodge* (NY, Arcade, 1989), Part IV.

25 See Verner W. Crane, "A Lost Utopia of the First American Frontier," in *The Sewanee Review Quarterly*, Jan.-Mar., 1919, pp. 48-61.

26 See for example Howard Zinn, *A Peoples' History of the United States* (NY, Harper, 1980), for its grand scope and its bibliography. I'm also indebted to Peter Linebaugh, author of *The London Hanged* (London, Penguin, 1991), who has begun to apply to America the methods of the English school of E.P. Thompson, C. Hill, N. Cohn, A.L. Morton, E. Hobsbawm, etc. See esp. Christopher Hill, *The World Turned Upside Down* (London, Penguin, 1972) and Norman S. Cohn, *The Pursuit of the Millenium* (NY, Oxford University Press, 1970), for English spiritual extremism of the Revolutionary period. I also found useful Norman S. Cohn, ed., *Civil Strife in America: A Historical Approach to the Study of Riots in America* (Hinsdale, IL, Dryden Press, 1972). For the general thesis of this essay I'm also indebted to Michael Taussig, *Shamanism, Colonialism and the Wild Man: A Study in Terror and Healing* (Univ. of Chicago, 1987).

27 P. Linebaugh, "Jubilating: Or, How The Atlantic Working Class Used the Biblical Jubilee Against Capitalism, With Some Success," in "The New Enclosures" edition of *Midnight Notes*, #10, Fall, 1990, p. 89.

PETER CORNELIUS PLOCKHOY AND THE BEGINNINGS OF THE AMERICAN COMMUNAL TRADITION

Timothy Miller

OMMUNAL LIVING IS ONE OF AMERICA'S GREAT ALTER-
native traditions. In a country largely devoted to laissez-faire
individualism, there has for centuries been a small but stalwart
counterflow—a principled minority who have argued that cooperation
is healthier than competition, that helpfulness is better than hostility,
and that living in community with others is a concrete way in which
one can contribute to a better and brighter human future.

How did the communal countertradition get started? Some surveys of American communes seem to presume that the genre began
with the Shakers.[1] Others push the beginnings back a bit further, to
the Ephrata Cloister in Pennsylvania.[2] Still others acknowledge the
existence of even earlier communal groups, but do little more than
mention them.[3] The pioneers of communal living are prophets little
honored in their own land.

In a protohistorical sense communitarianism is ancient: the original Americans all lived communally. No known tribe of the thousands
that inhabited the hemisphere in pre-Columbian times is known to
have believed in private ownership of real estate. They were all organized into clans in which group values and interests utterly super-

seded the selfish desires of individuals.

In terms of Euro-American history, the communal tradition has been dominated by religious visionaries. The majority have been Christian. They generally have deemed communal living the will of God and therefore an imperative for humans. The account in Acts 2, 4, and 5 of early Christians holding "all things in common" has been taken as a divine mandate by some who have worked it out in a variety of communal experiments. By far the most successful of them, at least in terms of numbers and stability, have been the Hutterites, who have lived communally most of the time since 1528 and in the United States since 1874. Starting with three tenuous colonies in South Dakota, they have spread throughout the upper Midwest and the prairie provinces, and now inhabit hundreds of colonies with their nearly 40,000 members.

The origins of Euro-American communitarianism can be traced to the earliest British settlers. The two earliest loci of English colonization, Virginia and Massachusetts, saw early forays into communitarianism at Jamestown and Plymouth, although the communities were not entirely voluntary in nature. A pooling of money and labor was mandated both by harsh circumstances (the settlers were, after all, trying to survive in the wilderness) and by the demands of the venture capitalists who financed their settlements, but it was not regarded as essential or even desirable by those participating in it. In the case of Plymouth, most historians of New England regard the relatively brief communism of the Pilgrims as a pooling of means for survival, immediately, and for profits to be distributed to individuals in the longer term. In any event, the communitarian arrangement was quite unpopular among most of those involved in it. As William Bradford (by no means an impartial observer) wrote in his history of the colony,

> The experience that was had in this common course and condition, tried sundry years and that amongst godly and sober men, may well evince the vanity of that conceit of Plato's and other ancients applauded by some of later times; that the taking away of property and bringing in community into a commonwealth would make them happy and flourishing; as if they were wiser than God. For this community (so far as it was) was found to breed much confusion and discontent and retard much employment

> that would have been to their benefit and
> comfort....The strong, or man of parts, had no more in
> division of victuals and clothes than he that was weak
> and not able to do a quarter the other could; this was
> thought injustice....And for men's wives to be com-
> manded to do service for other men, as dressing their
> meat, washing their clothes, etc., they deemed it a
> kind of slavery, neither could many husbands well
> brook it.[4]

A similar situation obtained at Jamestown. Once the terms of the
agreement of settlement allowed it, both groups of settlers moved to
individual holdings.

* * *

GIVEN THE SHORT LIVES AND UNPOPULARITY OF THE
Jamestown and Plymouth communal sojourns, the real history of
intentional community among Euro-Americans begins with one Peter
Cornelius Plockhoy, to use the Anglicized version of his name.
Plockhoy, despite his eminent status as communal leader, remains
historically obscure. A number of surveys of American communal history fail altogether to mention him, and neglect seems to breed
neglect.[5] Even most of the fairly comprehensive lists and studies mention Plockhoy only in passing and provide little information other
than the presumed name of the settlement.[6]

Fortunately, at least one survey, that of Arthur Bestor,[7] gives
Plockhoy a full page, and a few other older documents have survived
that give us some notion of what ideas fueled this communitarian
experiment, even if we know very little about the colony itself due to
its untimely extinction at the hands of enemies.

A century ago one would have had trouble learning very much at
all about Plockhoy. Fortunately, however, by 1899 the Pennsylvania
historian Samuel W. Pennypacker had managed to locate a copy of a
1662 Plockhoy pamphlet, written in Dutch, that outlined his ideas on
communal living, and a digest of another Plockhoy tract published in
1659.[8] About 1933 John Downie discovered another version of the earlier Plockhoy pamphlet, in English, in the British Museum, and published it along with his own commentary on it.[9] From these documents we can construct an outline of Plockhoy's communal philosophy.

First, Plockhoy argued for the essential equality of all people—this in an age of manifest inequality—and insisted that oppression of persons must cease. People, he insisted, must abandon the goal of achieving superiority over others, and follow the Christian ideal of service. With inequality eliminated, the world (or at least that part of it where such ideals were practiced) would see the end of jealousy and deception. Second, Plockhoy argued that the enlightened must voluntarily join into associations. That would make for much greater efficiency in labor, and all would gain correspondingly.[10]

Under Plockhoy's proposal, all in the community would labor six hours a day at work each member found suitable and acceptable. Private property could be retained, although the community would own the land and working capital. The naturally generous souls who would constitute the community would voluntarily donate their capital, which would be secured by a first mortgage. All would live simply; any finery, as in dress, would be forbidden.

The community would be housed in two large dwellings, one in or near a city, where the community's merchants could ply their trades, and the other in the country near a navigable river in order to provide access as well as transportation of goods. The city house would provide an outlet for the community's produce, the output of whatever agricultural or industrial projects the community might undertake; the country house would be headquarters for the agricultural enterprise as well as for industries which might range from shipbuilding to blacksmithing. Members of the community would live in both houses, which would have private bedrooms and many common rooms—kitchens, storage cellars, libraries, nurseries, infirmaries, guest rooms and the like. There would be a school which would be open to children from outside the community as well as those within it. There would also be a great room in the form of an amphitheater in which the community could gather to hear each other expound briefly on religious or secular topics of the day under a system of complete freedom of speech and encouragement of the exchange of ideas.[11]

Plockhoy also specified the form of government of the community. A governor over all would be chosen by vote. The governor would have three assistants. There would be lesser officials as well, and all would be subject to annual elections.[12] Women were apparently not contemplated as holding such positions. If you add this discrimination against women to his apparently unexamined plans to found a settlement on Indian lands, Plockhoy's egalitarianism seemingly did not transcend the usual limitations of his age.

Plockhoy, who realized that his utopian community would not necessarily prove amenable to everyone who joined, proposed to be unusually generous with those who would leave the community. They would "not only receive that which they brought, but also a share of the profit which hath been made since they came to the Society. If no profit hath been made in their time, they shall receive none, that so they that come into us may not seek their own private gain."[sic][13]

In all Plockhoy's was a finely detailed plan, one which envisioned a community of equals laboring together with the broadest of vision and the warmest of hearts to build a little sample of the Kingdom of God on earth. Plockhoy was incredibly optimistic about human nature, and was likewise optimistic about the material success of the venture, since he managed to describe at length how the community would dispose of surplus production, by dividing it up among the members to donate to the poor or give as presents to their outside friends.[11] He did recognize, however, that not just anyone could function effectively in such a community, and told the public that "we desire no wild cursers, drunkards or other such strange people in our community."[14]

Plockhoy came from a Dutch Mennonite family, and he was powerfully attached to his own church. Yet he also decried the sectarianism of the age. He urged that the church be one, a great community of men and women of all ages, in all lands.[15] His community would be open to all kinds of ideas, and there would be no exclusive orthodoxy in it.

Surveying the world about him, Plockhoy concluded that the leader who could most help him prepare the way for the ideal commonwealth was Oliver Cromwell, the Protector of England. So Plockhoy left his Dutch home at Zierik Zee for London, where Cromwell received him in 1658 and listened to his ideas in some detail. Plockhoy thereupon wrote two letters to Cromwell outlining his ideas in written form, letters which apparently formed the basis of his pamphlets published shortly thereafter.[16] Things seemed to be going well enough that Plockhoy told his readers that the community should be founded in London, and eventually move to Ireland, where land was cheap.[17]

But then the unexpected occurred: Cromwell died in September, 1658, and Plockhoy was left without the man he figured to be his most useful advocate. Plockhoy continued to promote his plan to

Parliament and to the public via his pamphlets, but circumstances were different than those upon which he had counted. The Digger uprising, for example, had occurred ten years earlier. The communitarian Diggers had attracted wide interest with their contention that private property was contrary to natural law and that the universe itself was on the side of communal ownership.[18] Unfortunately, now the tide was turning in English public opinion. The country that had shown some receptivity to change in recent years was becoming noticeably more conservative.[19]

So Plockhoy returned home to the Netherlands to pursue his plan. Since the Dutch authorities were actively promoting colonization of New Netherlands at the time, soon Plockhoy had official approval of a plan to establish a little utopia at the mouth of the Hoorn Kill on the Delaware River, where the town of Lewes, Delaware, now stands. Plockhoy turned to the printing press again, and produced a small volume outlining his communal plan, which had changed little since it had been proposed in England.[20] Again he despaired of the alienation and economic disadvantages inherent in normal family living, and outlined a community of full equals who would cultivate the land, engage in fishing, and develop trades and industries in the "new world." Each person would be granted a great deal of individual liberty. All would work six hours a day for the community, and as much more for private gain as each might choose. In turn, everyone would have his or her basic needs supplied. The community's government would be democratically elected by secret ballot. There would be a progressive school for the children. Although the presumption was that the members of the society would be predominantly Christian, complete freedom of conscience would prevail. Slavery would be outlawed. Those who left the colony would be free to take back whatever they had put in originally.[21]

This time Plockhoy had a concrete proposal for getting started: all those who would participate in the project were to gather at a particular time and place in Amsterdam in mid-September, 1662. Once a count of participants had been taken, the group could secure supplies for a year.[22] The public authorities of Amsterdam liked the plan, and contracted with Plockhoy on June 6 to advance 100 guilders for each of up to 25 persons in the company. They also granted a 20-year tax exemption to the community.[23]

And so off the expedition finally sailed, in May, 1663, reaching its appointed destination in the Delaware Valley later that year.[24] Now, one would expect, our story should begin in earnest. However, this is actually the end of it. We don't know how the colony fared in its year or so of existence. What we do know is that war broke out between England and Holland; the settlement of the conflict involved Holland's ceding of New Netherlands to England in return for being allowed to retain the presumably more valuable East Indies. Before the war was over, Sir Robert Carr entered Delaware Bay for the English, and he sent a small group of troops to demolish the settlement and carry off "what belonged to the Quaking Society of Plockhoy to a very naile."[25] What happened to the settlers has never been discovered.

There is, however, a postscript on Plockhoy, who apparently did not perish at the hands of the English. Samuel Pennypacker tells the story thus:

> In the year 1694 there came an old blind man and his wife to Germantown. His miserable condition awakened the tender sympathies of the Mennonites there. They gave him the citizenship free of charge. They set apart for him at the end street of the village by Peter Klever's corner a lot twelve rods long and one rod broad, whereon to build a little house and make a garden, which should be his as long as he and his wife should live. In front of it they planted a tree. Jan Doeden and William Rittenhouse were appointed to take up "a free will offering" and to have the little house built. This is all we know, but it is surely a satisfaction to see this ray of sunlight thrown upon the brow of the hapless old man as he neared his grave. After thirty years of untracked wanderings upon these wild shores, friends had come across the sea to give a home at last to one whose whole life had been devoted to the welfare of his fellows. It was Peter Cornelius Plockhoy.[26]

We may not know anything about Plockhoy's actual colony, but we do know enough about his ideas to realize that they were impressive. Centuries ahead of his time, this Dutch Mennonite preached compassion for the poor, uplifting education for all children, freedom of conscience, separation of church and state, and the abolition of slavery.

* * *

THERE WERE OTHER EARLY COMMUNES THAT HAVE escaped very much historical notice. The next one after Plockhoy's was the Labadist colony at Bohemia Manor, a large estate in Maryland. Much longer-lived than the Plockhoy venture, the Labadist colony was the first intentional community that influenced the subsequent course of American communalism. The 3,750-acre domain, founded in 1683, was the American outpost of a strict, austere movement instigated by the seventeenth-century Jesuit priest turned Protestant minister Jean de Labadie, who preached a stern millenarian and mystical faith.

It would be difficult to imagine harder lives than those led by the American Labadists. Colony head Peter Sluyter refused to let the colonists heat their rooms, although firewood was abundant. He deliberately had the colony's food made unpalatable, and those who complained had to eat the foods they liked the least. Meals were taken in silence. New members had to donate all their worldly goods to the group upon joining, but could take nothing out if they left. There were different rules for Sluyter, however; he kept his quarters comfortably warm and generally indulged himself in pleasures forbidden to the rest. Somehow the group made converts and kept enough members to continue its communal existence at least until Sluyter's death in 1722. Sometime thereafter things dissolved; all we know for sure is that a traveler looking for the Labadists in 1727 found that they were gone. Nevertheless, in terms of longevity the community was a rousing success, lasting for some four decades.[27]

Other communal experiments gradually appeared, and a counter-tradition began to take shape. A community of hermits most commonly known as the Society of the Woman in the Wilderness was begun near Germantown, Pennsylvania (the location is today a part of Fairmount Park in Philadelphia) in 1694 by a group of Rosicrucians and Philadelphians who scanned the heavens with a telescope from their observatory, looking for signs of the Second Coming. Their community, led by Johannes Kelpius, lasted for some decades, dissolving slowly after Kelpius's death in 1708. Johann Conrad Beissel, arriving in America with three companions in 1720 in the hope of joining the Woman in the Wilderness, was disappointed to see only a few isolated hermits at the site, so he went inland and founded a community that came to be called Ephrata in Lancaster County, Pennsylvania.[28] Other groups flourished as well in succeeding decades, and finally, in 1774, the first Shakers arrived and soon thereafter put communal history firmly on the map. Since then the United States has seen the founding of thousands of communal settlements, hundreds of them quite substantial. The tradition has continued without interruption for centuries, and today, with thousands of individual communities of a wide variety of types, may be as strong as it has ever been.

REFERENCES

1 See, for example, William Alfred Hinds, *American Communities* (Oneida, N. Y.: Office of the American Socialist, 1878).

2 See, for example, Ernest S. Wooster, *Communities of the Past and Present* (Newllano, Louisiana: Llano Colonist, 1924).

3 See, for example, Everett Webber, *Escape to Utopia: The Communal Movement in America* (New York: Hastings House, 1959).

4 William Bradford, *Of Plymouth Plantation*; edited by Samuel Eliot Morrison (New York: Knopf, 1953), 120-21.

5 See, e.g., Mark Holloway, *Heavens on Earth* (New York: Dover, 1966); Kenneth Rexroth, *Communalism* (New York: Seabury, 1974).

6 See, for example, Robert Fogarty, *Dictionary of American Communal and Utopian History* (Stamford, Connecticut: Greenwood Press, 1980), 236.

7 Arthur Bestor, *Backwoods Utopias*, 27.

8 Samuel W. Pennypacker, "The Settlement of Germantown," *Pennsylvania-German Society Proceedings and Addresses* (Lancaster, Pennsylvania), v. 9, 1899, p. 249.

9 John Downie, *Peter Cornelius Plockhoy: Our First Cooperative Hero* [sic] (Manchester: Cooperative Union, [1933]), p. 1. Pennypacker (p. 234) knew of the earlier pamphlet, but had never found a copy of it.

10 Pennypacker, "Settlement", 234-236.

11 Peter Cornelius Plockhoy, *A Way Propounded* (1639) as published by Downie, in *Plockhoy*, 4-20. A useful digest of the document is provided by Pennypacker, "Settlement," 234-245.

12 Plockhoy, *Way*, 11.

13 *Ibid.*, 6.

14 Quoted by Pennypacker, "Settlement", 257.

15 *Ibid.*, 230.

16 *Ibid.*, 232-234.

17 *Ibid.*, 245.

18 For a brief summary of the Digger position see Michael Mullett, *Radical Religious Movements in Early Modern Europe* (London: George Allen and Unwin, 1980), 53-54.

19 Bestor, *Backwoods Utopias*, 27.

20 The long title of the Dutch booklet began, "Kort en klaer ontwerp, bienende tot Een onderling Accoort," or, in English, "Short and clear plan,

serving as a mutual contract...." (Amsterdam, 1662). See Pennypacker, "Settlement", 248ff.

21 Pennypacker, "Settlement," 250-58.
22 *Ibid.*, 258.
23 *Ibid.*, 260.
24 Bestor, *Backwoods Utopias*, 27.
25 Quoted in Pennypacker, "Settlement," 262.
26 *Ibid.*, 262.
27 Probably the best overview of the Labadist colony is Bartlett B. James, "The Labadist Colony in Maryland," *Johns Hopkins University Studies in Historical and Political Science*, series XVII, no. 6, June, 1899, pp. 7-45.
28 On Beissel and Ephrata, see James E. Ernst, *Ephrata: A History* (Allentown: Pennsylvania Folklore Society, 1963). Ephrata's main buildings have been preserved as a state park in Pennsylvania, and are the oldest large material artifacts of American communal history.

FREEDOM OF CONSCIENCE MONUMENT
Commemorating the passage on April 21, 1649 of the "Act Concerning Religion."
Sculpted by Baltimore artist Hans Schuler and erected in 1934 by Maryland counties.

THE MANY HEADED HYDRA
Sailors, Slaves, and the Atlantic Working Class in the Eighteenth Century

Peter Linebaugh
Marcus Rediker

INTRODUCTION

THROUGH THE HARSH WINTER OF 1740-41, AS FOOD RIOTS broke out all over Europe, a motley crew of workers met at John Hughson's waterside tavern in the city of New York to plan a rising for St. Patrick's Day. The conspirators included Irish, English, Hispanic, African, and Native American men and women; they spoke Gaelic, English, Spanish, French, Dutch, Latin, Greek, and undoubtedly several African and Indian languages. They were a mixture of mostly slaves and wage laborers, especially soldiers, sailors, and journeymen. During their deliberations, David Johnson, a journeyman hatter of British background, swore that "he would help to burn the town, and kill as many white people as he could." John Corry, an Irish dancing-master, promised the same, as, apparently, did John Hughson himself and many others, a large number of African-Americans among them.

Eventually they put at least part of their plan into action, burning down Fort George, the Governor's mansion, and the imperial armory, the symbols of Royal Majesty and civil authority, the havens and instruments of ruling-class power in New York. They did not succeed, as evidenced by the 13 burned at the stake, the 21 hanged, and the 77 transported out of the colony as slaves or servants. The corpses of two of the hanged dangled in an iron gibbet on the waterfront as a lesson to others. As the bodies decayed in the open air, observers noted a gruesome, yet instructive, transformation. The corpse of an Irishman turned black and his hair curly while the corpse of Caesar, the

African, bleached white. It was accounted a "wondrous phemenonon."[1]

One of the many remarkable things about this upheaval is the way in which it confounds much of contemporary historical understanding. Here we have a polyglot community of workers who by current wisdom should never have been able to conceive, much less execute, a joint rebellion. Here we have "white" Europeans pledging themselves to the destruction of "the white people" of New York, by which they obviously meant *the rich people*. Here we have, not a slave revolt or a "great Negro Plot" (as it has long been called), not a mutiny by soldiers and sailors nor a strike by wage laborers, but rather a many-sided rising by a diverse urban proletariat—red, white, and black, of many nations, races, ethnicities, and degrees of freedom.[2]

The events of 1741 were part of a broader history of the Atlantic working class in the eighteenth century, a class that suffered not only the violence of the stake, the gallows, and the shackles of a ship's dark hold, but now the violence of abstraction in the writing of history. For concepts such as "nationality," "race," and "ethnicity" have obscured essential features of the history of the working class in the early modern era. Historians who consciously or unconsciously posit static and immutable differences between workers black and white, Irish and English, slave and free in the early modern era, have frequently failed to study the actual points of contact, overlap, and cooperation between their idealized types. Without such cooperation, of course, the economy of the transatlantic world could never have functioned.

Our study starts from the material organization of many thousands of workers into transatlantic circuits of commodity exchange and capital accumulation and then proceeds to look at the ways in which they translated their cooperation into anti-capitalist projects of their own, as did those who gathered and whispered 'round the fire at Hughson's tavern in New York. It is thus a study of *connections* within the working class—connections that have been denied, ignored, or simply never seen by most historians. It is also an effort to remember, literally to *re-member*, to reconnect as a way of overcoming some of the violence, some of the dismembering, the Atlantic working class has undergone. Our effort to remember begins with a myth about dismemberment.

THE MYTH OF THE MANY-HEADED HYDRA

THE SLAYING OF THE HYDRA WAS THE SECOND OF THE twelve labors of Hercules. A Greek version of the story is perhaps best known. Confronted with the monstrous, many-headed Hydra, a water snake with nine to a hundred heads, Hercules found that as soon as he cut off one head, two grew in its place. With the help of his nephew Iolaus, he learned to use a firebrand to cauterize the stump of the beast's neck. Thus they killed the Hydra. Hercules dipped his arrows in the blood of the slain beast, whose venom thus gave to his arrows their fatal power.

Allusions to the story appear often in the annals of European conquest in the seventeenth and eighteenth centuries. For instance, in 1751, a former governor of Surinam returned to Holland, where he wrote poetic memoirs recollecting his defeat at the hands of the Saramaka, the victorious maroons:

> There you must fight blindly an invisible enemy
> Who shoots you down like ducks in the swamps.
> Even if an army of ten thousand men were gathered, with
> The courage and strategy of Caesar and Eugene,
> They'd find their work cut out for them, destroying a
> Hydra's growth
> Which even Alcides would try to avoid.

Mauricius was a European conqueror writing to and for other Europeans assumed to be sympathetic with the project of conquest. They likened their labor to that of Hercules, here called Alcides. Hydra is identified with the former slaves who had freed themselves, and who in subsequent war assured their freedom—a first permanent victory over European masters in the New World, preceding by a generation the victory of the Haitian people.[3]

The Hydra comparison came easily to the pens of slaveholders worried about rebellion. Thus, in the aftermath of Bussa's Rebellion (Barbados, 1816) a planter wrote that Wilberforce and the African Institute "have pierced the inmost recesses of our island, inflicted deep and deadly words in the minds of the black population, and engendered the Hydra, Rebellion, which had well nigh deluged our fields with blood."[4]

The Hydra analogy was restricted, however, neither to the West Indies, nor only to Afro-American slaves. In 1702 when Cotton Mather published his history of Christianity in America (*Magnalia Christi Americana*) he entitled his second chapter on the sectarian opposition to the New England Puritans, "Hydra Decapita." "The church of God had not long been in this wilderness, before the dragon cast forth several floods to devour it," he wrote of the antinomian controversy of the 1630s. The theological struggle of "works" against "grace" subverted "all peaceable order." It prevented an expedition against the Pequot Indians; it raised suspicions against the magistrates; it confused the drawing of town lots; and it made particular appeals to women. To Cotton Mather, therefore, the Hydra challenged legal authority, the demarcations of private property, the subordination of women, and the authority of ministers who refused to permit open discussions of sermons. The antinomians of America had begun to call the King of England "the King of Babylon." The struggle in Massachusetts was then a theological dress-rehearsal for the English Revolution of the 1640s.

Thus, in many different contexts did various ruling classes use the ancient myth of the many-headed Hydra to understand their metropolitan and colonial problems, usually referring to the proletariat whom European powers were either conquering or disciplining to the life of plantation, regiment, estate, workshop, and factory. In this sense, the capitalists of London, Paris, and the Hague thus cast themselves as Hercules. Why did they do so? One might consider the question unimportant, since after all was not this a "Classical Age" in European history when allusion to classical myth was commonplace? Yet this begs the question, for why was it a "Classical Age"? Part of the answer lies in a project common to Roman and European ruling classes, both of which sought by conquest and tribute to control the rest of the world.

Part of the answer lies too in the fact that the European bourgeoisie of the early modern era was only beginning to develop an understanding of its time and place in the world, and—aside from Christianity and its myths—the only tools available to them for understanding social development were those classic texts rediscovered and made available during the Renaissance, which on the one hand assisted the "scientific revolution" through the revival of neo-Platonism and other hermetic traditions, and on the other provided examples and models of social formations, or modes of production, which supported the doctrine of European progress in social development.[5]

Hercules could be seen as revolutionary. It is not just that his labors were immense, gigantic, and inter-continental; they seemed to summarize, as myths often do, an enormous transition in human history. Indeed, taking the Neolithic Revolution as the beginning of history, Hercules belonged, as the oldest of the deities in the Greek pantheon, to the dawn of the ages. Thus, by the end of the nineteenth century, the generally accepted interpretation of the myth was that it expressed the transition to agrarian civilization. A myth that summarized the neolithic revolution might well be used to summarize the revolutionary rise of capitalism.

By the beginning of the eighteenth century the geographic zones of this latter Herculean struggle were the four corners of the North Atlantic, or the coast of West Africa, the Caribbean islands, the North American colonies, and the maritime powers of northwestern Europe. Within these zones the experience of human labor was organized in seven basic ways. First, there were those who hunted and gathered their subsistence, like some of the Indians and European hunters of North America and the poor commoners and scavengers of countryside and city in England and Ireland. Second, the women, servants, and children whose work was consigned to domestic settings of kitchen and cabin. Third, the unwaged but "independent" farmers who themselves presented a variety of types, from the poor tenants and *klachan* farmers of Ireland, to the villages of west Africa, to the communal cultivators among the Iroquois and the small-holders of America. Fourth, the unfree indentured servants who had been compelled to leave their vagabonding ways to be transported to the west Atlantic. Fifth, the artisanal craftworkers of town and plantation who have been so carefully studied in recent historiography. Sixth, the sailors and navies of the mercantile powers who formed the mass of eighteenth-century wage labor. And, seventh, the unfree, unwaged slaves whose mass, cooperative labor cleared the forests, drained the swamps, built the infrastructure of roads and ports, and labored in the plantations of sugar, tobacco, coffee, and cotton. Our remarks here are restricted to two zones—Europe and the North American colonies—and to two kinds of workers—wage laborers (especially sailors) and slaves.[6]

We will look at four moments in the history of the many-headed hydra in the eighteenth century: 1747, when, in the Knowles Riot in Boston, sailors and slaves fought the King's press gangs and in so doing created one of the central ideas of the "Age of Revolution"; 1768, when, in the London port strike, sailors, Irish coalheavers, and others pioneered one of the central ideas and activities of the modern working-class movement, the strike; 1776, when, in the American Revolution, sailors and slaves helped to instigate and then to win the world's first colonial war for liberation; and 1780, when, in the Gordon

Riots, the polyglot working class of London liberated the prisons amid the greatest municipal insurrection of the eighteenth century. All of these moments were in crucial ways the work of "a motley crew"— a multi-racial, multi-ethnic, transatlantic working class, whose presence, much less agency, is rarely, if ever, acknowledged in the historiographies of these crucial events.

1747: SEAMEN, SLAVES, AND THE ORIGINS OF REVOLUTIONARY IDEOLOGY

FREE WAGE LABORERS, MOSTLY SEAMEN AND OTHERS WHO congregated in urban areas, and unfree unwaged laborers, slaves who lived in city and countryside, were two of the rowdiest heads of the Hydra in Britain's North American colonies. Their numerous revolts were not only connected in important ways, they were, taken together, much more crucial to the genesis, process, and outcome of the American Revolution than is generally appreciated.

Jesse Lemisch made it clear years ago that seamen were one of the prime movers in the American Revolution. They played a major part in a great many of the patriot victories between 1765 and 1776. Seamen led a series of militant riots against impressment between 1741 and 1776, and indeed their agency was acknowledged by both Tom Paine (in *Common Sense*) and Tom Jefferson (in the Declaration of Independence), both of whom listed impressment as a major grievance and spur to colonial liberation.[7]

What has been less fully appreciated is how the sailor's involvement in revolutionary politics was part of a broader, international cycle of rebellion that spanned the better part of the eighteenth century. Merchant seamen entered the revolutionary era with a powerful tradition of militancy well in place. They had already learned to use portside riots, mutiny, piracy, work stoppage, and desertion to assert their own ends over and against those mandated from above by merchants, captains, and colonial and royal officials. They would soon learn new tactics.

After the declaration of war against Spain in 1739, struggles against impressment took on a new intensity as seamen fought pitched battles against press gangs all around the Atlantic. Seamen rioted in Boston twice in 1741, once when a mob beat a Suffolk County Sheriff and a Justice of the Peace for their assistance to the press gang of *H.M.S. Portland* and again when 300 seamen armed with "axes, clubs, and cutlasses" attacked the commanding officer of the *Astrea*. They rose twice more in 1745, first roughing up another Suffolk County Sheriff and the commander of *H.M.S. Shirley*, then, seven months later, engaging Captain Forest and *H.M.S. Wager* in an action that resulted in two seamen being hacked to death by the press gang's cutlasses. Seamen also animated crowds that attacked the Royal Navy and its minions in Antigua, St. Kitts, Barbados, and Jamaica throughout the 1740s.[8]

The most important early development in the seaman's cycle of rebellion took place in Boston in 1747, when Commander Charles Knowles of *H.M.S. Lark* commenced a hot press in Boston. A mob, initially consisting of 300 seamen but ballooning to "several thousand people," quickly seized some officers of the *Lark* as hostages, beat a deputy sheriff and slapped him into the town's stocks, surrounded and attacked the Provincial Council Chamber, and posted squads at all piers to keep naval officers from escaping back to their ship. The mob was led by laborers and seamen, black and white, armed with "clubs, swords, and cutlasses." The "lower class," observed Thomas Hutchinson, "were beyond measure enraged." The sailors originally assembled for "self-defense," but there was a positive element to their protest as well. As Knowles remarked:

> The Act [of 1746] against pressing in the Sugar Islands, filled the Minds of the Common People ashore as well as Sailors in all the Northern Colonies (but more especially in New England with not only a hatred for the King's Service but [also] a Spirit of Rebellion each Claiming a Right to the same Indulgence as the Sugar Colonies and declaring they will maintain themselves in it.

Maintain themselves in it they did: sailors defended their "liberty" and justified their resistance in terms of "right."[9]

This was the essential idea embodied in the seamen's practical activity, in their resistance to unjust authority. Sam Adams, who watched as the maritime working class defended itself, began to translate its "Spirit of Rebellion" into political discourse. According to historians John Lax and William Pencak, Adams used the Knowles Riot to formulate a new "ideology of resistance, in which the natural rights of man were used for the first time to justify mob activity." Adams saw that the mob "embodied the fundamental rights of man against which government itself could be judged." But the self-activity of some common tars, "zealous abetters of liberty," came first. Their militant resistance produced a major breakthrough in libertarian thought that would ultimately lead to revolution.[10]

This was only the beginning, for both the cycle of seamen's rebellion and for the articulation of a revolutionary ideology in the Atlantic world. In the aftermath of the 1740s, Jack Tar proceeded to take part in almost every port-city riot in England and America for the remainder of the century. Whether in Newport, Boston, New York, Philadelphia, Charleston, London, Liverpool, Bristol, or in the Caribbean, tars took to the streets in rowdy and rebellious protest on a variety of issues, seizing in practice what would later be established as "right" by law.[11]

The years leading up to the Knowles Riot were ones in which the winds of rebellion also slashed through many of the slave societies of the New World. The struggles included the First Maroon War of Jamaica (1730-1740), slave rebellions on St. John in the Danish Virgin Islands and in Dutch Guyana (1733), a plot in the Bahama Islands (1734), a slave conspiracy in Antigua (1735-36), a rebellion in Guadeloupe (1736-38), the Stono Rebellion (1739), the St. Patrick's Day rising in New York (1741), and a series of disturbances in Jamaica (early 1740s). The connections among these events are not always easy to discover, but the life of a slave named Will, who took part in the rebellion of St. John, then the conspiracy of Antigua, and finally the plot of New York, suggests something important about the movement and exchange of subversive experience among slaves. Another Antigua conspirator, banished from his own island, turned up as a leader of a plot on the Danish Island of St. Croix in 1759.[12]

The movement toward rebellion among African-Americans accelerated after 1765, as demonstrated in some important recent work by Peter Wood, who has argued that "black freedom struggles on the eve of white independence" intensified as slaves seized the new opportunities offered by splits between imperial and colonial ruling classes. Running away increased at a rate that alarmed slaveholders everywhere, and by the mid-1770s, a rash of slave plots and revolts sent the fears of their masters soaring. Slaves organized risings in Perth Amboy, New Jersey, in 1772; in St. Andrews Parish, South Carolina; and in a joint African-Irish effort in Boston, in 1774; in Ulster County, New York; Dorchester County, Maryland; Norfolk, Virginia; and the Tar River region of North Carolina, in 1775. In the last of these, a slave named Merrick plotted with a white seafarer to get the arms that would make the intended revolt possible.[13]

Such conspiracy and exchange was facilitated by the strategic position that many urban slaves or free blacks occupied in the social division of labor in the port towns, as day laborers, dockworkers, seamen, and river pilots. Northern ports, with their promise of anonymity and an impersonal wage in the maritime sector, served as a magnet to runaway slaves and free blacks throughout the colonial period and well into the nineteenth and even twentieth centuries. Many found work as laborers and seamen. Slaves too were employed in the maritime sector, some with ship masters as owners, others hired out for a given time. By the middle of the eighteenth century, slaves dominated Charleston's maritime and riverine traffic, in which some 20 percent of the city's adult male slaves labored. The freedom of Charleston's "Boat Negroes" had long upset Charleston's rulers, at no time more than when they involved themselves in subversive activities, as alleged against Thomas Jeremiah, a river pilot, in 1775. Jeremiah was accused of stockpiling guns as he awaited the imperial war that would "help the poor Negroes." Jeffrey J. Crow has noted that black pilots were "a rebellious lot, particularly resistant to white control."[14]

Peter Wood concludes that between 1765 and 1776 North American slaves generated a "wave of struggle" that became "a major factor in the turmoil leading up to the Revolution": "It touched upon every major slave colony, and it was closely related to—even influential upon—the political unrest gripping many white subjects in these years." Wood's treatment of this cycle of rebellion as "a significant chapter in the story of worker and artisan political unrest" invites us to link it to the revolutionary struggles of other workers.[15]

1776: The Mob and the "Many-Headed Power" in America

REVOLUTIONARY CROWDS, ROWDY GATHERINGS OF THOUsands of men and women, began in 1765 to create an imperial crisis of unprecedented dimensions. Mobs were crucial to the effective protests against the Stamp Act, the Townshend Revenue Act, the increased power of the British customs service, the Quartering Act, the Tea Act, the "Intolerable Acts," and therefore in the revolutionary rupture itself. All of this we can now appreciate because of important recent scholarship.[16]

What has not been appreciated is that most of these mobs were interracial in character, and that these potent if temporary unions of free waged and unfree unwaged laborers were instrumental in winning many of the victories of the revolutionary movement. The "Sons of Neptune" (themselves both black and white), other free blacks, and slaves were probably most united and most effective in their battles against impressment. The crucial Knowles Riot of 1747, which witnessed the birth of the revolution's language of liberation, was led by "armed Seamen, Servants, Negroes, and others." Later, as the revolutionary movement began in 1765, some 500 "seamen, boys, and Negroes" rioted against impressment in Newport, Rhode Island, and in 1767 a mob of armed whites and blacks attacked Captain Jeremiah Morgan in a press riot in Norfolk. Lemisch noted that after 1763, "Armed mobs of whites and Negroes repeatedly manhandled captains, officers, and crews, threatened their lives, and held them hostage for the men they pressed."[17]

Workers, white and black, also participated in the popular upsurges against the Stamp Act, whose successful repeal was perhaps the key moment in the development of a revolutionary movement. In 1765 "disorderly negroes, and more disorderly sailors" rioted against the Stamp Act in Charleston. A few months later, Charleston slaves (some of whom may have taken part in the earlier action with seamen) assembled and cried for "liberty," which moved city elders to keep the city under armed guard for ten days to two weeks. One protest led to another in which the slogan took on a different, more radical meaning.[18]

Seamen, again assisted by African-Americans, also led the militant opposition to the renewed power of the British customs service in the late 1760s and early 1770s. As Alfred F. Young has shown, seamen even drew upon the custom of the sea to forge a new weapon in the arsenal of revolutionary justice, the tarring and feathering that intimidated a great many British officials in the colonies. We can hear the clunk of the brush in the tar bucket behind Thomas Gage's observation in 1769 that "the Officers of the Crown grow more timid, and more fearfull of doing their Duty every Day."[19]

Seamen also led both the Golden Hill and Nassau Street Riots of New York and the King Street Riot, better remembered as the Boston Massacre. In both instances, sailors and other workers resented the ways in which British soldiers labored for less than customary wages along the waterfront. In New York they also resented the soldiers' efforts to destroy their 58-foot liberty pole, which, not surprisingly, resembled nothing so much as a ship's mast. Rioting and street fighting ensued. Thomas Hutchinson and John Adams, among others, believed that the actions in New York led directly to the "Fatal Fifth of March" in Boston. Adams, who defended Captain Preston and his soldiers in trial, called the mob that assembled on King Street nothing but "a motley rabble of saucy boys, negroes and molattoes, Irish teagues, and outlandish Jack Tarrs." Seamen also took part in the Tea Party, provoking Britain to a show of naked force in the Intolerable Acts, and an eventual confrontation that proved irreconcilable. During the revolution itself, tars took part in mobs that harrassed Tories and rendered their efforts less effective.[20]

Occasionally we get a glimpse of radical ideas and practices in transit, how the oppositional ideas of "these most dangerous people" actually spread from one port to another during the imperial crisis. Governor William Bull of South Carolina, facing Stamp Act protests in Charleston, found that the "Minds of Men here were universally poisoned with the Principles which were imbibed and propagated from Boston and Rhode Island." Soon, "after their example the People of this Town resolved to seize and destroy the Stamp Papers." In explaining this development, Bull noted that "at this time of Year, Vessels very frequently arrive" from Boston and Newport, where seamen and slaves had helped to protest the Stamp Act, just as they would do in Charleston. "Principles" as well as commodities were transported on those ships![21]

Those Adams called boys (apprentices), negroes and mulattoes, Irish teagues, and outlandish Jack Tars made up a huge portion of the urban population that was linked by tenacious cultural ties. A subculture of "apprentices, servants, slaves, and perhaps some journeymen, laborers, and sailors," revolved around common work experiences and a common cultural life of revels, masques, fairs, May-day celebrations, street parties, taverns, and "disorderly houses." "Apprentices, servants, and even negroes" drank together in Hell Town in Philadelphia, just as "seamen and Negroes" caroused "at unseasonable hours" in Charleston, and workers black and white congregated at Hughson's tavern in New York. Magistrate Daniel Horsmanden suggested that such taverns provided

> opportunities for the most loose, debased, and abandoned wretches amongst us to cabal and confederate together and ripen themselves into these schools of mischief, for the execution of the most daring and

> detestable enterprizes. I fear there are yet many of
> these houses amongst us, and they are the bane and
> pest of the city. It was such that gave the opportunity
> of breeding this most horrid and execrable conspiracy.

Grogshops, tippling houses, and dancing cellars existed in every Atlantic port, much to the despair of colonial ruling classes, who sought to criminalize and otherwise discourage contact between the free and unfree workers who used such settings to hatch conspiracies and even form a "maritime underground railroad" through which many escaped to freedom. There was, therefore, a history of interracial cooperation that underlay the joint protests of sailors and slaves against impressment and other measures during the revolutionary era.[22]

Seamen and slaves thus expressed a militant mood summed up by Peter Timothy when he spoke of Charleston, South Carolina, in the summer of 1775: "In regard to War & Peace, I can only tell you that the Plebeians are still for War—but the noblesse [are] perfectly pacific." Seamen in particular and wage workers in general were foremost among the most radical parts of the colonial population, who pushed the revolutionary vanguard to more extreme positions and eventually to independence itself. Contrary to the recent argument of scholars who claim that sailors, laborers, slaves, and other poor workingmen were in no position to "shape the revolutionary process," it is clear that these groups provided much of the spark, volatility, momentum, and the "sustained militance" for the attack on British policy after 1765. In the process they provided an image of interracial cooperation that should cause us to wonder whether racism was as monolithic in white society as is often assumed.[23]

Paul Revere's famous but falsified account of the Boston Massacre quickly tried to make the "motley rabble" respectable by leaving black faces out of the crowd and putting into it entirely too many fancy waistcoats. It is not, therefore, surprising that well-to-do colonists often fearfully called the mob a "Hydra," a "many-headed monster," a "reptile," and, more sympathetically, a "many-headed power," using the same mythic terms that other parts of the Atlantic bourgeoisie had long used to describe and interpret their struggle against a diverse Atlantic working class.[24]

Such fears are understandable, for the politicized mob was one of the three most important "mass organizations" (along with the militia and the army) in the revolutionary movement, and it was probably the hardest of these to control. Moreover, it was in most instances quintessentially democratic—not only could anyone join, but working-men could even rise to positions of momentary or long-term leader-ship. Given these facts, and the way in which such mobs were absolutely crucial to the making of the revolution, their subsequent suppression by former revolutionaries can be seen as part of an American Thermidor, their condemnation by big landowners, mer-chants, and even artisans as part of a literal "enclosure movement" designed to move politics from "out of doors" to legislative chambers. When Sam Adams, who helped to draw up Massachusetts's Riot Act of 1786, ceased to believe that the mob "embodied the fundamental rights of man against which government itself could be judged," he cut himself off from an important source of democratic creativity and expression, the force that years ago had given him the best idea of his life.[25]

Of the five workingmen killed in the Boston Massacre in 1770, John Adams said: "the blood of the martyrs, right or wrong, proved to be the seed of the congregation." Adams thus made clear the working-class origins of the revolution and the new nation, for the blood of the martyrs, as everyone knew, was the blood of a journeyman, an apprentice, and three wage laborers: a ropewalker and two seamen, one of whom was a half-black, half-Indian runaway slave who lived in the Bahama Islands. His name was Crispus Attucks. Of this martyr John Adams had said earlier, his "very looks would be enough to terri-fy any person," or at least any person like Adams himself. He might well have said the same about the "motley rabble" Attucks had led into battle, thereby speaking the fearful mind of the moderate leader-ship of the revolutionary movement. It would not be long before work-ing men and women all over America would be marching against the British under flags that featured a serpent and the motto, "Don't Tread on Me."[26]

1768: FROM IRELAND TO LONDON,
WHERE THE SERPENT LEARNS TO STRIKE

PATRICK CARR, ANOTHER BOSTON WORKER WHO WAS TO BE a martyr of the coming revolution, represented that part of the Atlantic working class that hailed from Ireland. Carr, like many oth-ers, left Ireland in the 1760s well-experienced in the ways of mobs and their confrontations with British military power. Many of his compatriots went to London, where they helped to make the London port strike of 1768.[27]

Indeed, the strike in London cannot be understood apart from Ireland, where the hangman's noose and the woodsman's axe had centuries before been the principle tools of the English Ascendency. Following the Williamite confiscations of the 1690s, the forests, and the human culture dependent upon them, were largely destroyed; the agrarian policy subsequently introduced into Ireland promoted pasturage for the export of cattle rather than an arable farming that could feed the population. As a result, a large population, having neither forests nor lands to subsist upon, either left the land altogether or submitted to a standard of subsistence so utterly mean that it beggared the powers of description of independent observers and caused even the rulers to wonder at how an oppressed population could tolerate such conditions. The Irish language was "banished from the castle of the chieftain to the cottage of the vassal," from whence in hard times it migrated to the boozing kens of London and the "low tippling houses" of American and Caribbean ports. The "Hidden Ireland"—its conspiratorial tradition and willingness to act outside the law—was carried along in the diaspora within people like Patrick Carr.[28]

The "Whiteboy Outrages," the name given to the largest and longest of agrarian rebellions in Ireland (1761-1765, with sporadic outbursts through 1788), was a major part of the subversive experience of the mobile Irish. These protests took place in a period of increased expropriation and accumulation, intensified by the demands of two world wars. With the outbreak of cattle disease, the murrain, in continental Europe, and the passage in 1759 of the Cattle Exportation Act, the value of Irish land increased greatly. The poorest of the cottiers who had a potato patch or a cow kept on the common land, suddenly found that even these were to be denied, as landlords, their agents, and bailiffs evicted them in search of new grazing lands, taking over whole baronies, and erecting walls, hedges, and fences to keep their herds in and the former tenants out. Against this, the Irish cottier and laborer reacted with what Lecky called "an insurrection of despair."[29]

In October, 1761, nocturnal bands of 200-400 people, dressed in flowing white frocks and white cockades, threw down fences enclosing lands in Tipperary. The movement quickly expanded to new areas in Cork, Kilkenny, Limerick, and Waterford, and to actions designed to redress other grievances, such as the manifold tithes (of potatoes, agistment, turf, or furze) imposed by an alien religious establishment. Sounding horns, carrying torches, and riding commandeered horses, the Whiteboys opened gaols, rescued prisoners, attacked garrisons, stole arms, released 'prentices, maimed cattle, ploughed wasteland, prevented export of provisions, burned houses, reduced prices, and everywhere tore down walls, fences, hedges, and ditches. These rebels were originally known as, and often called, "the Levellers."

The overall strength of the Whiteboys remains unknown, though it was reported that 14,000 insurgents lived in Tipperary in 1763. Their largest gatherings, 500-700 strong, took place in 1762 in Cork and Waterford. Using military techniques, the poorest cottiers and laborers (many of them spalpeens, or migratory laborers) formed themselves into an autonomous organization quite separate from the middling and upper classes. Indeed, the proletarian experience of the hundreds of thousands of Irishmen who had soldiered in the French army since 1691 lay behind the Whiteboy movement.[30]

Of necessity much of their movement was anonymous and mysterious. It was conducted "under the sanction of being fairies," it was said in 1762, and led by mythological figures such as "Queen Sieve" who wrote,

> We, levellers and avengers for the wrongs done to the poor, have unanimously assembled to raze walls and ditches that have been made to inclose the commons. Gentlemen now of late have learned to grind the face of the poor so that it is impossible for them to live. They cannot even keep a pig or a hen at their doors. We warn them not to raise again either walls or ditches in the place of those we destroy, nor even to inquire about the destroyers of them. If they do, their cattle shall be houghed and their sheep laid open in the fields.

Whiteboy captains who would carry out these threats called themselves "Slasher," "Lightfoot," "Fearnot," and "Madcap Setfire."[31]

Theirs was a movement inspired by strong notions of justice. The High Sheriff of Waterford, for instance, could find no person willing to whip a convicted Whiteboy, though he offered 20 Guineas and though a large body of troops was present for the occasion. When English law was enforced, as in the hanging of Father Sheehy in 1766, the people undermined its effect. The earth over his grave was treated as holy ground; a "Sheehy Jury" became proverbial for partiality. Four years later his executioner was stoned to death and ten years later his prosecutor killed, by people who refused to forget.[32]

The Whiteboy movement attacked tithes and alarmed many Protestants, but it ought not be interpreted as a sectarian phenomenon, since both Catholics and Protestants were present among both the Whiteboys and their victims, and since wealthy Catholics and Protestants cooperated to stop the risings.[33] And although it began in rural settings against enclosures, the movement ought not be interpreted exclusively as "agrarian unrest." Just as the creation of a landless proletariat is a necessary corollary to the expropriation of land, so the forms and experience of that struggle will move with the wandering, roving proletariat thus created. An historian of the transported convicts to Australia wrote, "The Whiteboy Associations were, in a sense, a vast trades union." Whiteboy sabotage, according to Constantia Maxwell, was taken up by Dublin journeymen. The Friendly Society of Philadelphia's ship carpenters, its historian avers, was also associated with the Whiteboys. Therefore, when in the late 1760s, the terms of exchange between England and Ireland included one and a half million pounds in remittances to absentee landlords, three million pounds worth of exports, and thousands of hungry laboring people, we need to add to such material commerce, a cultural exchange that is broader than choleric playwrights and sad balladeers, and which includes the rebellious organizations of "hidden Ireland," because these surfaced in London in 1768 with great effect.[34]

Proletarian labors in London were characterized by high turnover, by absence of guild fellowships, by ethnic heterogeneity, and by working conditions that were seasonal, dangerous, and subject to harsh discipline. The productive power of such social labor arose from the assembly of many people in one place at one time. Harvesting and road-making, canal-digging and soldiering required such labor, as did the loading, sailing, and unloading of ships. The Irish concentrated in the mass labor of coalheaving, a hot, filthy, back-breaking line of work, but crucial to the energizing of England's greatest city. Individually weak and pitiful, as a collective mass such wage laborers had power and posed danger. "A body of men working in concert has hands and eyes both before and behind, and is, to a certain degree, omnipresent," wrote Karl Marx.[35]

In the 1760s it took more money to eat, and the hungry people of London began to act directly against price increases. River workers led the groups who stole fresh vegetables, forced vendors to sell their wares at popular prices, and intimidated merchants into both closing down their shops/exchanges and burying their plate. On 11 May a group of sailors assembled at the Stock Exchange "and would not suffer any Person except their own Body to enter it." These actions were not peaceful: murder was a frequent occurrence during the spring and summer. Thomas Davis, for instance, said he "did not care who they killed, rather than his family should starve." When a "Gentleman" asked a young man whether it was foolish for people to risk their lives, he was answered: "Master, Provisions are high and Trade is dead, that we are half starving and it is as well to die at once, as die by Inches."[36]

Otherwise, the hungry took indirect actions to increase their wages. The sailors petitioned and marched upon Parliament to increase their wage payments. The shoemakers met often in mass meeting in Moorfields as part of their attempts to get greater wages. The bargemen struck for more money. The sawyers were threatened by the recent introduction of a steam-powered engine installed in Limehouse. They destroyed it. A thousand glass grinders petitioned for higher wages; thousands of London tailors did the same. Leaders were sent to prison, like the three tailors sent to Bridewell "for irritating their Bretheren to Insurrection, abusing their Masters, and refusing to work at the stated prices."[37]

In many ways, the riots of the spring and early summer of 1768 appear to be classic instances of the eighteenth-century plebeian "mob" in action: the forms (petitioning, marching, illuminations, smashing of windows), the heterogeneity of the "trades" (tailors, shoemakers, carpenters), and, generally, the subordination of its demands and actions to the middle-class reform movement led by John Wilkes. Yet the activities of that year need to be seen not only as the licensed outrages of the plebeian mob, but as something new, unlicensed, insurrectionary, and proletarian. "The Extremities to which the Cry of Liberty is carried, seem to threaten the Destruction of all Civil Society," as one newspaper put it. Wilkes and his men could not control the protests of 1768, as demonstrated when some sailors chanted, "No Wilkes, No King." Nor did artisans lead these events. The river workers led them, closing river shipping for a time, and almost causing a general strike. In July "A Spectator" observed the pattern of recent months: "Thus Sailors, Taylors, Coopers, Lightermen, Watermen, &c. follow one another, the adventurous Coalheavers leading the Van."[38]

The leaders of the coalheavers, many knew, were "of the Gang of

White Boys in Ireland, driven out from thence for the most Enormous Crimes, as they have bragg'd and given it out themselves," to quote the Solicitor-General of England. The involvement of Whiteboys among the coalheavers was reported by several newspapers and assumed by Samuel Foote, who wrote *The Tailors; A Tragedy for Warm Weather* about the strikes of '68-'69. Horace Walpole, the Earl of Orford, noted that the coalheavers "are all Irish Whiteboys"; his certainty of this fact allowed him to use the terms coalheavers and Whiteboys interchangeably. Thus the hydra-head slain by the noose and the axe in Ireland re-appeared with doubled force in London, as insurgent Irish wage labor. It may have been little enough solace to John Brennan's wife, who had carried the severed Whiteboy's head through the streets and shops of Kilkenny "collecting money from the populace" after his execution. But the inescapable truth remained, as recognized by the Chief Baron of Ireland's Exchequer: in Ireland, "England has sown her laws like dragon's teeth, and they have sprung up, armed men."[39]

The working men and women of riverside London came out of 1768 armed in a new way. The sailors, who collectively decided to "strike" the sails of their vessels and thereby halt the commerce and international accumulation of capital in the empire's leading city, had in conjunction with Irish coalheavers and others made a major addition to the political language and activity of the working-class movement: the strike.[40]

1780: INSURRECTIONARY LONDON

AS SEVERAL HEADS OF THE HYDRA FOUGHT FOR "INDEPENdence" beneath the symbol of the serpent in America, several others—"*a motley crew, and of every color*"—struck against British power in the Gordon Riots, the most serious municipal insurrection of the eighteenth century. The riots of 6 June 1780 were named after Lord George Gordon, a Scottish peer who led the Protestant Association, a mass organization dedicated to the repeal of an Act passed two years earlier for the "Relief of Roman Catholics." Parliament and the Bank of England were attacked; aristocrats found their houses demolished and their persons besieged. London parks became military encampments; strategic points were defended by artillery; the municipal bourgeoisie armed itself. Between four and five hundred people were killed. To the London working class the 6th of June 1780 was a glorious day because the prisoners of Newgate were liberated.[41]

Exact estimates of the number of prisoners freed on the night of 6-7 June 1780 must vary because of the disorders of the night and because of the many different prisons, jails, and other places of confinement that were opened. More than twenty crimping houses (where impressed sailors were confined prior to embarkation) and spunging houses (where debtors were held at the pleasure of their creditors) were forcibly opened in Southwark. The prisoners of Newgate, the largest and most terrible dungeon, were liberated amid such fire and destruction that one spectator felt "as if not only the whole metropolis was burning, but all nations yielding to the final consummation of all things."[42]

The prisoners "delivered from the Gaol of Newgate" were of several ethnicities—English, Irish, African-American, but also Italian, German, and Jewish. Of those liberated whose original cases can be found, five had been charged with crimes against the person (a rapist, a bigamist, an anonymous letter writer, and two murderers), two charged with perjury; the overwhelming majority were imprisoned for crimes against property: two counterfeiters, six burglars, ten highway robbers, and fifty larcenists escaped; most were propertyless. Several inside Newgate had American connections; they, like others both inside and outside the prison walls, had been affected by the revolutionary war under way for independence and the pursuit of happiness. Continuing the struggles sailors had waged over the previous forty years against impressment, the rioters fought for freedom against confinement. They did so in a "Republican Phrenzy" and a "levelling spirit."[43]

In fact, sailors themselves were prominent among the rioters, as indicated by the frequent mention of cutlasses and marlin spikes as principle weapons in the armory of the crowd. It had been a terrible year for sailors—the winter was cold, the war had been a fatigue, and the press gangs marauded the streets. The incidence of mutiny in the Royal Navy had begun to increase soon after the American Revolution broke out. A seaman by the name of Richard Hyde was tried for the liberation, or "delivery," of the Newgate prisoners. One of the Newgate turnkeys insisted that Hyde had insulted him, calling him "one of Akerman's Thieves," and threatened him by saying he would "cut his Throat and kill his Master." Other sailors broke into prison-keeper Akerman's house, where they obtained the keys to the gaol's main gate.[44]

Two other deliverers of Newgate, "not having the Fear of God before their Eyes but being moved and seduced by the Instigation of the Devil," to use the language of the indictments against them, were named John Glover and Benjamin Bowsey. They were African-Americans, and former slaves. Their activities at Newgate were decisive, and for that reason their importance to the subsequent history of Atlantic working people can be likened to the more well-known leaders of the Afro-London population, Ottobah Cugoano and Olaudah Equiano, whose fame partly arises because they were writers. Glover and Bowsey were activists.[45]

John Glover lived in Westminster where he was reputed to be a "quiet, sober, honest" man. He worked as a servant to one Philips, Esq., who was evidently an attorney, for during the afternoon of 6 June he sent Glover to his chambers in Lincoln's Inn to fetch some papers. The streets were full of people and news: the day before "the Mobbing of the Lords" had taken place, petitioners were returning from Parliament, the ballad singers were exhausting their talents, the clerks and law men of the Inns of Court had begun to arm themselves to do duty against the mob. Ignatius Sancho, a well-to-do African grocer, wrote from Westminster that evening observing "at least a hundred thousand poor, miserable, ragged rabble...besides half as many women and children, all parading the streets—the bridge—the Park—ready for any and every mischief." The day was a moment of truth when none could avoid taking sides. Glover did not gather the law papers, but instead joined one of the columns forming toward Newgate whose approach filled him with determination, for on Snow Hill he was seen striking the cobblestones with a gun barrel and shouting "Now Newgate!" He was one of the first persons who showed his face at the "chequers of the gate" whose keeper was addressed by him as follows, "Damn you, Open the Gate or we will Burn you down and have Everybody out," a threat he made good, for he was later observed "to be the most active Person Particularly in piling up combustible matters against the Door and putting fire thereto."[46]

The London Black community (10,000-20,000 people) was active during the week of 6 June. Later, Ottobah Cuguoano spoke from, of, and for this community when he said "the voice of our complaint implies a vengeance." Such voices were the voices of 6 June. While Glover and others were busy at Newgate, Charlotte Gardiner, "a negro," marched with a mob ("among whom were two men with bells, and another with frying pan and tongs") to the house of Mr. Levarty, a publican, in St. Katherine's Lane, near Tower Hill. Charlotte Gardiner was a leader of this march, shouting encouragements ("Huzza, well done, my boys—knock it down, down with it"), and directions ("Bring more wood to the fire"), as well as taking two brass candle sticks from the dining room. She did not even attempt to defend herself at the Old Bailey, and on 4 July she was found guilty and sentenced to die. The following Tuesday she was hanged.[47]

John Glover was identified well enough at the Old Bailey for purpose of hanging. But for historical purposes, his identification, like that of the nameless millions of the African diaspora, is much more difficult. Yet there is evidence to suggest that he took his name from an early member of the Committee of Correspondence of Marblehead, Massachusetts, a General John Glover who raised an American military regiment in 1775 among the multi-ethnic mariners and fishermen of this important Atlantic port. The John Glover who helped to deliver Newgate was probably a captured prisoner from General Glover's regiment.[48]

The problem of identification arises again when we consider a second African-American, Benjamin Bowsey, a man who came as close as any to being the leader of the 6 June delivery. His voice was apparently exciting, encouraging, and capable of arousing indignation. He was among the group of thirty who first approached the prison, marching three abreast, armed with spokes, crows, and paving mattocks. Later, he was indicted on three bills, one for riot, one for pulling down Akerman's house, and one for breaking, entering, and stealing. Bowsey had been in England for six years, and had probably been a slave in Virginia.

Men like Glover and Bowsey and women like Gardiner arrived in growing numbers in London, where they found work as fiddlers, lovemakers, cooks, boxers, writers, and especially domestic servants, day laborers, and seamen. The overall coherence (learned on plantation and shipboard) of the African population posed a police problem in London where it was expressed in clubs for dance, music, eating, and drinking, or in knots of American runaways and London servants. John Fielding, the Chairman of the Westminster Quarter Sessions whose office was attacked during the riots, was some years earlier already alarmed at the growing immigration of this population. The plantocrats, he said,

> bring them to England as cheap servants having no
> right to wages; they no sooner arrive here than they

> put themselves on a footing with other servants,
> become intoxicated with liberty, grow refractory, and
> either by persuasion of others or from their own incli-
> nations, begin to expect wages according to their own
> opinion of their merits; and as there are already a
> great number of black men and women who made
> themselves troublesome and dangerous to the fami-
> lies who have brought them over as to get themselves
> discharged, these enter into societies and make it
> their business to corrupt and dissatisfy the mind of
> every black servant that comes to England.

The Afro-London community by the 1770s had began to fight for the freedom of a proletarian—mobility and money.[49] They continued the fight in attacking Newgate, one of the chief symbols of state power and repression, amid a war across the Atlantic that continued a discussion of popular rights inaugurated generations earlier by the Levellers and other radicals of the English Revolution.

CONCLUSION

BY LOOKING AT THE REVOLTS OF THE MANY-HEADED HYDRA — laborers black and white, Irish and English, free and enslaved, waged and unwaged—we can begin to see how the events of 1747, 1768, 1776, and 1780 were part of a broad cycle of rebellion in the eighteenth-century Atlantic world, in which continuities and connections informed a huge number and variety of popular struggles. A central theme in this cycle was the many-sided struggle against confinement—on ships, in workshops, in prisons, or even in empires—and the simultaneous search for autonomy. The circulation of working-class experience, especially certain forms of struggle, emerges as another theme, linking urban mobs, slave revolts, shipboard mutinies, agrarian risings, strikes, and prison riots, and the many different kinds of workers who made them—sailors, slaves, spalpeens, coal-heavers, dockworkers, and others, many of whom occupied positions of strategic importance in the international division of labor. That much of this working-class experience circulated *to the eastward*, from American slave plantations, Irish commons, and Atlantic vessels, back to the streets of the metropolis, London, cannot be overemphasized. This interchange within a predominantly urban, portside proletariat took place over, around, beneath, and frequently against the artisans and craftsmen who are generally credited with creating the early working-class movement.

What consciousness pertained to this motley proletariat? We do not have a complete or definite answer to this question, although it is important that some points be raised despite the fact that we have in this segment of our longer study only concerned ourselves with slaves and maritime wage-workers. First, we need to emphasize that consciousness arose from experience. The struggle against confinement led to a consciousness of freedom, which was in turn transformed into the revolutionary discussion of human rights. The experience of cooperation on plantation, ship, and waterfront led to a consciousness of interdependence and produced perforce new means of communication in language, music, and sign. Second, the various workers we have considered here brought with them the traditions of their own histories, which were preserved and amplified within the Atlantic world of the eighteenth century. Thus, pan-Africanism originated in Africa, not on the slavers, and became a potent Atlantic force by the 1780s. The antinomian and anti-authoritarian traditions of self-government, a heritage of the English Revolution of the 1640s, was preserved and expanded in North America. Finally, a third point arises from our investigation. At its most dynamic the eighteenth-century proletariat was often ahead of any fixed consciousness. The changes of geography, language, climate, and relations of family and production were so volatile and sudden that consciousness had to be characterized by a celerity of thought that may be difficult to comprehend to those whose experience has been steadier.

We hope our conclusions will be of interest to all those who think that a working class did not exist in the eighteenth century (before the rise of the factory system), and to all those whose conceptions of nation, race, and ethnicity have obscured both a field of force in which all history unfolds and a popular world of vital cooperation and accomplishment. The many heads of the transatlantic hydra may be likened to a popular drink of the eighteenth century called "All Nations," a compound of all the different spirits sold in a dram shop, collected in a single vessel into which the dregs and drainings of all the bottles and pots had been emptied.[50] We shall have to study all nations to understand the beast who has called forth such great violence, physical and conceptual, down through the ages.

REFERENCES

1 Quotation in Daniel Horsmanden, *The New York Conspiracy* ed. Thomas J. Davis (Boston: Beacon Press, 1971), 309. See Peter Linebaugh, "A Letter to Boston's 'Radical Americans' from a 'Loose and Disorderly' New Yorker, Autumn 1770," *Midnight Notes*, 4 (1983) and T.J. Davis, *Rumor of Revolt: The "Great Negro Plot" in Colonial New York* (New York: Free Press, 1985).

2 Davis, *Rumor of Revolt*, 194.

3 This article, which represents work-in-progress, is a continuation of themes we first struck in Marcus Rediker, "Good Hands, Stout Heart, and Fast Feet: The History and Culture of Working People in Early America," and Peter Linebaugh, "All the Atlantic Mountains Shook," both in Geoff Eley and William Hunt (eds.), *Reviving the English Revolution: Reflections and Elaborations on the Work of Christopher Hill* (London: Verso, 1988). Richard Price, *To Slay the Hydra: Dutch Colonial Perspectives on the Saramaka Wars* (Ann Arbor: Karoma, 1983), 15, quotes Mauricius. Our work has received much encouragement from Christopher Hill, whose essay, "The Many-Headed Monster," in *Change and Continuity in 17th-Century England* (Cambridge, Mass.: Harvard University Press, 1975), we particularly value.

4 Quoted in Hilary Beckles, *Black Rebellion in Barbadoes: The Struggle Against Slavery, 1627-1838* (Bridgetown, Barbados: Antilles Publications, 1984), p. 107.

5 The ideological fabrication and the essentially racist project represented by the "Classical Age" is elaborated in wonderfully exact scholarly thoroughness by Martin Bernal, *Black Athena: The Afroasiatic Roots of Classical Civilization*, Volume I: *The Fabrication of Ancient Greece 1785-1985* (New Brunswick, N.J.: Rutgers University Press, 1987).

6 These paragraphs, as well as those that follow, owe much to our previous work, viz., Marcus Rediker, *Between the Devil and the Deep Blue Sea: Merchant Seamen, Pirates, and the Anglo-American Maritime World, 1700-1750* (Cambridge: Cambridge University Press, 1987), and Peter Linebaugh, *The London Hanged: Crime and Civil Society in the 18th Century; Or, History By the Neck* (London: Penguin, 1991). The discussions in these books of the class relations of work, among seamen, coalheavers, and many others, are indispensable background to all that follows in this article.

7 Peter H. Wood, "'Taking Care of Business' in Revolutionary South Carolina: Republicanism and the Slave Society," in Jeffrey J. Crow and Larry E. Tise (eds.), *The Southern Experience in the American Revolution* (Chapel Hill: University of North Carolina Press, 1978), 276. Jesse Lemisch, "Jack Tar in the Streets: Merchant Seamen in the Politics of Revolutionary America," *William and Mary Quarterly*, 3rd series, 25 (1968), 371-407.

8 Gary B. Nash, *The Urban Crucible: Social Change, Political Consciousness, and the Origins of the American Revolution* (Cambridge, Mass.: Harvard University Press, 1979), 221, 222; John Lax and William Pencak, "The Knowles Riot and the Crisis of the 1740s in Massachusetts," *Perspectives in American History* 19 (1976), 166-167; Dora Mae Clark, "The Impressment of Seamen in the American Colonies," *Essays in Colonial History Presented to Charles McLean Andrews by his Students* (New Haven: Yale University Press, 1931), 217; Carl Bridenbaugh, *Cities in Revolt: Urban Life in America, 1743-1776* (New York: Capricorn Books, 1955), 115; Richard Pares, "The Manning of the Navy in the West Indies, 1702-1763," Royal Historical Society *Transactions* 20 (1937), 48-49).

9 Knowles quoted in Lax and Pencak, "Knowles Riot," 182, 186; emphasis added. On the relationship between "liberty" and "right," see Lemisch, "Jack Tar in the Streets," 400.

10 See Lax and Pencak, "Knowles Riot," 205, 214; Rediker, *Between the Devil and the Deep Blue Sea*, 251-253. The interpretation offered here, stressing the ways in which the seamen's actions generated revolutionary ideology, is exactly the opposite of that proposed by Bernard Bailyn, who sees the ideas of revolutionary movement as giving meaning to the seamen's "diffuse and indeliberate anti-authoritarianism." See his *Pamphlets of the American Revolution* (Cambridge, Mass.: Belknap Press of Harvard University Press, 1965), 583.

11 Rediker, *Between the Devil and the Deep Blue Sea*, ch. 5.

12 David Barry Gaspar, *Bondmen and Rebels: A Study of Master-Slave Relations in Antigua, with Implications for Colonial British America* (Baltimore: The John Hopkins University Press, 1985) 37, 210; Michael Craton, *Testing the Chains: Resistance to Slavery in the British West Indies* (Ithaca: Cornell University Press, 1982), 335-339; Peter H. Wood, *Black Majority: Negroes in Colonial South Carolina from 1670 through the Stono Rebellion* (New York: Norton, 1974); Davis, *Rumor of Revolt*, 158.

13 See Wood, "Taking Care of Business," 276, and his more recent "'The Dream Deferred': Black Freedom Struggles on the Eve of White Independence," in Gary Y. Okihiro, ed., *In Resistance: Studies in African, Caribbean, and Afro-American History* (Amherst, Mass.: University of Massachusetts Press, 1986), 170, 172-173, 174-175; Jeffrey J. Crow, "Slave Rebelliousness and Social Conflict in North Carolina, 1775 to 1802," *WMQ* 3rd ser. 37(1980), 85-86; Herbert Aptheker, *American Negro Slave Revolts* (New York: Columbia University Press, 1943), 87, 200-202.

14 Gary B. Nash, *Forging Freedom: The Formation of Philadelphia's Black Community, 1720-1840* (Cambridge, Mass.: Harvard University Press, 1988), 72; Benjamin Quarles, *The Negro in the American Revolution* (Chapel Hill: University of North Carolina Press, 1961), 84; Lemisch, "Jack Tar in the Streets," 375. For the percentages of black workers in the maritime sector in the early nineteenth century see Shane White, "'We Dwell in Safety and Pursue Our Honest Callings': Free Blacks in New

York City, 1783-1810," *Journal of American History* 75 (1988), 453-454; Ira Dye, "Early American Merchant Seafarers," *Proceedings of the American Philosophical Society* 120 (1976), 358. On South Carolina, see Philip D. Morgan, "Black Life in Eighteenth-Century Charleston," *Perspectives in American History* New ser., 1 (1984), 200; Wood, "Taking Care of Business," 276; Crow, "Slave Rebelliousness," 85. On the black seamen in the West Indies, see Gaspar, *Bondmen and Rebels*, 109-111.

15 Wood, "The Dream Deferred," 168, 181. Wood argues that the cycle entered a new phase (to last until 1783) when Lord Dunmore made his famous proclamation (November 15, 1775) that offered freedom to any slave who would fight in the king's army (177).

16 It is important to note that early American mobs acted within relatively undeveloped civil societies that lacked police forces and usually lacked standing armies; local militias could not easily be mobilized against them, because militiamen were often part of the crowds. Urban mobs thus created enormous disequilibrium because there were so few other institutions or corporate groups to counterbalance them and guarantee social stability. Local authorities were too close to the action at hand, imperial authorities too far away. Crowds were, therefore, extremely powerful. They often succeeded in achieving their aims and usually managed to protect their own, which meant that individual members of the crowd were rarely arrested and prosecuted. Crowd activity itself was thus infrequently criminalized (even when it was condemned), a singular fact that makes it difficult for the historian to establish the precise social composition of early American crowds, as, for example, George Rude has done for crowds in England and France in the eighteenth century. (See, for example, his *Wilkes and Liberty: A Social Study of 1763-1774* [Oxford: Clarendon Press, 1962].) But such difficulties do not make it impossible to understand the role of sailors and slaves, for the power of the crowd insured that it would be the object of extensive commentary, if not the kind of direct legal analysis that would have come in the wake of repression.

17 Thomas Hutchinson, *The History of the Colony and Province of Massachusetts-Bay* ed. Lawrence Mayo Shaw (Cambridge, Mass.: Harvard University Press), vol. II, 332; Lemisch, "Jack Tar in the Streets," 386, 391; Bridenbaugh, *Cities in Revolt*, 309. For specific accounts of the riots, see *Newport Mercury* July 16, 1974 and June 10, 1765; *New York Gazette, Weekly Post-Boy*, July 12, 1764 and July 18, 1765; *Weyman's New York Gazette*, July 18, 1765.

18 Arthur Meier Schlesinger, "Political Mobs and the American Revolution," *Proceedings of the American Philosophical Society* 99(1955), 244; Bridenbaugh, *Cities in Revolt*, 313-314; Morgan, "Black Life," 233; Pauline Maier, "The Charleston Mob and the Evolution of Popular Politics in Revolutionary South Carolina, 1765-1784," *Perspectives in American History* 4 (1970), 176; Wood, "Taking Care of Business," 277.

19 Alfred F. Young, "English Plebeian Culture and Eighteenth-Century

American Radicalism," in Margaret Jacob and James Jacob, eds., *The Origins of Anglo-American Radicalism* (London: George Allen & Unwin, 1984), 193-194. See also Steven Rosswurm, *Arms, Country, and Class: The Philadelphia Militia and the "Lower Sort" during the American Revolution* (New Brunswick: Rutgers University Press, 1987), 32-33; Dirk Hoerder, *Crowd Action in Revolutionary Massachusetts, 1765-1780* (New York: Academic Press, 1977), 241. Gage quoted in Schlesinger, "Political Mobs," 246.

20 Lee R. Boyer, "Lobster Backs, Liberty Boys, and Laborers in the Streets: New York's Golden Hill and Nassau Street Riots," *New York Historical Society Quarterly* 57 (1973), 289-308; Hiller B. Zobel, *The Boston Massacre* (New York: Norton, 1970); L. Kinvin Wroth and Hiller B. Zobel, eds., *Legal Papers of John Adams* (Cambridge, Mass.: Belknap Press of Harvard University Press, 1965), vol. III, 266; Hoerder, *Crowd Action*, ch. 13; Rosswurm, *Arms, Country, and Class*, 46-48.

21 Bull quoted in Bridenbaugh, *Cities in Revolt*, 313-314; see also 114-115; Eric Foner, *Tom Paine and Revolutionary America* (New York: Oxford University Press, 1976), 54. Lemisch, "Jack Tar in the Streets," 391, Nash, *Forging Freedom*, 38-39, and Philip S. Foner, *Blacks in the American Revolution* (Westport, Conn.: Greenwood Press, 1975), 37- 38, are among the few historians who have noted the presence of African-Americans in revolutionary crowds. Others have not, perhaps because they distrusted some of these descriptions of "boys, sailors, and negroes" in colonial crowds, seeing them as self-serving efforts to protect well-to-do citizens who participated in mobs or as means to criticize mob activity by blaming it on the poorer parts of urban society. This seems to be the position of Dirk Hoerder, who admits that seamen and boys were common members of Boston crowds but argues that the presence of blacks was "negligible" (*Crowd Action*, 374). Sometimes the descriptions of crowds cannot be taken at face value, as when the Boston town meeting sought in 1747 to lay all blame upon "Foreign seamen, Servants, Negroes, and other Persons of Mean and Vile Condition" for the Knowles Riot, when in fact these groups could not have made up the "several thousand" who took part in the protest (even if these "Persons of Mean and Vile Condition" did in fact lead the riot, especially in its early stages). See the resolution of the Boston Town Meeting in *Boston News-Letter*, Dec. 17, 1747. Something similar was going on in John Adams's famous characterization of the mob involved in the Boston Massacre in 1770 quoted above. And yet other sources, written with less tendentious purposes, make it clear that such descriptions of various colonial crowds contained a strong element of truth.

22 Gary B. Nash, Billy G. Smith, and Dirk Hoerder, "Laboring Americans and the American Revolution," *Labor History* 24 (1983), 418, 435. (Nash, Smith, and Hoerder note that social structure varied by city as they delineate common occupational patterns.) See also Nash, *Urban Crucible*, 260, 320-321, and Sharon V. Salinger, *"To Serve Well and Faithfully": Labor*

and Indentured Servitude in Pennsylvania, 1682-1800 (Cambridge: Cambridge University Press, 1987), 101-102, epilogue; Foner, *Tom Paine*, 48-50; Rosswurm, *Arms, Country, and Class*, 37; Morgan, "Black Life," 206-207, 219; Davis, *Rumor of Revolt*, 81, 194, 248 (quotation of Horsmanden); Linebaugh, "A Letter to Boston's `Radical Americans'"; Gaspar, *Bondmen and Rebels*, 138, 204; Rediker, *Between the Devil and the Deep Blue Sea*, ch. 1; N.A.T. Hall, "Maritime Maroons: *Grand Marronage* from the Danish West Indies," *WMQ* 3rd ser. 42(1985), 491-492; Linebaugh and Rediker, "The Many-Headed Hydra," paper presented to the American Studies Association, 1988, 22.

23 Hermann Wellenreuther, "Rejoinder" to Nash, Smith, and Hoerder in "Labor in the Era of the American Revolution: An Exchange," *Labor History* 24 (1983), 442. Timothy quoted in Maier, "Charleston Mob," 181; Edward Countryman, *A People in Revolution: The American Revolution and Political Society in New York, 1760-1790* (Baltimore: Johns Hopkins University Press, 1981), 37, 45 (quotation).

24 Linebaugh, "A Letter to Boston's 'Radical Americans' "; William Godard quoted in Charles G. Steffen, *The Mechanics of Baltimore: Workers and Politics in the Age of Revolution, 1763-1812* (Urbana: University of Illinois Press, 1984), 73; Gouverneur Morris to Mr. Penn, May 20, 1774, in Peter Force, ed., *American Archives* 4th ser. (Washington, D.C., 1837), vol. I, 343; Governor William Bull of South Carolina, quoted in Maier, "Charleston Mob," 185; *Poor Richard, 1747* in Leonard W. Labaree, ed., *The Papers of Benjamin Franklin* (New Haven: Yale University Press, 1961), vol. III (1745-1750), 106.

25 Maier, "Charleston Mob," 181, 186, 188, and *idem*, "Popular Uprising and Civil Authority in Eighteenth-Century America," *William and Mary Quarterly* 3rd ser. 27(1970), 33-35; Hoerder, *Crowd Action*, 378-388. Gordon Wood notes that "once-fervent Whig leaders began to sound like the Tories of 1775" when confronted by the mobs, popular committees, and "People Out-of-Doors" in the 1780s. See his *The Creation of the American Republic, 1776-1787* (Chapel Hill: University of North Carolina Press 1969), 319-328, 326 (quotation).

26 Wroth and Zobel (eds.), *Legal Papers of John Adams*, vol. III, 269, and Kaplan, *The Black Presence in the Era of the American Revolution* (New York: New York Graphic Society, 1973), 8; Edward H. Richardson, *Standards and Colors of the American Revolution* (Philadelphia: University of Pennsylvania Press, 1982).

27 Zobel, *The Boston Massacre*, 192, 199.

28 This section depends on chapter nine of *The London Hanged*, "If You Plead for Your Life, Plead in Irish." W.E.H. Lecky, *A History of Ireland in the Eighteenth Century* (London, 1893) is the best traditional account, but it should be checked against modern scholarship summarized in Kerby A. Miller, *Emigrants and Exiles: Ireland and the Irish Exodus to North America* (New York: Oxford University Press, 1985). This section is indebt-

ed to Daniel Corkery, *The Hidden Ireland: A Study of Gaelic Munster in the 18th Century*, (Dublin, 1925), which describes what we think is unique, viz., aristocratic verse forms applied to a proletarian experience whose consequent feeling—nostalgia—has been so successfully exploited by bourgeois nationalism on both sides of the water.

29 Lecky, *History of Ireland*, vol. II, 226. Richard Musgrave writes that the Whiteboy movement began around 1759; see his *Memoirs of the Different Rebellions in Ireland* (Dublin, 1802, 3rd ed.), vol. I, 36-54. But most modern historians agree that the Whiteboys first appeared in 1761. Although their movement waned by 1765, their name lived on to describe a variety of agrarian movements throughout the 1780s and well into the nineteenth century. The best modern studies are Maurine Wall, "The Whiteboys," in Desmond T. Williams, ed., *Secret Societies in Ireland* (Gill and Macmillan: Dublin, 1973), 13-25 and especially James S. Donnelly, Jr., "The Whiteboy Movement, 1761-5," *Irish Historical Studies* 21 (1978-9), 21-54. Lecky's pages on the Whiteboys are especially valuable because they preceded the destruction of the Castle archives in 1916; see also Miller, *Emigrants and Exiles*, 61-67. M.R. Beames, *Peasants and Power: Whiteboy Movements and their Control in Pre-Famine Ireland* (New York, 1983), provides a useful study of the Whiteboy movements of the nineteenth century. Elsewhere we have discussed the Irish-African connection as it appeared in the seventeenth-century Caribbean. That experience only grew with the momentus migrations of the eighteenth century, and it spread to as yet unstudied areas in Ireland and in West Africa. We think that it was a major development as the two societies had much in common—a pastoral economy, the relative absence of a commercial sector, the predominance of large kinship groupings as the social basis of production, the absence of "individualism," and the emphasis upon collective mores, identities, music, and culture. These commonalities represented a basis for exchange when these two peoples found themselves occupying the most cooperative forms of eighteenth-century work—gang labor. See Linebaugh and Rediker, "Many-Headed Hydra."

30 Donnelly, "Whiteboy Movement," 26, 24, 34-35, 37-38, 39, 41-43; Beames, *Peasants and Power*, 33-34; "A Succinct Account of a Set of Miscreants in the Counties of *Waterford, Cork, Limerick*, and *Tipperary*, called *Bougheleen Bawins* (i.e. White Boys)," *The Gentleman's Magazine* 32 (1762), 182-183, in which is noted the capture of a man who "has been some time in the *French* service." Many thousands of Irishmen served in French armies in the century after 1691; see Linebaugh, *The London Hanged*, ch. 9.

31 T.W. Moody, et al., *A New History of Ireland* vol. VIII: *A Chronology of Irish History to 1976* (1982); J.A. Froude, *The English in Ireland in the 18th Century* (New York, 1874), vol. II, 25; Wall, "The Whiteboys," 16; Donnelly, "Whiteboy Movement," 28.

32 Lecky, *History of Ireland*, vol. II, 41-45; Wall, "Whiteboys," 19, 20. It is

worth noting that Sheehy was the only priest known to have been involved with the Whiteboys. The overwhelming majority of priests were strongly opposed, which, according to Maurine Wall, helps to explain the increasing popular intimidation of priests in the 1770s.

33 Wall, "Whiteboys," 18; James Connolly, *Labour in Irish History* (London: Bookmarks, 1987), 43. Richard Aston, chief justice of the Court of Common Pleas in Ireland, noted that "papist and protestant were promiscuously concerned" in the Whiteboy movement; see Donnelly, "Whiteboy Movement," 46.

34 Constantia Maxwell, *Dublin under the Georges, 1714-1830* (1936), 270; A.G.L. Shaw, *Convicts and Colonies: A Study of Penal Transportation from Great Britain to Australia and Other Parts of the British Empire* (1966), 173; James H. Huston, "An Investigation of the Inarticulate: Philadelphia's White Oaks," *William and Mary Quarterly* 3rd ser. 18 (1971); Thomas Prior, *A List of Absentees in Ireland* (Dublin, 1769), 3rd ed. The drought of 1765 and ensuing starvation in Ireland forced many to migrate to London and to America. See Donnelly, "Whiteboy Movement," 52-53.

35 Karl Marx, *Capital: A Critique of Political Economy* ed. Dona Torr (London, 1972), 315. T.S. Ashton, and Joseph Sykes, *The Coal Industry in the Eighteenth Century* (Manchester, 1964), 2nd edition.

36 T.S. Ashton, *Economic Fluctuations in England, 1700-1800* (1959), 181; William Beveridge, *et al.*, *Prices and Wages in England from the Twelfth to the Nineteenth Century*, vol. I, *Price Tables: Mercantile Era* (1939), 292; *Berrow's Worcester Journal*, 19 May 1768; *The Westminster Journal*, 14 May 1768; *Public Advertizer*, 14 May 1768.

37 "The Information of James Brown," *Sessions Papers*, Corporation of London Record Office, London, Bundle 1768.

38 *Berrow's Worcester Journal*, 12 May 1768; *The Public Advertizer*, 21 July 1768; "Memorials of a Dialogue betwixt several Seamen a certain Victualler & a S—l Master in the Late Riot," *Shelburne Papers*, vol. XCXXX, William L. Clements Library, University of Michigan.

39 *The Westminster Journal*, 16 July, 1768; *Berrow's Worcester Journal*, 23 June 1768, 14 July 1768; T.S. 11/818/2696, Public Record Office, London; Foote, *The Tailors; A Tragedy for Warm Weather* (1778), 31; Horace Walpole to Strafford, June 25 1768, in W.S. Lewis, *et al.*, eds., *Horace Walpole's Correspondence* (New Haven: Yale University Press, 1973), vol. 35, 324; see also vol. 23, 33; Donnelly, "Whiteboy Movement," 50.

40 It may be true, as John Rule has recently pointed out, that the verb "to strike" was already in circulation among the working class of London by 1765. This would not alter the accepted etymology of the term, its origins among the labors of seamen, nor would it lessen the importance of the events of 1768, which represented the greatest strike then known in Britain. See the *Oxford English Dictionary*, s.v. "strike," and the *Bulletin for the Society for the Study of Labour History* 54 (1989), 103.

[41] J. Paul de Castro, *The Gordon Riots* (1926), and Christopher Hibbert, *King Mob: The Story of Lord George Gordon and the Riots of 1780* (1958) are two good monographical introductions. They may be supplemented by the materials in John Stevenson, *Popular Disturbances in England, 1700-1870* (1979), Tony Hayter, *The Army and the Crowd in Mid-Georgian London* (1978), and George Rude, "The Gordon Riots: A Study of Rioters and their Victims," in his *Paris and London in the Eighteenth century* (New York: Viking Press, 1973), 268-292. The story as presented here draws upon the fuller treatment and the sources presented in Linebaugh, *The London Hanged.*

[42] *The Morning Post,* 9 June 1780.

[43] "London Prisoners," *Sessions Papers,* 1780, Corporation of London Record Office, London; *The Proceedings...of the Old Bailey,* 8 December 1779 and 14 April 1779; *The London Chronicle,* 6-8 June 1780.

[44] On the incidence of mutiny, see Arthur N. Gilbert, "The Nature of Mutiny in the British Navy in the Eighteenth Century," in Daniel M. Masterson, ed., *Naval History: The Sixth Symposium of the U.S. Naval Academy* (Wilmington, Del.: Scholarly Resources, Inc., 1987), 111-121.

[45] *The Proceedings,* 28 June 1780; Indictment Bills, Gaol Book, *Sessions Files,* vol. 28, June 1780, Corporation of London Record Office. See also Ottobah Cugoano, *Thoughts and Sentiments on the Evil and Wicked Traffic of the Slavery and Commerce of the Human Species* (1787), and Olaudah Equiano, *The Interesting Narrative of the Life of Olaudah Equiano, or Gustavus Vassa, the African, Written by Himself* (1789), both edited and republished in Francis D. Adams and Barry Sanders (eds.), *Three Black Writers in Eighteenth Century England* (Belmont, California, 1971). It should be noted that Glover, Bowsey, and Hyde (the sailor) represented half of those tried, presumed by the state to have been the ringleaders, for the attack on Newgate.

[46] Ignatius Sancho *Letters* (1782), republished in Adams and Sanders, *Three Black Writers* (Belmont, Ca., 1971).

[47] Cugoano, *Thoughts and Sentiments*, in Sanders, *Three Black Writers*, 106; Gradiner's activities reported in *The London Chronicle*, 4-8 July 1780. Discussions of the size of the London Black population may be found in Peter Fryer, *Staying Power: The History of Black People in Britain* (London: Pluto Press, 1984); James Walvin, *The Black Presence: A Documentary History of the Negro in England, 1555-1860* (New York, 1971); F.O. Shyllon, *Black People in Britain* (1977), and by the same author, *Black Slaves in Britain* (1974).

[48] In "A list of Massachusetts Soldiers and Sailors in the War of the Revolution" several "John" or "Jonathan" Glovers are listed as deserting or captured before 1780, and some are described as of dark complexion. For a fuller discussion of Glover's identity, and of Bowsey's, discussed below, see Linebaugh, *The London Hanged*, ch. 10.

49 Fryer, *Staying Power*, ch. 4; John Fielding, *Extracts from the Criminal Law* (1768); Frank Lorimer, "Black Slaves and English Liberty: a Reexamination of Racial Slavery in England," paper presented to the International Conference on the history of Blacks in Britain (1981), quoted in Fryer, *Staying Power*, 203, 541.

50 Francis Grose, *A Classical Dictionary of the Vulgar Tongue* (London, 1785).

"ANARCHY" IN THE AMERICAN REVOLUTION

David Porter

SEVERAL YEARS BEFORE PUBLISHING THE FIRST EXTENsive history of the American revolution, David Ramsay informed a friend, "This revolution has introduced so much anarchy that it will take half a century to eradicate the licentiousness of the people."[1] This brief statement alone reveals the problematic issue of "anarchy" in the American revolution. In using the "anarchy" label expansively, a huge range of reforms were conveniently, though incorrectly, lumped together by their opponents. As today, all who felt threatened by change found "anarchy," in a pejorative sense, a useful rhetorical threat. However, as the old order crumbled and before the new one could be fully raised in its place, *within* that vast array of change were genuine anarchical experiences and expressions which well deserved the name.[2]

Since populist social change—including actual anarchic phenomena—was a threat for Ramsay and other elite republicans, it had to be "eradicated" no matter how long it took. This became the political task of the new centralized system created in 1787, and the goal of those committed to "republican law and order" at state and local levels as well. Eradicating "licentiousness of the people" also became a task for the new order's cultural elite—including, like Ramsay, historians of the American revolution itself. In all of these dimensions—image, actuality, political repression and cultural censorship—the issue of "anarchy" in the American revolution continues to the present.

Derived from common religious and secular allusions during and after the English civil war of the mid-17th century, "anarchy" was a convenient Anglo-American epithet signifying the social chaos some perceived as the old order broke down. Hobbes, Locke and others described anarchy as a state of nature, which for the former was a state of "war of each against all," and for both, a condition preceding and motivating a socially-compacted hierarchical political order. The latter would supposedly preserve and enhance personal liberties impossible to maintain in the state of nature. Referred to as well in theories and histories of the Greeks and Romans, loosening the bonds of stable political order, it was thought, led potentially to "anarchy." That, in turn, would produce tyranny to counteract the inevitable violence and destruction involved.

Those who feared *any* increase of popular involvement in governance, as well as those who favored republican forms but feared direct democracy, both found "anarchy" a useful image to attack the credibility of advocates of greater change. In today's terms, the spectrum of those using this term pejoratively thus would (and does) include all from arch-conservatives to liberals and state socialists. Denouncing partisans of "anarchy" was as common then as attacks on "socialists" and "communists" in the twentieth century by those who feared a wide range of populist or social welfare reforms.

A British writer in 1775 denounced "those zealots of anarchy, who have denied to the Parliament of *Britain* the right of taxing the *American* Colonies."[3] A year earlier, American Tory Thomas B. Chandler criticized republicanism's refusal to respect established government, stating that "the bonds of society would be dissolved, the harmony of the world confounded, and the order of nature subverted."[4] In Pennsylvania, an editorial writer accused the Whig elite's efforts to substitute new political bodies for the colonial assembly as "setting up anarchy above order; it is the beginning of Republicanism."[5] Said American preacher-historian Jonathan Boucher in the late 1790s, the principles of the American revolutions were directed "clearly and literally against *authority*." They were destroying "not only all authority over us as it now exists, but any and all that it is possible to constitute."[6]

Republican elites so denounced, of course, had no intent of destroying hierarchy or social order generally. At best, they merely wished to substitute achievement for ascribed status (especially for those like themselves) to determine leadership of American society. John Adams, for example, wrote in 1775 of the need "to contrive some Method for the Colonies to glide insensibly, from under the old Government, into a peaceable and contented submission to new ones."[7] One year later he wrote, "There must be a Decency, and Respect, and Veneration introduced for Persons in Authority, of every Rank, or We are undone."[8] From this perspective, almost by definition, frontier areas were places where "all sorts of wickedness was carried on to excess, and there was no appearance of morality or regular order," where settlers thought themselves "beyond the arm of government and freed from the restraining influence of religion."[9] In effect, frontier conditions dramatized as well as anything the "dangers" of going beyond the elitist republican model. Alexander Hamilton claimed that when the people were "loosened from their attachment to ancient establishments," they were likely "to grow giddy" and "more or less to run into anarchy."[10] As time went on, republican elitists argued for stronger central authority, claiming, as did Washington in 1783, that "anarchy and confusion" would result if this were not done,[11] a view echoed by Hamilton's *Federalist No. 15* which stated that the proposed federal constitution would "rescue us from impending anarchy."

As the revolution produced populist initiatives from below, republican elites who had sought to channel such energies toward merely a break from England in turn denounced grassroots challenges in familiar terms. As early as 1775, the Albany, New York Committee of Safety declared that courts should continue to operate and in the King's name, because otherwise the country would be reduced to "anarchy and confusion."[12] In 1777, "Patriot" conservatives claimed that the 1776 "radical" Pennsylvania constitution they bitterly opposed was inadequate to counter the British threat to Philadelphia; therefore, the Continental Congress would have to interfere to save the city and state from anarchy and ruin.[13] In 1787, Benjamin Rush insisted that the common republican phrase of "popular sovereignty" properly meant only that all power is derived from, not literally seated in the people. "They possess it only on the days of their elections. After this, it is the property of their rulers, nor can they exercise it or reserve it, unless it is abused."[14] By 1784, Samuel Adams, earlier "radical" leader of the subversive Boston Committee of Correspondence, denounced "popular Committees and County Conventions" as "not only useless but dangerous" for they would "bring Legislatures to Contempt and Dissolution."[15] The demand for popular review of all legislation and potential annulling of that which was disapproved seemed to one Pennsylvania republican in 1784 as leading "to anarchy and confusion," tending "to dissolve and render nugatory every civil compact."[16]

Major upheavals from below, as the Shays Rebellion in Massachusetts (1786-87) and the Whiskey Rebellion throughout the western Appalachian frontier (early 1790s), caused the greatest alarm yet. A Boston town meeting in 1786 declared that a "state of anarchy is to be dreaded above all other calamities because there is no evil which it does not involve."17 In the critical month of February 1787, George Washington wrote Henry Knox:

If government shrinks, or is unable to enforce its laws; fresh manoeuvres will be displayed by the insurgents, anarchy and confusion must prevail, and every thing will be turned topsy turvey in that State; where it is not probable the mischiefs will terminate. . . . After what I have seen, or rather after what I have heard, I shall be surprized at nothing; for if three years [ago] any person had told me that at this day, I should see a formidable rebellion against the laws and constitutions of our own making as now appears I should have thought him a bedlamite, a fit subject for a mad house.18

LATER FRONTIER REVOLT OVER THE EXCISE TAX AND OTHER issues brought denunciations of "the busy and relentless sons of anarchy" and "vipers who would overturn all order, government and laws," as well as proclamations that "liberty is order" and "liberty . . . is reason."19

Occasionally in this era, writers acknowledged anarchy or pure direct democracy as a positive ideal. In this model, all citizens could meet together to personally and directly make decisions about their own public affairs. Said Thomas Paine: "Simple Democracy [is] society governing itself without the aid of secondary means." "In this first parliament every man, by natural right, will have a seat."20 Similarly, Thomas Jefferson privately stated, "I am convinced that those societies (as the Indians) which live without government enjoy in their general mass an infinitely greater degree of happiness than those who live under European governments."21 Examples of this model were cited among contemporary Native Americans, New England towns, ancient Athens and first millenium Saxons of Germany and England. But Paine, Jefferson and others dismissed their direct relevance because of inadequate "public virtue" (a self-restraining communitarian consciousness) and the larger scale of the new American republics. However slight, they argued, some degree of coercive legislation was necessary and some authority had to be given to elected representatives.

Since critics used the negative image of "anarchy" so generously, we should approach skeptically the phenomena so described. Despite such caution, however, anarchic examples appeared everywhere.

In some cases, an unintentional political void resulted when statist forms were not yet extended (as on the various frontiers) or were too weak to play a significant role. In such contexts, *de facto* forms of direct self-government emerged locally on their own. Of course, it could be argued, as it was at the time, that such areas attracted people who wanted no "Landlord or Law" anyway.[22] A second context for "anarchy" was in the original wave of anti-British revolution, as various forms of direct action and "dual power" emerged in the broad coalition of resistance and challenge to imperial structures. Popular initiatives from below were encouraged to develop needed momentum and legitimacy for the drive to independence. Roughly, this period extended from the late 1760s to 1776.

Gradually, republican elites began to consolidate personal privilege in alternative "dual power" structures which increasingly supplanted the old order. In response, large numbers of grassroots forces throughout the ex-colonies developed new forms of resistance and new political alternatives to challenge these original structures and "leaders" of "dual power." Often, as with enslaved Africans and tenants, they already knew the oppressive intent of republican elites from before the revolution. For many others, the first years of revolutionary experience taught that the "freedom" agenda of their elite or *arriviste* partners excluded the grassroots level, that a new social hierarchy would replace the old.[23] This third context of "anarchy" extended from roughly the early 1770s through the end of the century. It overlapped but was far from synonymous with Anti-Federalist opposition to the new U.S. constitution and with the Democratic-Republican movement of the 1790s.

To mention specific examples from each of these contexts is only illustrative. Anarchic energy filled the landscape. In Philadelphia in 1776, a void appeared as the old proprietary regime collapsed and before new structures had taken its place. As the son of the colonial chief justice described, "The Law business having languished from March to June totally stopt then, all the Courts declining to proceed; the Magistracy of the City also ceased & we have ever since continued without Justice in a State of nature."[24] In western Massachusetts, local communities forcibly closed the courts for at least six years, from 1774 on, and various towns described themselves as having returned to the "state of nature" as the colonial order was overthrown and before new state government was constitutionally legitimized.[25] In local meetings, residents explicitly pledged to avoid legal disputes and, if necessary, to resolve any conflicts through local extra-legal arbitration.26

Another void appeared when two competing regimes fought for the same territory and local residents refused to accept either. In the district southwest of Pittsburgh claimed by both Virginia and Pennsylvania, large numbers refused to join General George Rogers Clark's Virginia militia expedition in 1781, while at the same time Pennsylvania authority was too weak to establish a separate force of its own.27 Similar situations developed in western North Carolina (the state regime vs. authorities for a proposed state of Franklin), in Vermont (New York vs. New Hampshire), in the Wyoming Valley of Pennsylvania (Connecticut vs. Pennsylvania), and in both Carolinas, Delaware and Georgia (as "Loyalist" and "Patriot" forces fought to control each territory).

Throughout the frontier at this time, whether an area was obtained or not earlier by treaty with Native Americans, white settlers commonly moved in without purchase. "Improvement rights" became the basis for claims against any competitors—armed or not with official documents. Obviously, where unpurchased Native American land was concerned, anarchic behavior by white settlers occurred in a "void" of *white* government, not in an absence of territorial claims by societies generally. (Of course, even land "purchases" by white governments were obtained under duress.) This overall expansionist pressure and the frequently horrendous violence of white frontier settlers toward Native Americans fundamentally contradicted anarchic "egalitarian" and "communitarian solidarity" orientations *within* the white frontier in this period generally. In 1774, Iroquois chiefs confronted British Indian Superintendent Sir William Johnson about murders recently committed by the "lawless people" of the Pennsylvania-Virginia frontier. They told him, "We are sorry to observe to you that your people are as ungovernable, or rather more so, than ours."28

Of course, it was also no secret to Native Americans that when white *governments* chose to do so (as in "Lord Dunmore's War," the very frontier clash which caused the Iroquois critique), they often launched far more efficient genocide than the white frontier settlers themselves. Over time, Native Americans came to understand that British colonial and American "revolutionary" state regimes were committed, at least over the long range, to white territorial expansion at whatever cost. In this context, both governments and white settlers assumed that Native Americans lived in a "state of nature." As such, they were not seen as genuine participants in the European model of legal relations. Supposed treaty purchases and boundaries were viewed as mere temporary pragmatic expedients to avoid more costly wars of conquest. By contrast, when white settlers on the frontier argued that they themselves "entered the state of nature and created property in advance of the social compact,"[29] in many cases, such rights later gained *de facto* acceptance by colonial and state courts. At the least, they were defended by settlers through violent or non-violent resistance—with little moral appreciation of the fact that Native Americans were in the same "extra-legal" defensive position. Among and between whites on the frontier, peer pressure by itself resolved many disputes. In some areas, as in central and possibly southwestern Pennsylvania, in Tennessee, Kentucky, and North Carolina, settlers established more regular, but extra-legal processes of grassroots arbitration based on local community standards.[30] In terms of relations with colonial and state governments, the direct action of 18th century white frontier settlers had much in common with presentday illegal peasant occupiers of land in Latin America or city squatters in abandoned buildings of North America and Europe. Only later, did formal judicial structures and processes of the Eastern establishment attempt to define the frontier context by legalistic form.

From 1774 until 1780, for the ex-colonies as a whole, *no* central coercive government replaced the old authority of the Crown. Even during the 1780s, the finally-ratified Articles of Confederation established only the loosest of central regimes—with no enforcement machinery of its own.

From the late 1760s, a broad anti-imperial movement gradually developed throughout the colonies, incorporating activists from all social classes (except colonial officials themselves) and with demands ranging from immediate economic grievances to, eventually, separation from Britain itself. Various forms of grassroots, extra-legal, anarchic direct action emerged during the early period—from the familiar Boston Tea Party to social expropriation of Tory property and price freezes imposed on merchants by angry crowds of women.[31] While nominally the thirteen colonies remained for a time under British authority, in fact there emerged a classic example of "dual power." Local "committees of correspondence" and "committees of public safety" gained increasing allegiance and created alternative political networks within and between colonies, eventually culminating in a

"Continental Congress" which was totally illegitimate by terms of the old system. Apparently, both Tory and Whig elites were amazed that mere recommendations from these unofficial bodies were voluntarily followed as fully as they were.[32]

Of course, there is nothing necessarily anarchic about "dual power" and "direct action" in themselves. Hierarchical, coercive processes and individual power mongers can thrive through "alternative" power networks as much as in official state institutions. The federal constitutional convention and the subsequent extra-legal alteration of the then-existing confederation are classic illustrations of "dual power" with conservative intent. So, also, in Pennsylvania, was the defiant refusal of conservative Whig lawyers to practice and officials to hand over records to new appointees of the "radical" 1776 regime.[33] However, because they initially delegitimize official authority and usually require significant grassroots involvement, contexts of "dual power" with egalitarian goals can have substantial anarchic effects.

In the American revolution, once formerly apolitical people "had seen and even taken part in hounding, humiliating, perhaps killing men known to them as social superiors, they could not easily reacquire the unthinking respect for wealth and status that underpinned the old order."[34] Likewise, rigid sex roles for women quickly broke down in army encampments and battlefields as did previous domestic deference when women assumed greater decisionmaking responsibility in the absence of males.[35] The very presence and spread of an alternative power network, in this case, caused established power structures to become all the more paralyzed, thus offering more autonomous space in general for a wealth of alternatives from below.

The 1776 Congressional Declaration of Independence merely stated the "Patriot" elite's "official" validation of already-changed consciousness and practice throughout the colonies. From that point on, aside from British officials and Loyalist followers, the pretense of central government with powers of its own dissolved into thirteen politically independent societies. Within some of the latter, there was *no* commonly-recognized statewide governmental regime for years to come.

The late 1760s to the mid-1780s was a time of great solidarity within the movement. Like the mid-1960s for many today, it was the period frequently recalled later as the high point of egalitarian ideals.[36] Nevertheless, it was also a time when elites and power-seek-ers increasingly dominated revolutionary committees and when extra-legal "people-out-of-doors" movements became increasingly "regularized" and "legitimized" and sometimes far more intrusive than the previous colonial regime. As one historian described it, "The more moderate men in the emerging leadership learned quickly enough to use the devices and the language of revolution in order to achieve their own goal of keeping things under control."[37]

The early hierarchical, coercive intent of coopted "revolutionary" structures revealed itself sometimes most explicitly. In November 1775, the extra-legal North Carolina provincial congress met simultaneously in the same room with the official colonial legislature—a feat possible since it was largely the same men in each![38] In the same year, even the "ultraradical" Committee of Privates in 1775 in Philadelphia proclaimed that all should submit to every law.[39]

As the alternative power network of committees and congresses thus clarified its own orientation and began to become "official" state and local regimes, many at the grassroots level—now with a more wary and sophisticated perspective—began launching a new wave of anarchic energy and demands. A second wave of anarchic resistance was needed to protect the revolution from hierarchical "revolutionaries." In 1776, when an Albany County Committee of Safety ignored grassroots calls to place notorious royalists under restraint, members were made to run a gauntlet of local citizens in order to finally get the message.[40] Several months earlier, the same committee was told that if demands over economic grievances were not immediately answered, "we shall look upon it that you will not consider our oppression; and if we find that you will not vindicate our doleful Circumstances, we will without doubt be obliged to remove these ruinous circumstances ourselves."[41] In January 1781, unpaid regular forces of the Pennsylvania line finally mutinied when "revolutionary" officers refused to tell them of the terms of their enlistment while offering to pay those who would re-enlist.[42]

In contexts of political void or where slaveowners led state and local "revolutionary" regimes, revolts and the flight of thousands of enslaved Africans from their owners (mainly to the British) were a major anarchic force throughout this period. This, in turn, brought reactionary measures by supposed "revolutionary" regimes. George Washington, as early as October 1775, banned Afro-Americans from the "army of the revolution" to prevent it from becoming a "refuge of freedom" for runaways.[43] Yet frequently it was in areas of greatest slave population that the "revolutionary" hold was weakest. In St. Mary's County, Maryland, for example, a local colonel complained that patriot forces were poorly armed, "Negroes . . . in the lower part of the county are beginning to be very insolent," and militia men were threatening to shoot some of their officers. "It really begins to be high time to put our government in full force and some examples made or nothing but anarchy and destruction must ensue."[44] Similarly, pervasive tenant Loyalism and active defiance of landlord "revolutionaries" in the Hudson Valley were only logical extensions of that area's tenant revolts of prior decades. Surely, these liberatory attitudes and actions of tenants and enslaved Africans contributed much to the anarchic climate of this period generally.

Confronting supposed "revolutionary" state governments in each of the thirteen new republics—the transformed "dual power" alternative committees and congresses of the early 1770s—new extra-legal local committees and county conventions appeared, aiming to articulate grassroots grievances and, in some cases, to openly defy official "revolutionary" authorities. Most spectacular was Shays' Rebellion in Massachusetts in the mid-1780s. In western and central sections of that state, the great majority of people supported revolt against a Boston regime completely insensitive to the economic and judicial plight of small farmer debtors. Spontaneously-organized armed troops of men closed county courts (as they had in the 1770s), liberated jailhouses and came near to marching on Boston itself to burn that seat of oppression to the ground. Similar armed defiance occurred simultaneously in New Hampshire, Virginia, North Carolina, Georgia and elsewhere.

Those creating new government structures to replace the old usually tried more "democratic" formulas to gain popular legitimacy without seriously empowering those from below. Representation and suffrage were generally enlarged. The more "radical" the dominant politicians in each state, the more likely were other reforms such as mandatory rotation of office, short terms, unicameral legislatures, binding instructions on legislators from local constituents, weak executives, written constitutions and separate conventions to write these constitutions.

To the extent that such measures merely tried to legitimize statist structures, they had nothing to do with anarchy. But when decentralization, circulation of leaders, and greater accountability were forced on the new governing elite by intense grassroots pressure *as part of* an overall climate where local citizens disobeyed laws they didn't agree with anyway, such a model began to resemble confederal organizations which emerged in the historical anarchist movement of the past century.[45] In such an atmosphere, ideological conflicts over whether large scale communities required representation instead of deliberation by all, whether majorities could coerce minorities or whether governments had the right to coerce at all boiled down to a basic struggle for autonomous, self-governing political space. In the voluntaristic political context favored by many, legislative bodies at every level, with direct participation or representation, could be used simply to communicate and freely coordinate in meeting common needs. Indeed, this was the nature of both the early committees of correspondence and the continental congress.

Apparently in the spirit of moving toward that model, New York City's Body of Mechanics in early 1776 told the provincial congress that any constitution should be ratified by the people, that deputies to committees and congresses should be recallable whenever their constituencies saw fit and that the people generally should retain "an uncontrolled power to alter the constitution in the same manner that it shall have been received."[46] Likewise, the Virginia freeholders of Albemarle County declared that the power of "approving, or disapproving, their own laws . . . ought forever to remain with the whole body of the people."[47] As one historian suggested, "the intensity of a Whig's radicalism was measured not by his confidence in the representatives of the people but by his suspicion of them. Those in 1776 who voiced fears of the representative bodies' forming interests separate from those of the people constituted the most alienated and radical groups in America."[48] This movement toward "extreme actuality of representation," combined with rejection of the coercive claim of law, was a movement toward anarchical social organization.

It is in this particular sense that alarmist statements about the threat of "anarchy" from below were accurate. Whatever their distortion in tending to link all radical reforms of government, grassroots activism and disdain for the law in one package of imminent "anarchy," elites and power-mongers at national, state and local levels were increasingly anxious to repress populist currents. The 1787 federal constitution was precisely designed to replace "the present anarchical confusion prevailing almost everywhere" and to protect "the worthy against the licentious."[49] Though most likely opposed by a majority of the population, the new system was ratified through conventions that were chosen by limited electorates and subjected to intense political pressures. Many accepted it not only because of its skilled political guides and propaganda spin-doctors, but also because most Anti-Federalist writers and politicians themselves conceded a need for stronger central government generally and, more basically, sided with hierarchical politics instead of grassroots egalitarianism.

When anarchic forces and experiments re-emerged so defiantly in the Whiskey Rebellion despite this constitutional capstone of supposed "popular sovereignty," Washington, Hamilton and other centralizers reveled at the chance to suppress such "levelling" tendencies once and for all. Large numbers resisted militia mobilizations to aid the federal regime.[50] But, once again, centralizers had the willing assistance of elites at state and local levels who were incorrigibly wedded to statist principles. In his charge to a Washington County, Pennsylvania grand jury in December 1794, for example, state district judge Alexander Addison elaborated with typical Hobbesian imagery. If any part of a state, he said, decides to evade laws it doesn't like, then all will claim such rights. "Each man in the State will be free from all law but his own will. Government and society are then destroyed, anarchy is established, and the wicked and the strong, like savages and wild beasts, prey on the whole and on one another."[51]

The relative repressive success of statism was due to other factors as well. Most white frontier settlers of this period apparently refused to admit any commonality with anarchist political models of their own Native American neighbors—let alone, for many, any commonality with Native Americans whatsoever. Yet a genuine cross-racial anarchic political alliance and confederation in that region could well have produced and defended a prosperous anarchist culture and political society—which, of course, would also have changed the course of world history.

White racism was, however, too deep. In itself, this fundamental ideological contradiction prevented any growth and consolidation of longer-range anarchic communities out of America's revolutionary context. To the point, in late 1786 the Confederation Congress authorized money to militarily repress Shays' Rebellion under the "acceptable" guise of an anti-Indian campaign. British forces actively encouraged slave revolts and promised freedom to those who would flee to British lines, thus increasing reactionary, hierarchical tendencies among local white "revolutionary" regimes. Britain also encouraged aggrieved Native Americans to attack the white frontier, causing settlers to demand greater military presence—obviously antithetical to a genuine anarchist agenda.

To the extent that most women were discouraged from participating in public "revolutionary" activity, emerging anarchic formations were deprived of those energies and ideas women could have contributed as well. The inherent rationale for hierarchical power and privilege in racism and sexism alike fundamentally contradicted that anarchic logic emerging through experience in other realms. It opened the doors for statist forces to appeal directly and analogically to many who were contrarily inclined.

Statist arguments and appeals also gained strength because of the fears and demands of war—in the East and on the Appalachian frontier. As every government instinctively knows, military "threats" from "enemies" help to legitimize greater central power.[52] Even the Spanish anarchist movement, the strongest movement ever in the West committed to anarchist principles, organizationally succumbed to "crisis" logic in the civil war and revolution of the 1930s—with significant negative impact on movement morale and success.

A lack of coherent positive vision also diminished the longer-range potential for anarchic tendencies of the American revolution. Such images could have articulated more forcefully and convincingly the gut-level anarchic emotions and behavior of the day[53] and could have allowed anarchic forces in one area to communicate and coordinate with each other, as had the earlier movement against the British.[54] Elite claims (then as now) that the people lacked adequate political "virtue" to indulge in greater democracy can be dismissed as self-serving rationales to preserve their own power. At the most, they are best viewed as self-fulfilling prophecies produced by their own discouragement of grassroots self-responsibility. Yet evolution toward anarchist society (then as now) does require the nurturing of anarchist culture. The basic issue is how to promote and maintain a libertarian, egalitarian, and communitarian consciousness beyond the first stage of revolution.

Apparent political repression of one generation's "anarchy" does not preclude others, of later generations, from finding inspiration and models from a grassroots collective memory. It is here where cultural censorship has played its role through Orwellian denials of anarchic experience and aspirations during the revolutionary era and through doublespeak glorification of elitist accomplishments—culminating in the federal constitution—as "democratic" triumphs of the people. If anarchic phenomena could not be totally ignored, traditionally historians have dismissed them in all too familiar terms.[55] For example, well-known contemporary historian Page Smith once wrote:

> In every frontier community, the most essential task was to impose form on the chaotic elements that swirled around and through it....Law was form and in the several decades preceding the American Revolution, the founders and first citizens of frontier communities almost invariably became lawyers, because by doing so they were able to bring the whole awesome weight of English law to bear on the intractable and anarchical forces of the frontier.[56]

For those open to seeing it, much of the American revolution becomes a massive grassroots experience of anarchic tendencies and models. Many aspects could inform presentday anarchist activity instead of lying in the shadows of the bewigged Republican elite in our American equivalent of Lenin's mausoleum.

However, most new historians still frame the revolutionary period in ways which divert evidence of anarchic intiatives to other purposes. In *The Creation of the American Republic*, which many regard as the single best interpretive volume on the politics of that era, Gordon Wood includes abundant data on anarchic experiments and ideals. In his hands, however, these become a mere foil by which to dramatize the creative synthetic brilliance of elite theory and politicking, which somehow led to America's republican experiment that "has succeeded so well."[57] Wood describes the radical Whig perspective as a "paranoic mistrust of power," the aspiration for power to be *seated in* rather than abstractly *derived from* the people as a "bastardization" of the principles of the revolution, the crisis of the revolutionary period as the "abuse of republican liberty"—"licentiousness leading to anarchy," and the emergence everywhere of new men in politics and business as a more rapid rising of "the scum" than most revolutionary leaders could anticipate.[58]

A different, but equally serious diversion is offered by Edward Countryman, researcher of some of the finest evidence on grassroots activity in this period. In his book on New York state, Countryman refers to Marx, Lenin and Trotsky as the best non-academic analysts he could find. One wonders how long the credibility of this authoritarian holy trinity would have survived when judged by the educated, suspicious eyes of Virginia slaves, Hudson Valley tenant farmers or backcountry Shays rebels. Countryman correctly suggests that "the measure of the conservatives' triumph [since the American revolution] is the extent to which we have forgotten those revolutionary qualities" of grassroots radical activism.[59] Yet, while liberal and radical scholars increasingly reveal for us the genuinely revolutionary content of that era, their own reinterpretation of the American revolution might suggest that "the measure of the statist liberal and radical academic triumph is the extent to which the anarchic perspective is forgotten."[60] To uncover the history that these writers have found and to channel it academically into alternative statist categories of their own is to repeat the travesty of original statist manipulations of alternative "dual power" in the revolution. It is to participate, in their own way, in a continuing effort to brainwash the American people.

When Ethan Allen told a New Yorker, "God Damn your Governour, Laws, King, Council & Assembly,"[61] these general political sentiments were not his alone. Nor were those of saddletree maker James Chambers, "a person of wicked and turbulent mind and of evil name, fame and reputation" in Washington, Pennsylvania when, two years after the repression of the Whiskey Rebellion, he accosted Judge Addison with: "Damn you and the law too, you damned little scotch son of a bitch, I disregard you both!"[62] We must give voice to that hostile armed gallery in Redstone, Pennsylvania as they watched coopting local elites compromising their autonomy with federal commissioners while Washington's troops were being organized to repress them in the same rebellion.[63] These were the passions of large numbers. To perceive again their political actions and aspirations is to rediscover serious large-scale anarchic tendencies as an important legacy of American political tradition. In fact, much of what historians have labelled as the immature, chaotic dimensions of the early American experience seems to demonstrate many of the tactics, strategies and aspirations of the modern anarchist movement.

REFERENCES

1 Quoted in Gordon S. Wood, *The Creation of the American Republic, 1776-1787* (N.Y.: W.W. Norton and Co., 1972), p. 403.

2 I distinguish in this essay between "anarchic" and "anarchist," between "tendencies toward anarchy" and "anarchism." The first term in each set describes strong anti-hierarchical dispositions and implications, often confined to just one or two realms (usually the political and economic) and fre-

quently with little self-conscious linkage to others beyond the immediate community. The second term describes a conscious ideological commitment to liberty, communitarian solidarity and full egalitarianism in a multiplicity of realms and with universal inclusion. In personal terms, one's own "anarchic" beliefs and behavior can often lead to consciously embracing "anarchism." Historically, the more narrow religious, economic, social or political "anarchic" leanings of particular social groups could help to produce a multi-realm self-proclaimed anarchist movement.

[3] Quoted in Wood, *op. cit.*, p. 349.

[4] Quoted in *Ibid.*, p. 66.

[5] Richard Alan Ryerson, *The Revolution is Now Begun: The Radical Committees of Philadelphia, 1765-1776* (Philadelphia: U. of Pa. Press, 1978), pp. 61, 63.

[6] Quoted in Wood, *op. cit.*, pp. 66-67.

[7] Quoted in *Ibid.*, p. 131.

[8] Quoted in *Ibid.*, p. 67.

[9] Comments of easterners John Wilkins and David McClure, quoted in Thomas P. Slaughter, *The Whiskey Rebellion* (N.Y.: Oxford U. Press, 1986), p. 64.

[10] Quoted in Wood, *op. cit.*, p. 67.

[11] Quoted in Merrill Jensen, *The New Nation: A History of the United States during the Confederation, 1781-1789* (N.Y.: Vintage Books, 1950), p. 408.

[12] Quoted in Edward Countryman, *A People in Revolution: The American Revolution and Political Society in New York, 1760-1790* (N.Y.: W.W. Norton and Co., 1989), p. 146.

[13] Robert L. Brunhouse, *The Counter-Revolution in Pennsylvania, 1776-1790* (Harrisburg: Pennsylvania Historical and Museum Commission, 1971), p. 30.

[14] Quoted in Wood, *op. cit.*, p. 374.

[15] Quoted in *Ibid.*, p. 327. Adams also strongly denounced the Shays and Whiskey Rebellions both.

[16] Quoted in *Ibid.*, p. 368.

[17] Quoted in Myron F. Wehtje, "Boston's Response to Disorder in the Commonwealth, 1783-1787," in Martin Kaufman, ed., *Shays' Rebellion: Selected Essays* (Westfield, Mass.: Westfield State College, 1987), p. 55.

[18] Washington 2/3/1787 letter to Henry Knox, reprinted in John C. Fitzpatrick, ed., *The Writings of George Washington*, vol. 29 (Washington: U.S. Government Printing Office, 1939), pp. 151-53.

[19] Slaughter, *op. cit.*, pp. 133-34.

[20] Thomas Paine, *"Common Sense," "The Rights of Man," and Other Essential Writings of Thomas Paine* (N.Y.: New American Library, 1984), pp. 242, 25.

[21] Jefferson 1/16/1787 letter to Edward Carrington, quoted in Richard K. Matthews, *The Radical Politics of Thomas Jefferson: A Revisionist View* (Lawrence, Ks.: University Press of Kansas, 1986), p. 63. Benjamin

Franklin described Native American society in similar "anarchic" terms (Staughton Lynd, *Intellectual Origins of American Radicalism* [Cambridge: Harvard U. Press, 1982], p. 85).

22 Sir William Johnson 11/24/1767 letter to General Thomas Gage, in E.B. O'Callaghan, ed., *The Documentary History of the State of New-York*, vol. II (Albany: Weed, Parsons & Co., 1849), p. 886.

23 This impetus for a second wave of anarchic behavior and perspective typifies revolutions elsewhere as well, as in France, Russia (1917-21), Spain, Algeria and presentday Eastern Europe, and appeared in 60s upheavals in the West as well.

24 Quoted in Thomas R. Meehan, "The Pennsylvania Supreme Court in the Law and Politics of the Commonwealth, 1776-1790," Ph.D. dissertation, U. of Wisconsin, 1960, pp. 124-5.

25 A good example is the May 1776 petition of Pittsfield, Mass., reprinted in Robert J. Taylor, ed., *Massachusetts: Colony to Commonwealth* (Chapel Hill: The U. of North Carolina Press, 1961), pp. 26-29.

26 Resolutions of Worcester County Convention of Committees of Correspondence, Sept. 20-21, 1774 ("U.S. Revolution, 1754-1928" manuscript collection, box 1, folder 4 (1774), American Antiquarian Society, Worcester, Mass.). An apparent model "compact" for grassroots conflict resolution "during the present anarchy" is found in the "Westborough, Mass. Papers, 1724-1879," "Miscellaneous Manuscripts" folder, A.A.S. Though it is not dated, it was probably produced in 1774, perhaps as a direct response to Worcester County conventions of that year.

27 Boyd Crumrine, ed., *History of Washington County, Pennsylvania* (Philadelphia: L.H. Everts & Co., 1882), pp. 94-101, 227-29.

28 Quoted in Francis Jennings, "The Indians' Revolution," in Alfred F. Young, ed., *The American Revolution* (DeKalb: Northern Illinois U. Press, 1976), p. 338.

29 Alan Taylor, "'A Kind of War': The Contest for Land on the Northeastern Frontier," *The William & Mary Quarterly*, January 1989, p. 7.

30 George D. Wolf, *The Fair Play Settlers of the West Branch Valley, 1769-1784* (Harrisburg: Pennsylvania Historical and Museum Commission, 1969); Malcolm J. Rohrbough, *The Trans-Appalachian Frontier* (N.Y.: Oxford U. Press, 1978), pp. 45, 54-55.

31 Edward Countryman describes women's action in Ulster County, N.Y., for example, while Linda K. Kerber cites the same phenomenon across the river in Poughkeepsie (Countryman, *op. cit.*, pp. 182-83, and Kerber, *Women of the Republic* [N.Y.: W.W. Norton and Co., 1986], pp. 43-44).

32 Wood, *op. cit.*, p. 317. This is not to deny, however, that such structures also used extra-legal coercion as well.

33 Brunhouse, *op. cit.*, pp. 36-37.

34 John Shy, "The Military Conflict As A Revolutionary War," in Stephen G. Kurtz and James H. Hutson, eds., *Essays on the American Revolution* (N.Y.: W.W. Norton and Co., 1973), p. 154.

[35] Joan Hoff Wilson, "The Illusion of Change: Women and the American Revolution," in Young, ed., *op. cit.*, p. 422; Kerber, *op. cit.*, pp. v, 8-12; Mary Beth Norton, *Liberty's Daughters: The Revolutionary Experience of American Women, 1750-1800* (Boston: Little, Brown & Co., 1980), pp. 195-96, 216-17.

[36] Wood, *op. cit.*, p. 102.

[37] Countryman, *op. cit.*, p. 145.

[38] Wood, *op. cit.*, p. 315.

[39] Ryerson, *op. cit.*, p. 147. This committee was headed by James Cannon, the author of much of the 1776 Pennsylvania constitution (regarded, with that of Vermont, as the most radical among all the new states). He was a close associate of "radical" republicans Thomas Paine and Thomas Young.

[40] Countryman, *op. cit.*, pp. 170, 182.

[41] Quoted in *Ibid.*, p. 182.

[42] Jensen, *op. cit.*, p. 33.

[43] Benjamin Quarles, *The Negro in the Making of America* (N.Y.: Collier Books, 1964), p. 47. This policy eventually had to be discarded at the national level as the war went on and recruitment became more difficult. However, some "revolutionary" state regimes, as in Georgia and South Carolina, refused to accept this change despite their desperate position in the war.

[44] Ronald Hoffmann, "The 'Disaffected' in the Revolutionary South," in Young, ed., *op. cit.*, p. 284.

[45] Probably the best single English-language book on this issue is Juan Gomez Casas, *Anarchist Organization: The History of the F.A.I.* (Montreal: Black Rose Books, 1986).

[46] Countryman, *op. cit.*, pp. 162-63.

[47] Quoted in Wood, *op. cit.*, p. 366.

[48] *Ibid.*, p. 363. Obviously even more alienated were those, such as slaves, Native Americans, women and those men without suffrage, all of whom had not even a formal pretense of participation in self-governance.

[49] Statements of James Iredell and John Dickinson respectively, quoted in Wood *op. cit.*, pp. 474, 475.

[50] Slaughter, *op. cit.*, pp. 210-14.

[51] Quoted in Alfred Creigh, *History of Washington County from Its First Settlement to the Present Time* (Washington, Pa.: 1870), p. 99. This picture of extreme competitive individualism, of course, conveys far more the ethics of emerging capitalism than the social reality of those partisans of "anarchy" in the Whiskey Rebellion which Addison supposedly describes. Community solidarity and mutual aid among settlers was powerfully expressed at this time in many ways and was a constant reality of frontier life generally. Writers like Paine easily recognized this reality and acknowledged that the vast bulk of activities carried out by governments could be better accomplished by people on their own, in a non-governmental "state of society" (Paine, *op. cit.*, pp. 228-29).

52 I have not discussed principled resistance during this period to military enlistment and to demands of the war on civilians. However, in many respects, such resistance also no doubt left significant anarchic effects.

53 That ideological formulations of this sort were potentially then "in the air" is obvious from the writings of contemporaries Richard Price and William Godwin.

54 Statist "revolutionary" leaders were clearly aware of this potential, given their harsh denunciations of extra-legal political meetings and associations once they themselves came to power. The same calculation caused Washington's administration not to publicize the spread and depth of anti-excise revolt throughout the frontier, thus leaving each area feeling more vulnerable in its resistance to federal authority (Slaughter, *op. cit.*, pp. 118-19).

55 Neither Charles Beard nor Merrill Jensen, the leading "anti-federalist" critical historians of two earlier generations, went beyond the limits of the elite Anti-Federalist perspective. For Jensen, those who wanted no central government at all were "extremists" and were "not representative" of "the essence of the years both before and after 1789" (Jensen, *op. cit.*, p. 425). Probably their best-known successor of the present generation, Jackson Turner Main, offered additional, though limited clarity by stressing a "Cosmopolitan" vs. "Localist" dichotomy of perspectives in that period (*Political Parties Before the Constitution* [N.Y.: W.W. Norton and Co., 1974]) and by acknowledging that only a few Anti-Federalist leaders "came from the small farmers or truly represented them." Says Main, "They frequently defended views somewhat less democratic than those of their constituents, and they were often out of sympathy with the economic demands of the rank and file." Furthermore, Anti-Federalists "drew their greatest strength" from the middle class. (*The Antifederalists* [N.Y.: W.W. Norton and Co., 1974], p. 5.) But like Beard and Jensen before him, and another more recent work in the same vein, John F. Manley and Kenneth M. Dolbeare, eds., *The Case Against the Constitution* (Armonk, N.Y.: M.E. Sharpe, Inc., 1987), a statist perspective still blinds Main to the anarchic implications of his own research.

56 Charles Page Smith, *James Wilson: Founding Father, 1742-1798* (Chapel Hill, The U. of North Carolina Press, 1956), p. 45. Despite the almost altruistic motivation implied here, then as now, ideologically and professionally supporting "law and order" had its material rewards. "...Lawyers almost everywhere [on the frontier] prospered. ...Success in law became the basis for investment in lands or a career in politics or both" (Rohrbough, *op. cit.*, p. 54).

57 Wood, *op. cit.*, p. 123.

58 *Ibid.*, pp. 17, 374, 411, 476.

59 Countryman, *op. cit.*, p. xix. His remarks on Marx, Lenin and Trotsky appear on pp. xviii, 133-35, 183-84.

[60] Staughton Lynd's *Intellectual Origins of American Radicalism* is the only well-known work I've found on this period which consciously shows connections between themes and experiments of that context and those of modern anarchism.

[61] Edward Countryman, "'Out of the Bounds of the Law': Northern Land Rioters in the Eighteenth Century," in Young, *op. cit.*, p. 47.

[62] From the indictment sent by the Washington County (Pa.) Court of Quarter Sessions of the Peace to the Pennsylvania Supreme Court, December 12, 1796, in "Washington County, Pennsylvania Circuit Court Transcripts and Miscellaneous Papers," microfilm #1, Washington County courthouse, Washington, Pa.

[63] Slaughter, *op. cit.*, p. 201.

HENRY TUFTS, LAND PIRATE

Neal Keating

...There must have been distributed throughout a
large part of the narrow region known as the United
States, in those days, a stratum of society like that
still found in some isolated and degraded settlements
among the mountains,—hamlets whose wandering
inhabitants are habitually called gypsies, although
without gypsy blood.

Colonel Thomas Wentworth Higginson[1]

While law-abiding people were greatly in the majority, respecting the lives and property of one another,
there was throughout a drifting element of the lawless and reprobate, largely recruited from the runaway servants and convicts I have described, who
roamed from province to province commiting crimes...

James Schouler[2]

These men cannot live in regular society. They are too
idle, too talkative, too passionate, too prodigal & too
shiftless to acquire either property or character.
Finding all their efforts vain, they become at length
discouraged and then under the pressure of poverty,
the fear of a gaol and consciousness of public contempt, leave their native places, and betake themselves to the wilderness.   Timothy Dwight[3]

...lawlessness inevitably arose in a population that
contained, along with stable homesteaders and
tradesmen, many shiftless vagrants and ne'er-do-
wells who found the frontier an ideal setting for their
mischiefmaking.   Ralph Nadinghill[4]

THE CHARGE

PRE-REVOLUTIONARY NEW ENGLAND MUST HAVE CONtained a significant proportion of people who cared not a bit for the law, nor property, work, or God. Furthermore, these same people generally recognized their common interests and acted on them. The individualistic character that so famously personifies the people of the United States was not invented until after the nineteenth century was well under way. Before this invention, life had a much more communal, perhaps medieval flavor. Not everyone was a lonely predestined puritan. Thieves, fugitives, drifters and disaffected strangers made up a part of a loose network of people who connected and associated within the context of lawless desire. I have named these people *land pirates*. If we were to assign these land pirates an ideological label, it would be that of egoistic anarchy. Of this network there is not much record. There are some hints and observations; and then there is Henry Tufts' narrative, which, in addition to being one long, great brag, is a key document of evidence of the existence of this network.

Mark Twain immortalized (and to a degree, romanticized) the ethos of land pirates in his books about life on the Mississippi River. He was not just imagining things. He was also describing a reality, one in which those people who did not fit into the power structure were still able to slip through it more or less successfully. It can still be done, and those who do it continue the tradition of secrecy. Although land pirates may oppose power, and slip through its grid, they are nevertheless implicated in the general order as much as any cop. They can achieve different effects, but they cannot entirely escape.

The American Revolution not only removed the rather tentative grid of power-relations that England maintained in the colonies. It also initiated a much more insidious power structure from within the colonies themselves. Over time, this structure would come to contain the land pirates in the ever-growing institution of incarceration. Today, the United States incarcerates a proportion of its people that is higher than any other nation on Earth.

The lost history of Henry Tufts is found. It has much relevance for the lived present.

I wake the dead.

GOING THERE

IN THE YEAR 1807 IN THE TOWN OF DOVER, NEW HAMPSHIRE, the printer and eminent citizen—Samuel Bragg, Jr.[5]—produced a book very different from anything he had ever published before or after. Titled *A Narrative of the Life, Adventures, Travels and Sufferings of Henry Tufts*, this book differed from Bragg's usual titles on science and religion. This book was the autobiography of an infamous vagabond criminal. It is also a work of classic American literature, or it would be if anyone knew about it.

Why Bragg published this book—so out of character with everything else he did—remains something of a mystery. He may have done it for the money that scandal often brings, but this is at best only a partial reason. Bragg was a successful printer and publisher of books and newspapers—none of which could be called deviant in any way. Maybe he was bored with pious works, and publishing Tufts' narrative relieved the monotony of routine. It is likely the mystery will never be solved. Three years after publishing Tufts' narrative, Bragg's entire operation burnt to the ground. Bragg died but a year after that, it is said, of a broken heart.[6]

Many copies of this book must have been destroyed in the fire, but many more were destroyed by the relatives of the author, who sought to preserve the good upstanding family name of Tufts (Tufts University in Boston was founded by one of Henry's relatives).[7] As a result, there are few copies still in existence. One copy was auctioned off in the 1920s, fetching some $30. Another copy, in 1984, went for $800.[8]

In 1930, a second edition of Tufts' narrative was published, edited by the odd librarian, Edmund Pearson. Some forty pages were cut from this edition, and a new title, *Autobiography of a Criminal*, affixed. Of the editing, Pearson states that he didn't "bowdlerize" the text, and that Tufts "is allowed to recite his crimes, and smugly describe his lechery without interference."[9] Yet, upon comparison of the two editions, this does not seem to be so. Pearson does cut out some significant portions, including a notorious incident where Henry disguises himself as Satan in order to evade the authorities (he was wanted at the time for desertion from the Revolutionary Army).[10] Nevertheless, the text of the second edition runs some 350 pages.

Like most criminal narratives, Tufts' is written by a ghostwriter, a fact admitted to on the title page.[11] As to who the ghostwriter is, there are two educated guesses. One puts the blame on a Colonel Tash,[12] who was something of a hero in the Revolution; while the other attributes it to a clever young lawyer of Dover.[13] There is no confirmation on either of these names, and it seems that this too will remain a mystery.

Henry Tufts was born in 1748. He was over fifty years old when he orally recited his autobiography. While it is doubtless that he lies about some of the events he relates (lying is the central device in his long, colorful career as a student of "the science of deception"), it is nevertheless a narrative that has the overall ring of truth to it. Many of the names, dates and places he mentions can be confirmed. He may embellish and slant his stories, but he does not appear to have simply imagined them. His narrative, therefore, is also an important historical document, for it shows a very different world than what is usually shown as a representation of late eighteenth-century New England. The world Henry Tufts shows us is from the perspective of the underground marginalized disaffected outcast. Henry Tufts is the first counter-cultural anti-hero of the United States.

He played many roles in the course of his career as a land pirate. He was a legendary horse-thief, a capable burglar, a part-time bigamist and full-time philanderer, a convincing conjuror, an aimless vagabond, a good doctor, a pilfering parson, a palmist, a work resistor, a dropout, a soldier, a draft-dodging fugitive, a prisoner, an unknowing agent of genocide, and forever a ne'er-do-well. He even did a stint as a slave-driver for a few months when he drifted south to Virginia. Apparently he was no good at this profession. He complains about the slaves being too disinclined to work, which is of course something he could relate to all too well. It was probably too much work for Henry to get the slaves to work. Besides, all he was really concerned with was seducing the plantation owner's daughter.

Throughout his adventures, Henry displays a fondness for his fellow humans, even while he cons and seduces them. This, in part, contributes to an understanding of his failure as a slave-driver. He was not a violent man. He appears to have had an exceptional sense of humor. Compassion illuminates his narrative, but it is of an existential sort, and not at all materialistic. He never seems to have things to give to others (indeed, he usually takes things), but he does give love to others, and the one legitimate skill he learns in life (although as we shall see, he learned it in a most questionable way) is healing.

Why Henry narrated his notorious life of crime, and thus broke the code of silence characteristic of land pirates, is a most interesting question. He certainly didn't do it for the usual reasons. I propose that his motives were, in keeping with his character, mischievous. To understand this requires some background in the tradition of this form.

THE ONTOLOGICAL BASIS FOR CRIMINAL NARRATIVES

HISTORY IS NOT MADE. IT IS CONSTRUCTED. THE GENERAL condition that gives rise to such production is that of conflict between desire and the law.[14] It is the law that benefits from the construction of history, because history provides the foundation—an understanding of the past—upon which to build up the consolidation of the law into the regulative structure of the state.

Desire in itself needs no such foundation. Desire needs no such structure. Desire does not need history. It is not concerned with order and organization. Desire lives in those instances of impassioned intensity. Once they are gone, it is not simply that they no longer exist. *They never did.* That is why those periods filled with "revolutions, nomadic wanderings, and the strangest mutations"[15] are not in the history books. There was nothing in these periods to suggest the necessity of an enduring record precisely because there was no cognizance of laws. To be outside of the law is to be outside of history, which connotes being outside of that most fundamental of laws: the law of time itself.

Desire contextualized within time becomes an historical subject for the law. This can only happen once the law is established to such a degree that desire is no longer perceived as a major threat to the general order. A shift can then take place, from a strategy of forbidding desire to one of allowing, even encouraging a limited discourse of desire, so as to make an example of it, to ridicule it, and thus recuperate it within the overarching structure of the law. Foucault delineated this process as it relates to sexuality.[16] It also relates to crime.

It is no accident that the criminal narrative began its proliferation in sixteenth-century Spain, when the crown was at the height of its power.[17] Crime, in the form of vagabonds and other disreputable characters roaming the countryside showing little respect for the sanctity of private property, was no longer a perceived threat. Indeed this same description of crime fit those agents of the crown busying them-

selves with plundering the New World. However, it was a very different story just a century prior, when the Inquisition was still in full
swing, burning people alive for much less than petty thievery or some
other flim-flam. During this earlier period, desire was still perceived
to be a threat, for the law was not fully established.

In England, the story was different, but the process was the same.
Particularly devastated by the black plague, England, in response to
the social chaos[18] that ensued, developed one of the most litigious
structures ever known, at one point featuring over two-hundred
offenses for which one could be sentenced to death. The criminal narrative did not catch on so well here, mainly because there were many
more real-life rogues than there were in Spain, and the majority of
them were not in the service of a king. Yet the discourse of desire blos-
somed in many other forms, such as songs and legends, of which perhaps the most enduring is the legend of Robin Hood.[19] Ironically, the
extensive legal structure of post-plague England, while foundationally
solid enough to allow a discourse of limited desire, was so overbearing
(particularly evidenced by the enclosure laws) as to bring about a real
conflict with desire; one that threatened to topple the structure. That
this result did not happen is probably due in no small part to the
demographic outlet provided by the colonies in the "New World."

In another irony, the discourse of desire was exported to New
England, and was transformed by the Puritans into a device designed
to terrorize the congregation onto the path of righteousness. The subjects of these narratives were not Robin Hoods. They were usually
very desperate murderers, or so they were portrayed. These early
American criminal narratives were usually recited orally to a minister, who would then write it up (after embellishing it substantially),
and have the narrator sign it. Often, the confessions were manipulat-
ed to fit into the traditional Christian themes of the fall, humiliation,
repentance, and redemption.[20] It was in this way that desire was
channelled into a discourse contextualized within time that served to
reinforce the general laws with which an unmonitored desire was in
conflict.

HENRY TUFTS' NARRATIVE

WHAT IS EXTRAORDINARY ABOUT TUFTS' NARRATIVE IS THE
constant intrusion of unmonitored desire into the formal discourse of
contextualized desire that his narrative assumes. In some ways the

narrative assumes the form of a typical Puritanized criminal narrative: the confessed fall, the stated humiliation, the alleged repentance and the hopeful redemption. Yet this form is utterly undermined by Tufts' sheer exuberance at his own cleverness as a thief, or a fakir, or a bigamist. He holds himself up too well for someone who has fallen. He is too proud to feel humiliated. He is too sensually inclined to ever repent, and in reality he is already redeemed. You cannot help but laugh at his pathetic apology at the end of the book. This is the most obvious, and probably the biggest lie of the entire narrative. That he can get away with it is perhaps the best proof of the general verisimilitude of his intensely-lived outlaw life.

Henry explains himself existentially: "Nor birth, nor parentage, or mean, or great, confers protection from the stroke of fate."[21] This is nothing less than the employment of the device of mysterious origins. The "depraved disposition"[22] which is developed in his "riper manhood"[23] is neither the result of nature (birth/genetics), nor of nurture (environment/childhood). It remains a mystery. At any rate, by the time Henry is fourteen, his "genius began to display itself."[24] This is when he commits his first theft: a dollar bill from a neighbor. He gets caught and word of his crime gets around. In no time at all, he is being taunted by his fellow playmates, who, along with the rest of the community, figure that his genius "might ripen into an aptitude for the perpetration of the worst of crimes."[25]

Henry says of himself, "My reveries were directed...to unprofitable objects, for instead of contemplating aright upon the doctrines of *meum* and *tuum*, as of age to have done in some measure; instead of considering the sanctity of individual property; weighing the vile and mercenary nature of my transgressions, or guarding against a further repetition of them, my mind was principally employed in adjusting the degrees of impunity, which might, or might not attend, the commission of such deeds in the future. Ideas of this kind were my frequent concomitants; and such is the prevalency of habit, that it naturally begets a mental alliance in its favor; an inclination in the human breast to cherish familiar objects, whether their complexion be virtuous or vicious, beautiful or deformed....The longer I digested the above subjects (the pleasures of crime), the more I became attached to favorite irregularities, and more strongly inclined to provide means for their gratification. Such being my case I gave into the indulgence of corrupt appetites and commenced a career of filching...."[26]

He would have made a good criminologist if it wasn't for his reliance on the device of mysterious origins for explaining the development of his "depraved disposition." It is hardly scientific, but it is key to the entire narrative, underscoring it with a robust sense of wonder. It is through this device that Henry achieves a structural observance of the Puritan narrative form, and it is through the abuse of this device that he subverts the same.

While Henry filched in general, he was especially successful as a horse thief, stealing more than fifty horses in the course of his narrative. He was rarely apprehended. On one occasion, he had stolen a farmer's horse in one town and sold it in another. When the farmer caught up with Henry, he was talked into going back with Henry to the town where Henry had sold his horse. Henry stole the farmer's horse back, and stole another one for himself as well. The two rode off together into the night. Another time, a man bragged to Henry (knowing full well his penchant and skill as a horsethief) that his horse was so well guarded that there was no way he could steal it. It was really a simple thing to do. Henry laced some rum with opium, gave it to the guards, who subsequently slipped into a stupor, making Henry's theft child's play. Once more, he rode off happily into the night. As a "master of deception,"[27] Henry was able to paint spots on a stolen horse with enough skill so as to make the horse unrecognizable to its rightful owner. He regularly carried a little kit of paints and tools for such needs.

While he got away with many thefts, he was also caught and thrown into jail many times. However, he was usually able to break out.

OF LAND PIRATES & THE AMERICAN REVOLUTION

HENRY MAY HAVE HAD EXCEPTIONAL ABILITY IN DOING ALL the nefarious things he did, but he was not so unusual for doing them. In virtually every town in which he commits some form of mischief, he is able to find a co-conspirator and/or a woman as promiscuous as he. This is one index of the land pirate network. A second index is revealed by examining the difficulties encountered by George Washington during the American Revolution, and comparing it with Henry's account. Henry enlisted in the Revolutionary Army on November 5, 1775, near Boston.[28]

In a letter to the provincial congress of New York, Washington writes, "It must give great concern to any considerate mind, that...there are men among us so basely sordid, as to counteract all our exertions, for the sake of a little gain."[29] From Washington's letters it is obvious that discipline and desertion were constant problems. Washington was not the only commander with these problems. Major General Schuyler almost resigned out of frustration brought about by "disregard of discipline, confusion and want of order among the troops."[30]

Henry, meanwhile, can only magnify such great concerns, as well as validate them, as he writes of joining the Revolutionary Army for the first time: "Being by nature volatile, and prone to novelty, I was strongly impelled to become acquainted with a military life. This my fancy portrayed, as the best method of supporting self and family, and in a way consistent with beloved ease, and at the same time, as, certainly more honorable than thievish pursuits, though a soldier in fact, may be a thief."[31]

Henry relates an incident which occurred in his second two-month enlistment. He goes out one night with two fellow soldiers. They steal "a number of dunghill fowls,"[32] and almost get caught by the owner, who, hearing the birds squawk, comes running out. In typical Tuftian fashion, Henry cons the farmer by walking up to him, looking very innocent and asking for some cider. When the farmer tells Henry that he thinks he has heard someone stealing his chickens, Henry replies that "there is nothing more likely, for just now I saw several fellows running down [the] street".[33] Cursing, the farmer invites him (and his cronies) in for cider. After the refreshment, they "bid him adieu"[34] and on the way back to army quarters, retrieve the stolen chickens, and manage to steal a few geese as well, from yet another farmer. The next day, when this farmer showed up at the commissary to complain to Henry's captain of his loss, the captain instructed him to search as he pleased. This being in vain, the captain then gave the privates permission to drive the farmer out of the camp, which they did, with snowballs, "pelting him unmercifully."[35] Henry concludes this little anecdote, mentioning that, "at the expiration of the two months I was dismissed with the commendation of having behaved as a good soldier".[36]

Imagine what the "father of our country" would have felt had he read of Henry's exploits. Just a few months before the above-related incident, Washington had "...required of all the officers, that they be exceeding [sic] diligent and strict in preventing all Invasions and Abuse of private property in their quarters, or elsewhere,...that every private soldier will detest, and abhor such practices, when he considers, that it is for the preservation of his own Rights, Liberty and Property, and those of his fellow countrymen, that he is now called into service...."37 What would Washington have said to a private soldier who bragged about drawing more than twice his company's ration of meat, through a ruse aided and abetted by his immediate superiors?

In fact, this happened more than once, even in companies that didn't have such a clever private as Henry. In another letter, Washington talks about having "broken"38 two captains for pulling just such a stunt. It was usually the officers that Washington complained about, as well as broke, or otherwise punished. For, while he hoped that every private would detest and abhor such practices, he was quite insistent that the officers *prevent* such practices. Clearly he expected more of the officers. In one of the more embarrassing letters he wrote, Washington states the problem rather bluntly: "...an unaccountable kind of stupidity in the lower class of these people...believe me, prevails but too generally among the officers...."39

It seems the officers were just too cozy with the rank and file. Indeed they were paid about the same, but more than that, they were generally from the same neck of the woods as the company they were put in command of, and were thus more comfortable with their neighbors than with strangers of equal rank. From Washington's point of view however, "...there is no such thing as getting officers of this stamp to exert themselves in carrying orders into execution—to curry favor with the men (by whom they were chosen, and on whose smiles possibly they may think they may again rely) seems to be one of the principle objects of their attention...."40

There wasn't any problem in Henry's company when it came to carrying orders into execution. When the young private returns with the double ration of meat, happy officers order Henry to go somewhere else and steal "a moderate quantity of rum"41 to wash down the meal. Henry executes this order with alacrity, after which, he says, alongside his captain, we "regaled ourselves like lords upon these goodly things, which we devoured with as keen avidity, as though they had been acquired ever so honestly, while I received the applause of every guest, as well for my zeal, as ingenious contrivance...."42

Although Henry is unique, the applause and approval he received for both his zeal and ingenious contrivance is not. He was particularly good at doing what many others were also doing, albeit at less advanced levels of dexterity. What they all shared was a profound lack of interest in what Washington called "the great and common cause in which we are all engaged...."[43] There was another cause more common than that of independence from England. The real common cause was self-interest, i.e., an immediate increase in autonomy whenever possible. To the view of this cause, putting the health of a large abstract power-grid like a United States before the health of your own situation was pretty much as stupid as putting the health of any other large abstract power-grid (e.g., England) before your own profit margin.

Certainly not every Yankee soldier saw things that way, but a significant proportion did—enough to almost lose the war. A good example of this is the mass desertion of the Connecticut regiments, who after doing their two-month stint, refused to stay a few extra days, until replacements (one of whom was Henry Tufts) could be mustered. Here we are speaking in the range of some five-thousand soldiers, all of them deserting en masse. The occasion would prompt Silas Deane, patriot, lawyer and Yale graduate, to write his wife, in disgust: "The behavior of our soldiers has made me sick; but little better could be expected from men trained up with notions of their right of saying how, and when, and under whom, they will serve."[44] Apparently, the desire for one's own autonomy does not blend very well with military regimentation—even if the stated purpose of said regiments is to gain independence. From the point of view of the leaders, such autonomy is less than desirable, and is usually called something else. In remarks on the desertion, Governor Trumbull of Connecticut put it thus: "Indeed there is great difficulty to support liberty, to exercise government, to maintain subordination, and at the same time to prevent the operation of licentious and levelling principles which many very easily imbibe."[45]

The mass desertion of the Connecticut regiments was perhaps exceptional for its dramatic nuances. More common were everyday abuses of property, lack of order, wasting of ammunition, casual desertion, and other petty scams. Washington had a hard time believing that "...some officers, under pretence of giving furloughs to men recovering from sickness, send them to work upon their farms for their own private emolument, at the same time that the public is taxed with their pay, if not with their provisions...."[46] Such things happened often enough to prompt an outraged Washington to write that "it is a matter of exceeding great concern that at a time when the united efforts of America are exerting in defense of the common rights and liberties of mankind, that there should be in an army constituted for so noble a purpose, such repeated instances of officers, who lost to every sense of honor and virtue, are seeking by dirty and base means, the promotion of their own dishonest gain...."[47]

I'll let you the reader be the judge here. I can only conclude that as liberty and autonomy had not yet been consolidated into a unifying and normalizing institution, many people thought of these ideas in much more immediate and practical terms. What Washington and other "leaders" refer to as dishonest gain and selfishness seems to me a healthy response to a regimented subjugation that never held any interest for land pirates and the like.

HENRY TUFTS AMONG THE ABENAKI

PRIOR TO THE OUTBREAK OF THE AMERICAN REVOLUTION, Henry had spent three years living with the Abenaki Indians in western Maine. His original reason for doing so was that he had accidentally stabbed himself in the leg during a knife game, and the wound had not healed well at all—in fact he was dying. It was his hope that the Abenaki, who had a reputation for the healing arts, would be able to heal him. I want to stress that Henry was a far cry from any sort of ethnographer. Nevertheless, the three chapters in his narrative that deal with this period do comprise a sort of ethnography. It is probably the only one there is for the western Abenaki in the eighteenth century.[48]

Like all ethnographies, Tufts' begins with the journey to the other.[49] He is frustrated and depressed. He's half dead. The journey through the pigwackett country is long and arduous. Yet he heads up his "study" with the following: "I far prefer a savage life/ to gloomy cares or vexing strife."[50] That's just the big picture. More specifically, and much more desperately, "By the time prefixed I was equipped for departure and had gathered (in my opinion) such a portion of health and strength, as might enable me to travel a few miles a day. So bidding adieu to family and friends, I set out on the precarious enterprise, but the most gloomy doubts of success and uncertainty of my return, were my constant attendants on the way. I proceeded by short and slow marches, traveling sometimes not more than a mile or two in a day. The people, whom I visited on the road, used me, for the most part, with much kindness, otherwise, of neccessity, I must have abandoned the expedition.

"I shall not here attempt to decipher the multiplicity of difficulties and discouragements, arising from pain, sickness, want, and sometimes almost despair, which I encountered during this long and tedious pilgrimage."[51] I have to laugh when he continues on with his sympathy-generating prose: "To render an adequate description of my sufferings and trials would far exceed my feeble ability...."[52]

Such puns can only ruin the intended effect, unless such ruination was itself the intended effect. Nevertheless, if his pain and sickness are not enough, his distress is made complete when he must "pass several uncomfortable nights in the howling wilderness, where the frequent yellings of the wild beasts inspired ideas of horror and amazement."[53] He gets a little bit of comfort when he has "the good fortune to procure the company of some English hunters a small part of the remaining way."[54]

At last he arrives at his destination: an Abenaki camp. Their wigwams appear to Tufts as "uncouth and wretched habitations"[55] and make him unsure of how he will be received by these "rude sons of nature."[56] Henry explains that they don't just live in the wigwams, but that they are their "inmates."[57] This suggests a jail, another kind of abode, but one with which Henry is infinitely more familiar.

The "uncultivated"[58] Abenaki proved to be both friendly and considerate towards Henry, who surely must have appeared a pathetic sight (after all that suffering). The language barrier was surmounted, not by clever Henry, but by the presence of several Abenaki, who were functionally bilingual. That they welcomed Henry, a stranger and a Yankee, in addition to being conversant in English, is understandable given both the traditional and historical context in which the Abenaki lived.

The traditional context (which was arguably the ultimate cause of their downfall) was the rule of hospitality towards strangers.[59] The historical context was the economic and biologic relations that developed between the Abenaki and the Europeans. By the time Henry arrived (probably sometime in 1772), they had been in contact with Europeans for over a century and a half. They were among the first tribes to be utterly destroyed by the encroaching "civilization," through both its profit-based economics and its civilized diseases. It is reasonable to assume that in the course of this genocidal catastrophe, there had been opportunities for the Abenaki to learn the meaning, not only of the Europeans' language, but also of their actions.

Perhaps they sought to assimilate Henry into the tribe. He appears to have been adopted by them (every ethnographer's dream, eh?). Not only was he taught some of the medical techniques by the renowned Indian "doctress,"[60] Molly Occut; he was regularly invited to participate in the hunting excursions. He usually declined, being far too inclined towards indolence. Apparently his room and board were free. He was taught how to trap, and enjoyed regular sexual relations with a chief's daughter (Polly). As time passed, he was thoroughly healed by the good doctress.

Henry developed a desire to learn "Indian physic" in a thoroughgoing way, but the Indian doctors were reluctant to teach Henry *all* their secrets. He explains that "Since beginning to amend in health under the auspices of madam Molly, I had formed a design of studying the Indian practice of physic, though my intention had hitherto remained a profound secret. Indeed I had paid strict attention to everything of a medical nature, which had fallen within the sphere of my notice. Frequently I was inquisitive with Molly Occut, old Plilips, Sabattus and other professed doctors to learn the names and virtues of their medicines. In general they were explicit in communication, still I thought them in possession of secrets they cared not to reveal."[61]

It is at this point in the narrative where I have the greatest difficulty with our hero Henry, who both before and after this juncture, was a perfect rascal and outlaw. There is an immense paradox in Henry's solution to getting these healers (who have so thoroughly and selflessly healed him) to teach him their secrets. It was a simple solution really. He gave them rum. It worked. At first he bought ten gallons of rum... "with which I regaled a number of my indian friends as long as it lasted. By this exploit I so far engaged their good will and gratitude, that no sooner did I acquaint them with my desire to learn the healing art, then they promised me every instruction in their power, which, subsequent to this I ever found them ready to afford."[62]

After he hit upon this "solution," he regularly procured rum for the Abenaki. It was for this reason that he began to accompany the hunting parties more often, i.e., so as to obtain furs that he could then trade for rum with which to ply the healers. This is what he called his "favorite scheme."[63] His reasoning was that by learning the art of physic, he might more be able to live a life suited to his "beloved ease."[64]

What is implied in the narrative is that the Abenaki are unable to procure rum for themselves. It was probably illegal for either the French, and especially the English, to sell rum to the Abenaki—on paper at least. Abenaki leaders had been petitioning the governor of Massachusetts for some time prior to Henry's stay there to forbid anyone to come near the Abenaki settlements with rum. It is widely accepted and readily apparent that alcohol has been a complete disaster for American Indians from the moment of its introduction. While there are some exceptions to this rule (e.g., the Tarahumara in northern Mexico, and several other groups which included non-distilled alcohol as part of their cultural configurations),[65] the Abenaki were not one of them. Alcohol devastated the communal and cognitive frameworks through which they obtained social cohesion. The nonordinary reality brought on through rum did not (unlike other nonordinary realities, brought on through use of organic hallucinogens such as psyilocybin mushrooms) refer back to Abenaki culture in any kind of affirming, reinvigorating way. Quite the opposite. Instead, it revealed the hidden problems of their life-styles without any means of their resolution.[66]

Henry had no problem in obtaining rum from "diverse English people" who "occasionally visit...to purchase furs and the like."[67] That is not to say it was impossible for the Abenaki to procure their own rum. However, it was probably more difficult, as well as more expensive, for them to do so. It is here that I am confronted with the overriding paradox of Henry Tufts' narrative. It is a problem with what T.S. Eliot called the "objective correlative," which refers to the notion that the objective of a given protagonist must correspond to the characterization of this protagonist. In the event that this correlation doesn't take place, we have on our hands either a faulty piece of fiction, or some other hidden process going on.[68]

For all the things Henry Tufts made himself out to be in the narrative (and there were many things, deviant and otherwise), he was consistently a compassionate character. He was a con man, but he did not seem to be capable of coercive behavior. The only other time in which he physically harmed another person occurred in the course of a wrestling match, in which he threw his opponent a bit too hard. Months later, he heard the man was still seriously ill. This caused Henry no small amount of grief. While it is true that the narrative is peppered throughout with expressions of remorse for doing this or that nefarious deed, rarely can such remorse be shown as genuine. This is one of those rare moments. He may have not given a damn for the difference between *"meum and tuum,"* but he seems to have had a fair sense of human suffering, and did not generally exhibit any interest in inflicting it on others.

Given this characterization, one cannot but be struck by the lack of compassion exhibited by Henry towards the Abenaki. Having benefitted from living and learning among this group of people, why would he then turn around and provide them with the means of their own destruction? Henry is way out of character here, even if his character is little more than a fiction invented by the narrator. It is a possibility that he didn't know what he was doing. After all, Henry was no teetotaller. He obviously had a penchant for the voluptuous and the sensual. Though his personal visions of excess tended towards the sexual or the felonious, he enjoyed the occasional bout with the bottle as well. It could be that he saw nothing wrong in the excessive use of alcohol among the Abenaki.

However this is too simplistic. He does seem to have a clear understanding of what is happening: "One pernicious practice to which those poor people were miserably addicted, as I had frequent opportunities of witnessing, and which was one great cause of their wretchedness, was their excessive fondness for spiritous liquors; with which they were supplied, for the most part, by the New England traders. Such was their insatiable thirst for the fatally intoxicating potion, that they would cheerfully barter away, in purchase of it, their most valuable furs, even after encountering every incredible hardship, of cold, hunger and fatigue, in their acquirement. Frequently I have remonstrated with them on the folly and impropriety of this conduct, but without making any lasting impression upon their minds."[69]

When was it, I wonder, that Henry remonstrated with them on the folly of their excessive fondness for liquors? Was it as he filled their cups with the same? Was it while they were riding out one of the usual three-day hangovers they would incur as a result of Henry's "generous sharing"[70] of his own rum, by which he was buying a medical education? Another possibility is that rum was relatively easy for the Abenaki to get ahold of, and it might have thus seemed to Henry that they were just going to get drunk and wretched anyhow, whether he gave them rum or not. So why should he have not profited from the inevitable?

A third possibility, and perhaps the most likely, is that the narrator Tufts was being very honest, and was thus able to contradict himself without even being aware of having done so. When we place the life of Henry Tufts in the context of the grid of power-flows characteristic of that epoch, we can perceive this contradiction. Doing this is rather tricky and not without problems. It involves interacting with the temporal duration. The presumption is that distance perceived (i.e., we are far enough away from Henry Tufts' world) allows us to delineate the grid as it was then manifest. We may not be able to objectively and conclusively state all the nuances of this grid, but from the biased perspective of subjective desire for freedom, we can at the very least interpret the totality of the grid. We can understand genocide. It is most likely that neither Henry the narrator, nor Henry the subject of the narration—who most certainly contributed to the extermination of his friends and teachers—understood the forces which not only made this specific paradox possible, but that were simultaneously re-shaping the entire world.

When we consider fully the paradox of Henry Tufts among the Abenaki, it gradually becomes clear just what we are staring at: the blank emptiness of power, both in the temporal duration as well as the lived present. While referring to the existence of a grid has some heuristic value (it is after all classificatory), it tends to be misleading. It is more accurately described as faceless and unremitting. That quality of facelessness is characteristic of power manifested in western cognition. It derives from disassociation from kin-based cosmologies. We ought to be awed by genocide instead of outraged. For it is in genocide that one is confronted with unceasing ignorance and the endless impotent stares of unknowing agents, who, even if they are anti-authoritarian in other ways, can with a simple shrug of their shoulders, unleash a universe of blameless annihilation.

Adam Smith was being anthropocentric when he spoke of an invisible "hand". Power has no such feature. It is blank; faceless—a smooth serenity. Rarely can it be perceived at all. Yet in those moments when the objective of a knowing subject (such as Henry) no longer corresponds to the capacities of the subject's desire, then can one glimpse power. Then can one witness the law in action. Nietzsche once wrote that if you have never lied, you can never know the value of truth.[71] Henry Tufts, the land pirate, was a big liar, but in the case of his "favorite scheme," we can only conclude that he was being very, very honest.

REFERENCES

1 Higginson, T.W.; *Travellers and Outlaws*, Boston, 1889; Lee & Shepard.
2 Schouler, J.; *Daily Life in Revolutionary America*, Williamstown, 1906, 1976; Corner House Publisher.

[3] Dwight, Timothy; *Travels in New England*, Cambridge, 1969 (first published in 1821); Harvard University.

[4] Nadinghill, Ralph; *Yankee Kingdom*, New York, 1973; Harper & Row.

[5] Moore, John; *Historical Notes on Printers and Printing, 1420-1886*, Concord,1886; Republican Press Association. Two reports about Bragg: one has him buying the Dover newspaper from his father; the other reports him buying it from his brother-in-law. Wadleigh, George; *Notable Events in the History of Dover*, Dover, 1913; pp.187-188. Listed here is a proclamation, signed by some of the "first citizens" of Dover, on April 4, 1798; Bragg's signature is one of these.

[6] *Ibid.*, p. 199: "He was a very industrious and enterprising man of steady habits and attention to his business... this disaster (fire) took such hold of his mind as, after a while, to produce a dejection of spirits, and invite a complication of disorders which has thus early put a period to his existence."

[7] Both Higginson and Pearson attest to this business of other Tufts destroying copies of Henry's narrative, but I've thus far been unable to corroborate this. It's quite possible. For example, Jay F. Tufts, who compiled an extensive geneaological history of the Tuft's family, wrote that "as Henry had a rather questionabe reputation, it is better to let old family skeletons die, and stay buried" (1963).

[8] *Bookman's Price Index*, New York; 1984.

[9] Pearson, Edmund; *The Autobiography of a Criminal, by Henry Tufts*, New York, 1930; Duffield & Co., p. xvi.

[10] Tufts, Henry; *Narrative of the Life, Adventures, Travels and Sufferings of Henry Tufts*, 1930; Duffield & Co., p. xvi.

[11] *Ibid.*, the exact quote on the title page is "in substance, as compiled from his own mouth."

[12] Pearson, *op. cit.*, p. xv: "a pencilled note in the copy of the book in the New York Pubic Library quotes David Murray in the *News Letter* as saying that it was written by Colonel Tash of New Durham."

[13] Thompson, Mary; *Landmarks in Ancient Dover*, Concord, 1892, Republican Press Association.

[14] White, Hayden; *The Content of the Form*, Baltimore, 1987; Johns Hopkins University.

[15] *Ibid.*, p. 12 quoting from Hegel, *The Philosophy of History*.

[16] Foucault, M.; *The History of Sexuality, Part I*, 1978, Random House. In a pill, the discourse on sexuality, which is presumed to be a liberating thing, increases in proportion to the extent in which bodies are made into subjects upon which power can then be brought to bear.

[17] Chandler, F.W.; *The Literature of Roguery*, Boston, 1907; Houghton, Mifflin & Co. The first criminal narrative is "La Vida de Lazarillo de Tormes" (1554).

[18] Miller, Henry; *On the Fringe*, 1991; Lexington Books.

19 Chandler, *op. cit.*
20 Williams, Daniel; "Doctor, Preacher, Soldier, Thief: A New World of Possibilities in the Rogue Narrative of Henry Tufts"; in *Early American Literature*, vol.XIX, 1984.
21 Pearson, *op. cit.*, p. 3.
22 *Ibid.*, p. 5.
23 *Ibid.*, p. 5.
24 *Ibid.*, p. 6.
25 *Ibid.*, p. 7.
26 *Ibid.*, pp. 7-9.
27 *Ibid.*, p. 232.
28 *Revolutionary War Rolls*, vol. 14, #1.
29 Washington, George; *Writings, Vo.III, 1775-1776*, New York, 1889; Putnam & Sons, p. 74.
30 *Ibid.*, p. 267.
31 Pearson, *op. cit.*, p. 97.
32 *Ibid.*, p. 99.
33 *Ibid.*, p. 99.
34 *Ibid.*, p. 99.
35 *Ibid.*, p. 100.
36 *Ibid.*, p. 100.
37 Washington, *op. cit.*, p. 5.
38 *Ibid.*, p. 98.
39 *Ibid.*, p. 98.
40 *Ibid.*, p. 97.
41 Pearson, *op. cit.*, p. 101.
42 *Ibid.*, pp. 102-103.
43 Washington, *op. cit.*, pp. 5-6.
44 *Ibid.*, p. 255.
45 *Ibid.*, p. 255.
46 *Ibid.*, p. 75.
47 *Ibid.*, p. 75.
48 Day, Gordon, (1974) "Henry Tufts as a Source on 18th Century Abenakis", in *Ethnohistory*, vol. 21, #3.
49 Pratt, Mary Louise; in *Writing Culture*, Berkeley, 1986; University of California; p. 39.
50 Pearson *op. cit.*, p. 59.
51 *Ibid.*, pp. 59-60.
52 *Ibid.*, p. 60.
53 *Ibid.*, p. 60.
54 *Ibid.*, p. 60.
55 *Ibid.*, p. 61.
56 *Ibid.*, p. 61.
57 *Ibid.*, p. 60.

58 *Ibid.*, p. 61.
59 Calloway, C.G.; *Dawnland Encounters*, Hanover, 1991; University Press of New England.
60 Pearson, *op. cit.*, p. 63.
61 *Ibid.*, p. 66.
62 *Ibid.*, p. 68.
63 *Ibid.*, p. 68.
64 *Ibid.*, p. 72.
65 Washburne, Chandler; *Primitive Drinking*, New York,1961; College and University Press.
66 Morrison, Kenneth M.; *The Embattled Northeast*, Berkeley, 1984; University of California.
67 Pearson, *op. cit.*, p. 62.
68 Eliot, T.S. "Hamlet and His Problems" in: *Selected Essays*, 1932; Harcourt, Brace & World.
69 Pearson, *op. cit.*, p. 62.
70 *Ibid.*, p. 67.
71 Nietzsche, F., *The Gay Science*, New York, 1974; Vintage.

KEEP YOUR POWDER DRY
Two Insurrections in Post–Revolutionary America

Paul Z. Simons

When you know, when you know, your history,
Then you would know where you're coming from
Then you wouldn't have to ask me,
Who the hell I think I am.

Bob Marley

The Country's a' in a greetin mood
An some are like to rin red-wud blood:
Some chaps whom freedom's spirit warms
Are threatning hard to take up arms,
And headstrong in rebellion rise
'Fore they'll submit to that excise
Their liberty they will maintain,
They fought for't, and they'll fight again.

Anonymous (1793)

I T HAS ONLY BEEN IN THE PAST THIRTY YEARS OR SO THAT historians of the American post-revolutionary period arrived at a mind-bending conclusion; the new citizens were as angry and contentious after the revolution as they had been before its advent. Most nineteenth and early twentieth century historical discussions of the period had dealt with the construction of the constitution of 1787 and the responses of the states to the document. By the middle of the twentieth century, scholars were beginning to realize that there exists a vast continent of data that firmly proves that the new citizens, particularly in the frontier regions, were dangerously alienated from the fledgling republic.

In addition, these frontiersman and yeomen farmers, having gone through the crucible of the revolution, were more than willing to take up arms to protect what they considered to be their rights. This is.

where their story diverges from other riots. Whereas most colonial riots had followed the English pattern of the violent redress of perceived wrongs, these Americans were planning out and out insurrection to ultimately topple their respective state governments.

In the following essay we will examine the chronology and contours of Shay's Rebellion and the Whiskey Rebellion for the purpose of annihilating the myth that the United States has *always* been a nation of sheep.

SOME BACKGROUND

POPULAR UPRISINGS IN THE AMERICAN COLONIES HAD become something of a commonplace occurrence prior to the revolution. Most of these risings were similar, if not identical, to riots that had been occurring in England since the mid-seventeenth century. There were a number of different strains of rioting in colonial American society. Perhaps the most pronounced was the occasional defense of local communal interests against governmental institutions, though more often in spite of these institutions. Perhaps the most widespread form of this type of insurgency in the colonies was the customs riot. After 1764 and the imposition of the Sugar Act, this form of riot reached almost epidemic proportions. For example, in 1767 at Falmouth (Portland), Maine, a customs official's home was subjected to a barrage of stones while "persons unknown and disguised" stole sugar and rum that had been impounded the same day. Customs' informers were particularly singled out by the mob for retribution and such enmity was shared by persons of higher station as well. In 1701 the attorney general of South Carolina publicly thrashed a known customs informer on the streets of Charleston.

Local economic interests spurred a number of incidents. The Boston mob, a virtual city institution by 1776, forcibly retrieved wagons laden with foodstuffs during times of dearth. Tobacco riots, where insurgents destroyed tobacco plants, were common in the Southern colonies during years of exceptional harvests in order to ensure a decent price for the crops that remained unharmed. The draining of manpower through impressment into the British Navy also proved to be an effective trigger for a riot. Impressment riots, in particular, seemed to be a direct outgrowth of the mob taking the job of colonial government into its own hands. Thus the 1765 Maidstone Riot in Newport broke out only after the governor's request for the return of the "pressed" seamen went unanswered.

There was an entire class of riots that defy any label at all. Among these was the annual Pope's Day celebration in New England which almost invariably degenerated into a wild, drunken brawl punctuated by an occasional burned building or smashed window. A singular example of what can only be called a scheduled riot. Other examples of such nondescript rioting include the Boston mob's repeated efforts to forcibly close "bawdy houses" (1734, 1737 and 1771) and the Norfolk, Virginia "Smallpox" Riot where a group of insurgents quarantined a number of infected persons against their will.

Colonial America then, was hardly the land of peace that it has been portrayed as in most secondary school primers. Indeed, the judgment of a North Carolina planter is probably far more appropriate: "scarce a decade passed that did not see the people in arms to redress official grievances."

SHAYS' REBELLION

THE POPULAR UPRISING THAT CAME CLOSET TO ITS STATED aim of toppling a state government occurred in western Massachusetts during the winter and spring of 1786-87. The rising would be named for one Daniel Shays, a yeoman farmer who found himself consistently in debt and occasionally in jail due to nonpayment. And therein lies our story...

Western Massachusetts at the time of the cessation of hostilities in the Revolutionary War was primarily a rural area. Small communities comprised of between ten and fifty families dotted the region, though the vast majority of the populace lived on small farms. The acreage of these farms provided for a subsistence level of production, with occasional surpluses used to barter for manufactured goods such as medicines, glass, and gunpowder. An example: Paul Smith of Whately, Massachusetts, at the age of twenty-nine years in 1784, had three dependents, fifty-six acres of land, one ox, two cows, and six pigs. In order to feed himself and his family for a full year, he required 60 bushels of flour, 500 pounds of pork, 200 pounds of beef, flax for home-spun, and small amounts of peas, turnips, potatoes, and fruit to round out his family's diet. Farmer Smith cultivated only fourteen acres and allowed the other forty-two to lie fallow. This was something of a typical arrangement in rural New England where yeomen rarely cultivated more land than they could work themselves. In the words of one of these farmers, "What need has the man who possesses 300 acres, to destroy the wood, or clear the land...any faster than he can make use of the soil?"

As should seem obvious from the above discussion, such a rural, subsistence economy was not conducive to the encroachment of what Marx termed the "general equivalent", to wit: money. Yet, money was the one thing of which the merchants of western Massachusetts were in dire need. After the end of the Revolutionary War coastal traders found themselves in a real predicament. While there were attempts to trade with the Baltic States, France, and the Mediterranean these came to nothing. Most of the tidewater merchant class found themselves renewing contracts with British firms with which they had once been associated. Now that independence had been achieved, however, Britain imposed serious restrictions on the markets to which the Americans had access. This was especially true for the lucrative British West Indies' trade in molasses and sugar, from which the Americans found themselves wholly excluded. The British also refused to extend any kind of credit to their American counterparts and demanded payment in specie (i.e., coin, gold, or silver) for all transactions. Thus, the long chain of debt that extended across the Atlantic, from London and Liverpool to Boston, eventually found its way into western Massachusetts where local merchants began demanding cash payment for goods for which they had once bartered.

Of course, the yeoman farmers had little or no money with which to pay for their purchases, so the extension of credit by domestic merchants became commonplace. Just as commonplace were legal prosecutions of recalcitrant debtors. Retailers were unmoved by moneyless farmers pleading for more time to pay their debts. In Hampshire County, from July 1784 to December 1786, seventy-three men were jailed for up to two months due to relatively small debts.

The first stage of the Shays' Rebellion juggernaut opens with the yeoman farmers petitioning state government for the issuance of paper currency and tender laws. Such supplications were rejected by lawmakers, however, as being frivolous and they urged the yeoman to purchase less rum and more seeds. It is important to note that the entire western section of the state was consumed in the debate over paper currency, large meetings were held in almost every town, and literally hundreds of petitions flooded the Boston General Court. Clearly, the lack of specie and the possibility of the debtor's cell had touched a very deep nerve in these post-revolutionary yeomen.

The initiation of mob action occurred during late August of 1786, as one might expect, after the final harvest of the season. On August 29, 1,500 farmers closed down the Court of Common Pleas at Northampton. A week later a similar occurrence put a debtor court out of business at Worcester. By the end of September trouble had spread as far as New Hampshire where a crowd of 200 malcontents surrounded the state house, and held the governor and assembled legislators hostage for over five hours. By the end of 1786, the uprising had spread to every New England state but Rhode Island and had involved upwards of 9,000 insurgent yeomen.

Who were these unhappy yeomen and how, in a era when the swiftest mode of communication was a messenger on horseback, did they affect such rapid mustering of far-flung participants? There was a great deal of social uniformity among the insurgents; most were farmers with an odd "country artisan" thrown in. Shaysites were primarily English and Scotish-Irish and adhered to the Congregational faith. The one large dissenting community in Massachusetts, the Baptists, were largely uninvolved in the turmoil due to the denunciation of the rioting by the popular preacher Isaac Backus.

A large number of Shaysites were related to each other. In the Hampshire County action, insurgents included 100 yeomen from Pelham; these included eight Johnsons, twelve Greys, and six McMillans. Sixty percent of the Pelham contingent attacked the debtor court with a father, brother or cousin. Shaysites were also accustomed to the honored tradition of helping out fellow yeomen, as required, on their farms. Thus, a barn raising or the digging of a root cellar became a social activity where neighbors got together, discussed common problems, and relaxed afterwards with food and drink.

Speaking of drink, local taverns provided another venue for the exchange of information and the building of linkages to other farming communities. Innkeepers would post news items from outlying towns and travellers would stop to gossip about events in other parts of the state. Some rural tavern owners opened their establishments to their more militant clientele, and a few Shaysite incursions were doubtless planned over a dram of rum and a clay pipe. Evidently as the insurrection gathered steam such practices became widespread. Hampshire County militia leader William Shephard complained that tavern owners, "have generally been very seditious, their houses have been the common rendezvous for the council and the comfort of these people [the Shaysites]."

A number of Shaysites fought during the Revolutionary War. This becomes particularly pronounced when one examines the lists of those militants the government branded as leaders. Although Daniel Shays and others repeatedly denounced the idea that leaders existed among the insurgents, they were men who had translated political and economic grievances into action on the field of battle. It is not surprising that they would do so again.

The response to the forced closure of debtor courts in the fall of 1786 by the mercantile elite in Boston and the General Court was swift and stupid. As opposed to allowing that maybe the Shaysites might have a point and introducing a modified monetarist policy by printing limited paper currency, the General Court stepped across the line into out and out repression. Habeas corpus was rescinded, summary arrest and imprisonment without due process was instituted, and a Riot Act that outlawed gatherings of over twelve individuals was passed. Finally, a militia of several thousand men was raised to put an end to the rebellion.

Such repressive measures in response to what the insurgents considered justified (though admittedly extra-legal) actions drove the Shaysites over the edge. Admittedly it was a pretty short road to begin with, but there had been room for compromise and the General Court had missed its chance. The tone and volume of Shaysite rhetoric began to lose its moderation. In early 1787, Isaac Chenery told Captain Webb of his intent to overthrow the state government: "I had rather be under the devil than such a government as this."

In early December of 1786 the Shaysites, through their network of taverns and familial relations, divided central and western Massachusetts into four regimental districts. Each district was administered by a "committee of the people." The heads of these committees were responsible for writing "to the several towns in their respective regiments in the name and behalf of this committee, requesting them to meet and organize." Messengers were designated to carry leaflets to small landholders in inland counties soliciting their support.

After having achieved a moderate amount of organizational success, the Shaysites began plotting the overthrow of the state government. The first strike was to be the capture of the federal arsenal at Springfield. The arsenal held some 7,000 muskets, 1,300 barrels of powder, and a large quantity of shot and shell. All told, the arsenal had some 450 tons of military hardware that would have gone a long way to ensuring the success of the rebellion. After having seized the arsenal and defeated the state militia, the Shaysites proposed to "march directly to Boston, plunder it, and then...to destroy the nest of devils, who by their influence, make the Court enact what they please, burn it and lay the town of Boston in ashes." So much for petitions solemnly asking for paper currency.

The actual attack on the arsenal was well planned with one exception, communication. The plan provided for three columns of insurgents to surround the arsenal, cut off bridges to isolate the structure from a large force of militia that were marching to relieve the surrounded garrison and then to storm and take the building. Unfortunately, communication between the three attack groups was poor and one column was misinformed as to the day of the assault. On January 25, 1787 1,500 yeomen, "came on impetuously but in good order with their pieces shouldered." They marched to within 250 yards of the arsenal and halted. Daniel Shays exchanged unpleasantries with the commander of the regiment and then ordered the insurgents to, "March, God Damn you, march!" The insurgents were routed after a brief barrage of grape shot. The Shaysites attempted to regroup some days later at Petersham, and along the way they harassed and abused merchants unlucky enough to have opened up shop on the road from Springfield. The final defeat of the Shaysites occurred outside of Sheffield at the hands of the state militia. After a six minute fire fight thirty yeomen lay dead and the rest dispersed post haste.

After the insurgency of the winter of 1787, and fearing reprisals by state government, most Shaysites migrated to eastern New York or Vermont. Though occasional punitive raids against militia commanders and particularly obnoxious merchants were carried out during 1787 and 1788, Shays Rebellion was, for all intents and purposes, over.

THE WHISKEY REBELLION

THE CONTROVERSY THAT WOULD EVENTUALLY MUSHROOM into the Whiskey Rebellion is complex. It was about a young federal government imposing its will, through taxation, on a frontier region that was interested in maintaining its autonomy. It was about frontiersmen seeking access to the Mississippi River to encourage trade and it was about constant warfare between Indians and settlers.

Finally, however, it was about taxes levied on a staple frontier potable, whiskey.

Western Pennsylvania was a particularly harsh place to thresh out a living during the last decade of the eighteenth century. While the soil was productive, and just about anything that was planted would grow, there were other problems to be dealt with on the frontier. The weather was a constant menace, winter would often arrive too soon, killing crops while still in the ground, and in the spring the Monongahela River would almost always flood drowning a hapless family or two. The chances of being massacred by hostile Indians were very real. The area itself was overrun with vermin, rats, mosquitoes, and lice. It is no wonder that the settlers of the region were a particularly belligerent lot.

Contemporary observers were horrified by both the living conditions and the people of western Pennsylvania. It was commonplace in the literature of the time for travelers to state that civilization had degenerated on the frontier in response to the harshness of local conditions. Virginian Arthur Lee, after a visit in the early 1780s, found "not a priest of any persuasion, nor church, nor chapel, so that they are likely to be damned, without the benefit of clergy." John Wilkins, another contemporary, concurred, offering as an explanation for the region's irreligiosity, "the Presbyterian ministers were afraid to come to the place, lest they be mocked or mistreated." William Winans did find meetings on Sundays but the frontiersmen gathered not for worship but, "to drink, to settle their differences, and to try their manhood in personal conflict. And many were the black eyes and bitten members which were the fruits of these... reunions of the neighborhood." One of the local entertainments mentioned by quite a few travelers was the proclivity of frontiersmen to gouge each other's eyes out. Evidently this mutilation was not only a test of bravery but hand-eye coordination as well.

Added to the violence and irreligiosity was the squalor in which most of the settlers lived. Mary Dewees, while traveling through the region with friends, recounted a single night in the home of a settler, "this night our difficulties began: we were obliged to put up at a cabin...perhaps a dozen logs upon one another with a few slabs for a roof, and the earth for a floor, and a wooden chimney. The people [were] very kind but amazing[ly] dirty. There was between twenty and thirty of us; all lay on the floor except Mr. Rees, the children and [myself]...and I assure you that we thought ourselves lucky to escape being fleaed alive."

One of the most interesting anecdotes about the region is of young John May, a merchant from Boston who had inadvertently read a pamphlet describing western Pennsylvania as a virtual paradise of rich inhabitants and cold, hard cash. He invested in a trading venture and set out in the spring of 1789 to make his fortune. When he arrived in Pittsburgh he found that specie, as in most western regions of the United States, was in great demand and people were unwilling to part with it. He described the inhabitants of the region as rude and ignorant and felt himself "surrounded with devils." During one of his trips into the outback May was stranded by floods and he took refuge in "a little cabin. Our inmates are all Dutch [i.e., German] excepting the beasts. She who was mistress is dead. The old man, a daughter of eighteen, two hired women a little older, three hired men, a number of children, besides a bear and five dogs make up our bedlam." May was told later that this was one of the more well-to-do families in the region.

There was also the continuing situation of hostilities with the local Indian tribes. Far from the currently perceived idea that the Indians were victimized by the unilateral violence of the white race, it cannot be stated too strongly that the Indians put up one hell of a fight in response to the westward momentum of settlement. This is not to absolve the whites, it merely puts forward a more accurate accounting of the actual nature of the warfare. Thus the Paxton Riots occasioned the massacre of a group of peaceful Christianized Indians by settlers in 1782. On the other hand, there were numerous incursions by Indians into white occupied territory where whole families were massacred. This would be one of the major points of contention in the Whiskey Rebellion. The settlers demanded protection against Indians, a responsibility that the newly constituted federal government would avoid for years.

The settlers also requested that the federal government grant access to the Mississippi and Ohio rivers in order to transport their goods in to international markets. John Jay and others in the foreign policy apparatus disregarded these demands in order to curry favor with both the British and Spanish governments, who both claimed possession of the area.

Ultimately, however, the frontiersmen wanted to be left alone. No one had helped the settlers in times of trouble, no collections were taken up in Philadelphia for their children in times of dearth, no one sent militias to protect them from rampaging Indians and no resources were made available by state governments to repair and improve the almost medieval road system that plagued their commerce. That was fine with them. If no one was going to help, the frontiersmen would take the responsibility themselves to fight Indians when and where they wished, to trade in markets unencumbered by "national" duties, and to spend their profits on whatever the hell they pleased.

Enter a newly formed federal government which had been granted broad powers of taxation in its constitution, and further, was having some problems balancing its budget. Alexander Hamilton, Secretary of the Treasury under Washington, had proposed an excise tax on whiskey and other luxuries since 1790 as a way to balance the debt that the new nation had incurred. Such proposals, however, met with a lukewarm response from both Congress and other cabinet officers, notably Jefferson. As the debate over the excise tax moved to the floor of the House in 1791, it became clear that the old Federalist/Anti-Federalist arguments had been given a new lease on life. Opponents of the bill considered it, "odious, unequal, unpopular and oppressive." It was stated that the excise would operate unequally and, "deprive the mass of the people of almost the only luxury they enjoy." The potential predations of excise officers were enumerated again and again, yet the bill passed Congress easily in March of 1791 and the excise on whiskey and spirituous liquors to be collected at the point of production, went into effect immediately. Of course, there is a difference between enacting legislation and enforcing it, as Hamilton and Washington would soon discover.

Short of attaching an excise to semen, Hamilton could have chosen no other commodity to tax that would have more infuriated the frontiersmen of western Pennsylvania. In the absence of specie, the farmers of the region had been using whiskey as a valuable equivalent for barter. In Washington County alone there were 500 stills in 1790, one for every ten families. The output from these stills was low, about 100 gallons a year, and provided for normal home consumption with a moderate surplus for trade. Whiskey was also part of the normal wage for day laborers in the area. Workers expected frequent draughts of spirits along with their pay, or they would move on to more favorable conditions. A modern equivalent of the whiskey excise then would be a tax on money itself.

Western Pennsylvania became the scene of increasing agitation during the next three years. A number of extra-legal organizations, like the Mingo Creek Society, were formed with the purpose of putting forward the political claims of the settlers. They also served as debating and informational societies, and one Federalist of the period called these groups "the cradle of... insurrection." Although no real efforts had been made by the federal government to collect the excise from small distillers until 1794, a full three years after the imposition of the tax there were some minor riots. On November 22, 1793 a group of men broke into the home of excise collector Benjamin Wells and forced him to surrender his commission. During March of the same year, John Neville, excise officer and one of the most cantankerous men then alive, journeyed through Washington County "to visit some of the most obstinate distillers." Neville later learned that a crowd of about sixty insurgents had followed him to check that no distillers had registered their stills. The unfortunate James Kiddoe had in fact registered his still after discussions with Neville. The crowd heard of Kiddoe's action and, in response, burned his still to the ground and fired upon his house. The only bit of luck Kiddoe had that day was that he escaped with his life.

Neville continued in his efforts to make the small distillers pay the excise and, in response to his efforts, violence sporadically erupted in the countryside. Finally, in June of 1794, Neville succeeded in establishing an excise office in Washington County. John Lynn agreed to sublet a part of his house to the excise inspector. Not long after Neville established the office, however, a group of twelve men with blackened faces visited Lynn. He barricaded himself in the upstairs portion of his home. The men stated that if he surrendered they would guarantee his person and property. Lynn agreed. The men seized him, abused him, and dragged him off to a remote section of forest where they stripped him, cut off his hair, and then tarred and feathered him. They left Lynn naked and lashed to a tree. The next morning someone "discovered" Lynn and released him.

By mid-May 1794, Hamilton, who had had about enough of the recalcitrant distillers in western Pennsylvania said, "there was no choice but to try the efficiency of the laws in prosecuting with vigor delinquents and offenders." To these ends District Attorney William Rawle secured processes from the federal court in Philadelphia and ordered sixty frontier distillers to appear before the magistrates in August, 1794. On June 22, United States Marshall David Lenox began his journey from Philadelphia to Pittsburgh and thence to the frontier regions to serve the processes. Lenox met up with Neville in Pittsburgh and together the two set out to do their duty.

Lenox writes of his first day, "in the first few hours I served process on four persons all of whom showed much contempt for the laws of the United States." By about noon that day, they were serving William Miller with a process when the whole situation began to degenerate very quickly. Miller refused a copy of the summons and exchanged sharp words with both Lenox and Neville. Having served the summons, they turned to leave and found a crowd of thirty to forty men approaching them. The settlers milled around the two men on horseback for a minute or two asking their purpose. Neville informed the crowd that they were serving summonses and had no intention of arresting the distillers, then directed them to disperse. Neville and Lenox rode off, Lenox to Pittsburgh and Neville to his home. All but one of the summonses for the region had been served.

By an unfortunate coincidence for Neville, the Mingo Creek militia had gathered nearby to drill on the same day. Rumor went around that a federal marshal had been sent to arrest recalcitrant distillers and the militiamen became enraged. The militia officers decided to send a company to apprehend Lenox, and another company to surround Neville's house, on the chance that Lenox had returned there.

At daybreak on July 16 John Neville thought he heard the sounds of movement coming from outside his house. Opening the door he realized the house was surrounded. Neville, upon seeing his situation, fired into the militia men and mortally wounded Oliver Miller. The militia returned his fire, and Neville sounded a horn which was the signal for his slaves to open fire as well. Several of the attackers fell wounded while Neville and his household went unharmed.

The killing of Oliver Miller, in conjunction with the serving of the summonses on distillers, galvanized the opinion of both frontiersmen and the more respectable elements from the towns. On July 17, at 5:00 pm a group of between 500 and 700 militia men paraded before Neville's house to the martial music of drums and fife. Present for the first time at any of the insurgent actions were a large number of community leaders. In the opposing camp, Neville had realized that the killing of Miller would lead to further difficulties, so he petitioned the garrison at Fort Pitt to assist him in defending his home. Major James Kirkpatrick with ten soldiers from the Fort agreed to come to his aid and on the afternoon of the 17th, they took up strategic positions.

After an hour of marching and posturing, the militia closed into tight ranks and James McFarlane, the commander of the expedition, strode forth to lay down the rebels' demands. In the meantime, Kirkpatrick had smuggled Neville into a ravine on the other side of the house for safety. McFarlane sent a written summons into the house demanding that Neville surrender himself, along with a written resignation of his excise post, and a promise never to engage in tax collection again. Kirkpatrick told McFarlane that Neville was not at home but that they could search the house and remove any papers they wished. McFarlane responded that the soldiers must evacuate the house and ground their weapons. Kirkpatrick refused and negotiations were halted. The militia surrounded the house at a distance of fifty to eighty yards and the firing began.

The fire fight itself lasted over an hour. The rebels started a number of fires in and around the house in order to dislodge the soldiers. At some point, a cry was heard inside the house and the rebels ceased firing. McFarlane stepped out to see if the soldiers were surrendering, a shot rang out, and he fell dead. This was the last straw. McFarlane was a Revolutionary War hero and was greatly respected throughout the region. The rebels set to with a frenzy, and as fire consumed the house, the trapped soldiers were forced to surrender. There is no accounting of how many died or were wounded during the fighting. What is certain is that several men did die and a number of insurgents expired within days from wounds sustained in the battle.

Later in the evening Lenox was captured by the militia and brought to Couche's Fort. There he was assaulted by frontiersmen with muskets, and others attacked him with knives. The rioters forced Lenox to relinquish all of the remaining summonses and the receipts of summonses he had already served. They then made him swear an oath not to return to the region and he was released.

The Whiskey rebels were stunned by their success. They had stopped the collection of the excise in western Pennsylvania and, with the exception of Pittsburgh, were in effective military control of the entire region. The question remained, however, what next? A meeting was called, then canceled, then called again for August 1, to be held on Braddock Field, with the purpose of marching on Pittsburgh, razing the town, and securing arms stored in Fort Fayette. The citizens of Pittsburgh were terrified but they developed a plan that would save their city. The most obnoxious citizens (i.e., representatives of the federal government) were expelled and large amounts of whiskey were secured from local distillers. When the militia arrived they were greeted warmly by the townspeople, toasted liberally with free whiskey, and sent home drunk and, probably, a little confused.

In the following months the country seethed with open rebellion. Liberty poles were raised, crowned by incendiary slogans. These raisings were attended by people from the surrounding countryside and they became the occasion for fiery speeches and physical intimidation of opponents. The farm buildings of Major Kirkpatrick were burned to the ground in a midnight raid. In fact, marauding bands roamed through the countryside at night, dressed in pseudo-Indian garb, held mock trials, banished those they pleased and brutalized tax collectors. Men in blackened faces screamed "Death to traitors" and threatened enemies with the guillotine. Perhaps most ominous for the federal government, a flag with six stripes, four representing counties in Pennsylvania and two for sympathetic counties in Virginia, was raised over rebel homes and even flew for a time in Pittsburgh. Indeed, as the summer of 1794 advanced the rebellion seemed to be spreading into Virginia, Maryland, Ohio, and even eastward towards central Pennsylvania.

The response from the federal government was two-fold and two-faced. While sending negotiators to attempt to smooth over the situation and to meet at least a few of the rebel demands, President Washington was busily raising and equipping an army to move as swiftly as possible into rebel-held areas before the onset of the Appalachian winter. Washington's army took the field in early October. The major action of the army was to march around the hills of western Pennsylvania and generally subdue the populace by its presence. This worked to an extent, yet underneath the veneer of submission, smoldering resentment could still be found. Liberty poles sprouted magically during the night around the pickets of the army and in the morning these poles lined the soldiers' paths. Yet by the end of the year the government had re-established order in all the insurgent counties, and slowly excise collectors crawled out from under the rocks to take advantage of the calm. The Whiskey Rebellion had not been so much crushed, as pushed underground. A number of rebels moved westward into Ohio and beyond in order to escape the long arm of the federal government, and the Rebellion came to a close.

A FEW FINAL THOUGHTS

UPON READING AN EARLY DRAFT OF THE ABOVE manuscript an associate of mine, well versed in post-industrial critical theory remarked on the seeming rightist nature of both rebellions. The comment struck me and I recall wanting to say, "Well, yes and no."

Certainly both rebellions are excellent examples of the extreme localist sentiment of the early Americans. In fact, up until the Civil War and the rapid and coerced centralization affected by the Republican Party, one might well say that the United States was more a "confederal" than a federal nation. There is sufficient evidence to state that the citizens were far less concerned with federal than state and local matters. The thirteen original colonies were at best ambivalent toward each other's economic and political necessities. When it came to territorial disputes, however, the colonists were far from indifferent and war between the colonies was averted only through the intervention of royal governors. Recall that these arguments carried into the post-revolutionary era; some of the most hotly contested phrasing of the Articles of Confederation concerned the designation of state boundaries. Such localist perspectives, however, if followed to one conclusion, can be turned into arguments for states' rights and, by extension to defend the "peculiar institution" of slavery. Yet, there is also the germ of insurrection in such arguments leading, as they do, towards the formation of both rural and urban communes.

Further, these rebels were well-versed in the rhetoric of legitimate insurrection; a tradition that reaches at least as far back as the English Revolution and was carried forward by the likes of Algernon Sidney and the great fence-sitter John Locke. The sense that it was the duty of the citizenry to topple unresponsive, tyrannical governments is pervasive in both Shaysite and Whiskey Rebellion thinking and action. This essential right of insurrection is one that has clearly been lost in the rhetoric of today's post-industrial theorists.

Finally, it must be noted that events such as the Shays' and Whiskey Rebellions belong to a rich fabric of contestation in the United States. When insurrectionaries forget their past, they also fail to postulate a vibrant future, and the tapestry of insurrection in this country is far from being complete...

REFERENCES

The primary sources for the Shays' Rebellion section include *Shays' Rebellion: The Making of An Agrarian Insurrection*, by David P. Szatmary (Boston: University of Massachusetts Press, 1980) and *The History of the Insurrections in Massachusetts in the Year 1786 and the Rebellion Consequent Thereon*, by George Richards Minot (New York: DaCapo, 1988, reprint of 1788 edition). The Szatmary text is concise and his conclusions, though tainted with a Hobsbawmist prejudice against agrarian radicalism, are at least supported by the historical record. The Minot text is pure fury from an unsympathetic eyewitness and functions equally well as an historical account or a Federalist rant. Take your pick.

The sources consulted for the Whiskey Rebellion component include *The Whiskey Rebellion: Frontier Epilogue to the American Revolution*, by Thomas P. Slaughter (New York: Oxford University Press, 1988) and *Whiskey Rebels: The Story of a Frontier Uprising*, by Leland D. Baldwin (Pittsburgh: University of Pittsburgh Press, 1968). The Slaughter book is exceptional in both depth of narrative and conclusions. Baldwin is an historian of the old American school; that is the subject matter is fascinating and the manner in which it is rendered is excruciating. Recommended for insomniacs.

The conclusions are based on the following works, *The Articles of Confederation*, by Merrill Jensen (Madison, Wisconsin: Madison House, 1991); *Intellectual Origins of American Radicalism*, by Staughton Lynd (Cambridge, Massachusetts: Harvard University Press, 1982); *The Origins of Anglo-American Radicalism*, ed., by Margaret C. Jacob and James R. Jacob (Highlands, New Jersey: Humanities Press, 1991); *Rebels and Democrats*, by Elisha P. Douglass (Chicago: I. R. Dee, 1989); *The American Revolution Considered as a Social Movement*, by J. Franklin Jameson, (Princeton, New Jersey: Princeton University Press, 1940) and *From Resistance to Revolution*, by Pauline Maier (New York: W. W. Norton, 1992). Of these, the best overall work is the Pauline Maier book; it is well-written and researched as she exhibits a sense of time, place and humor.

TRANSFORM & REBEL
The Calico Indians and the Anti-Rent War

Thom Metzger

THE REMAINS: A COSTUME AND MASK STORED BEHIND glass like a saint's garments in a reliquary. A scarlet linen vest, a gown of printed broadcloth, and a mask made of sheep skin. Fabric flowers ornament the mask, along with faded blue ribbons, leather fringe, mesh over the eye holes, a goatee, sideburns and eye brows made from fur.

In a photograph, sixteen men pose in similar costumes. Most brandish knives, all wear grotesque masks and gowns or jackets of brightly colored calico. Horns of leather, drooping mustaches, long false beards, wolf-like snouts, stag antlers, plumes of horse hair, tassels hanging from pointed ears, and hard fierce animal-like mouths.

They were farmers, many of them teen-aged boys, all of them little better than serfs. And for a few years in the early eighteen forties, while similar anti-authoritarian movements brewed in Europe, these self-styled Calico Indians roved the countryside of eastern New York State, flouting law, order and social norms.

After the American War of Independence, a semi-feudal system remained firmly in place along the Hudson River Valley, reaching from New York City to Albany, through the Catskills and to the Massachusetts border. Three hundred thousand farmers, working almost two million acres, lived like serfs with little hope of ever escaping their bondage to the land's owners. This patroon system had its origins in the Dutch colonial efforts of the 1600s, when huge blocks of land were "purchased" from the indigenous inhabitants, and tenants were brought in to secure Holland's hold.

In 1664, the Dutch colony was seized by the British, but the feudal system remained largely unchanged, farmers paying a yearly rent (in food stuffs or its equivalent in cash) yet never having the opportunity to actually own the land. In 1695, the governor granted a patent which transformed the patroonship of Rensselaerwyck into a manor and the patroon into its lord. At the same time, the British further entrenched the system by granting patents to millions of acres of new land. The last colonial governor of New York expressed the thinking of the time when he wrote that giving these huge tracts of land to the aristocracy would "counterpoise in some measure the general levelling spirit that so prevails," making reference to the antinomian and proto-anarchist Ranters, Diggers, and Levellers of Great Britain.

After the Revolutionary War, some land was taken from the Tories, but the most valuable tracts were given to Federalists as payment for their war claims, and other sections were sold to speculators. The most powerful landowning families—Van Rennselaer, Livingston, Schuyler, and Hamilton—continued to tighten their hold on the area through intermarriage and further purchases. In 1839, Stephen Van Rennselaer, known as the Good Patroon, died. Realizing that the patroon system was fragile and that only so much pressure could be put on it before it collapsed, he often had allowed tenants' rents to lapse during times of bad harvest or other ill fortune. At his death, it was found that he'd accumulated large debts. Owing him nearly a half million dollars in back rents, his tenants were seen by the Van Rennselaer heirs as a likely way out of their financial predicament. In the Helderbergs, on the west side of the Hudson, where farming was particularly difficult, resentment against the heirs' new demand for total payment rose quickly, developing within the year into what is now known as the Anti-rent War.

The first anti-rent meetings were called in Berne, the highest place in the Helderbergs. In a Declaration of Independence dated July 4th, which the newly-formed anti-rent association sent to Stephen Van Rensselaer IV, they compared his oppressive rent measures to the Stamp Act of 1765 and themselves to the self-named Sons of Liberty, who fought against British economic oppression by tarring and feathering the King's functionaries, ransacking their homes and hanging them in effigy.

Quickly, the anti-rent associations had thousands of dues-paying members and their influence was felt throughout all the leasehold lands. The governor of New York sent in armed militia to put down the rebellion and the Anti-rent War began in earnest. Disguising themselves in costumes of brilliant calico, covered with fur, feathers, and tin ornaments, wearing sheepskin masks, or with their faces painted red and black, parties of self-proclaimed Indians struck back against the patroons/underlings.

When sheriffs would approach a farmer's land, intending to sell off some of his livestock in order to pay back rents, the Calico Indians would surround the lawmen—usually on horseback—or ambush, disarm and drive them away. And on the few occasions when the auctions did occur, the Indians deployed snipers to kill all the cattle and sheep that had been sold. The Indians' tactics were a mixture of guerrilla warfare and adolescent playfulness. They kidnapped sheriffs and held them prisoner in taverns until they agreed to jump up and down three times and shout "Down with the rent!" They stole and destroyed legal papers, threatened farmers who paid their rents, and harassed sheriffs whenever they appeared.

Adopting pseudo-savage names (Red Jacket, Black Hawk, Yellow Jacket, Blue Beard, Little Thunder, White Chief) the Calico Indians bound themselves by an oath. "I do of my own free will and accord come forward to join this body of men and will reveal no secrets of the society made known to me necessary to be kept." Farm-wives and daughters were enlisted to make gowns and masks, the more outlandish the better. At their peak, the Indians numbered over ten thousand, yet no two costumes were alike. The chiefs' garments were the most flamboyant, however, because the anti-rent associations provided money to buy calico (as well as ornaments and pistols). Anyone was able to deck himself out as outrageously as he pleased. When a prominent Rennselaer county Indian died, an escort of his fellows—ninety-six men strong, mounted and in full battle dress—formed the vanguard of his funeral procession. In 1844, when Governor William Bouck held a conference to meet with local residents, over a hundred Indians stood at the edges of the crowd, shouting and jeering.

Armed with muskets, pistols, scythes, axes, clubs, hatchets and knives, the Indians were able to mobilize quickly whenever sheriffs approached to serve writs or seize property. As a primitive communication network, the Indians convinced (sometimes by the use of force) farmers to use their tin dinner horns only as a warning signal that the law was near. The message could be quickly relayed over many miles, the blaring of the horns (normally used to call workers in for their meals) reaching across the hills and valleys of the Catskills. The organization of the Indian bands followed the cell structure which one of the most important anti-rent leaders, Thomas Devyr, had used while a Chartist agitator in Scotland. The Indians divided into ten-to-fifteen man units, the identity of individuals known only to the chief of the cell, who was in turn known only by his mock-Indian name.

Devyr, born in Donegal, Ireland in 1805, published a pamphlet called "Our Natural Rights," in which he stated: "I saw that the earth if vigorously tilled would yield plenty of the comforts of life. Willing labor and fertile soil would produce plenty to eat, drink and wear." After publishing the pamphlet, he fled from Ireland, and went to work in London, working for the liberal papers in which he attacked Irish Landlordism. Working class rebels in Newcastle-upon-Tyne asked him to join them. He left London, calling it "that great social wen," and quickly rose to prominence among the Scots fighting for social and political reform. In 1840, he fled Scotland to avoid arrest and landed in New York. Within months, he was at the forefront of the anti-rent struggles in the Hudson Valley.

Another prominent anti-rent leader was Dr. Smith Boughton, who came to be known by his Indian name, Big Thunder. A brilliant public speaker and organizer, he traveled up and down the Catskills, addressing meetings, exhorting farmers to join or support financially the Indians' efforts. Targeted by the lords of Livingston manor, he was eventually arrested for robbery (after a sheriff was relieved of his warrants and writs by a band of Indians) and sentenced to life imprisonment at hard labor.

In 1844, the hostilities had increased to such a high pitch that Governor Silas Wright issued a proclamation declaring Delaware County (the epicenter of Indian activities) to be in a state of insurrection and ordered in the military to "preserve order." Then, in early 1845, he requested that the legislature pass a law making it illegal for any individual to appear with "his face painted, discolored, covered or concealed," or to refuse help to a law enforcement officer in the pursuit of "seizing, arresting, confining...every person with his face so painted." Though anti-rent forces were building strength in the legislature, the measure passed easily. The Calico Indians, however, continued their guerilla war. As in most insurgency movements, the rebels remained hidden and highly mobile, striking only when they had sufficient force to overcome their enemy, then evaporating as quickly as they'd gathered.

The Anti-rent War continued until August of 1845, when Sheriff Green More and Osman Steele (his jailor and undersheriff) rode to the farm of Moses Earle near Andes, to sell off some of Earle's livestock in order to satisfy a warrant for two years' back rent. The Indians gathered in force, blaring their horns, and surrounded the two sheriffs.

Steele resisted and shots were fired. Three bullets hit him and he died late that day. The Indians scattered. As soon as the news got out, public opinion turned against the rebels. The cells disbanded, thousands of masks were burned and buried, and the calico gowns were converted overnight into curtains and quilts. Mass arrests followed the death of Steele and eventually eighty-four men were convicted: two sentenced to the gallows and thirteen to prison terms.

Yet, though the Indians' violence was condemned by the general population, their goals were still popular and the anti-rent forces continued to work their way into state government. In 1846, John Young was elected governor of New York on an anti-rent platform and a few weeks after taking office, had pardoned all the Calico Indian prisoners still in jail. In 1848, the legislature abolished the tenure rent system.

In retrospect, it is clear that in order to throw off the two hundred year old feudal system, the Catskill and Hudson River Valley farmers needed to transform themselves, physically as well as emotionally. Like the "Indians" who took part in the Boston Tea Party, the Catskill rebels disguised themselves for practical purposes, to prevent being identified and punished. However, they also chose to transform themselves into creatures who could do what no law-abiding citizen would dream of doing. By putting on ridiculous costumes, taking false names, and swearing melodramatic oaths, they escaped centuries of social constraint.

The view of Indians that the farmers exhibited is clearly quite skewed. Boyish enthusiasm, romantic notions of the noble savage, and simple ignorance shaped the Calico Indians' idea of themselves. The costume itself points to a gross misunderstanding of what "Indian" meant. Looking more like animals dressed in women's clothing than the original inhabitants of the land they worked, the Calico Indians embraced freedom by embracing otherness. Decked out in gowns, flowers, wigs, ribbons and tassels, they allowed themselves, most likely without knowing it, to play at being women. Wearing masks made from animal parts (sheepskin, horse hair, stag horns, pig ears and feathers) they were more beasts than men. And a few of the most brave even played at being demons: wearing horns, fangs and scarlet talons. Half-drunk, converting their farm implements into weapons, they had strength where before they had only servitude and the prospect of endless toil.

For them the word "Indian" meant something far larger than Native American. It was a label that denoted wildness, lack of restraint, the ability to follow one's desires. Some took names that were overtly Arabic (The Prophet), or Mexican (Santa Anna). With their secret oaths, midnight forays, bizarre costumes, their violence mixed with grandiose heroics; they clearly believed that to be an Indian was not merely to be non-white, but also something bigger than life. Crossing racial, gender, even species lines, all expectations were overturned. Anecdotes were told of parents talking for hours with their sons, and of girls being overwhelmed by the kisses and caresses of their own brothers, without anyone suspecting their true identity. Drunken farm boys could be, for a few hours, powerful chieftains; warriors rather than serfs. Armed sheriffs could be mocked, humiliated and treated as buffoons. Even family ties meant nothing. Social, as well as political law was overthrown.

At the killing of undersheriff Osman Steele, the Indians shouted, "Down with the laws, we are here to break them." For a few years, they lived out the fantasy of the disenfranchised. By mixing their playfulness with criminality and righteous defiance, they were able to claim their land and a small, but significant, measure of dignity.

REFERENCES

Carmer, Carl. *The Hudson* (Farrar and Rinehart: 1939).
Christman, Henry. *Tin Horns and Calico* (Holt: 1945).
Ellis, David. *Landlords and Farmers in the Hudson–Mohawk Region, 1790–1850* (Octagon Books: 1967)
Gould, Jay. *History of Delaware County* (Keeny and Gould: 1856).
Kelsay, Isabel T. "The Trial of Big Thunder," *History,* #33 (7/35).

THE IROQUOIS INFLUENCE
ON WOMEN'S RIGHTS

Sally Roesch Wagner

[I]t behooves us women to question all historians,
sacred and profane, who teach by examples or pre-
cepts any philosophy that lowers the status of the
mothers of the race, or favors the one-man power in
government.[1]

THESE ARE THE WORDS OF ONE OF THE MAJOR THEO-
rists of the early women's rights movement, Elizabeth Cady
Stanton, written 100 years ago. Stanton, along with Lucretia
Mott, called the first women's rights convention in Seneca Falls, New
York in 1848, and is generally credited with being the "mother" of
early feminism.

Stanton and Matilda Joslyn Gage wrote the major documents of the
radical wing of the women's movement, and shared leadership positions in the National Woman Suffrage Association and authorship of
the monumental History of Woman Suffrage with Susan B. Anthony.
With the growing conservatism of the women's movement after 1890,
the name of Matilda Joslyn Gage was literally written out of history
by increasingly timid new woman suffragists who had taken charge. A
similar attempt to sever historical ties with Elizabeth Cady Stanton
was only partially successful.

As feminist historians restore Gage and Stanton to their rightful
place in history, we find a new history. This is especially true with the
rediscovery of Matilda Joslyn Gage, considered by some Women's
Studies scholars today to have been one of the foremost feminist theo-
reticians, and considered during her time as part of the suffrage "triumvirate" with Stanton and Anthony. The inclusion of Gage and
Stanton causes a rethinking of the origin of the nineteenth century

women's movement. Previously, twentieth century historians assumed the story of feminism began with the "discovery" of America by white men, or the political revolution staged by the colonists. The underlying assumption seems to have been that there was no seed of feminism in American soil when the first white settlers arrived. White people imported it.

Certainly there was a European foundation for American feminism. Suffragists documented the influence in the *History of Woman Suffrage,* edited by the "triumvirate" of the women's movement: Matilda Joslyn Gage, Elizabeth Cady Stanton and Susan B. Anthony Gage, regarded as "one of the most logical, fearless, and scientific writers of her day," traced the white Western history of feminism back to the early part of the fourteenth century. In her chapter on "Preceding Causes" in the first volume of the *History of Woman Suffrage*, Gage maintained that European women, along with their male supporters, had waged a four hundred year struggle for women's rights.[2]

She documented calls for women's rights during the Revolution which were ignored, as all the pleas by Western women had been for three hundred years. The United States revolutionaries, once they had cemented power, placed women into a political subordination more severe even than that of the colonial period.[3] Ironically, these decreased rights for women were a result of basing the new state laws on English law. The European tradition of church and law placed women in the role of property. Gage quoted Herbert Spencer's "epitome of English history," *Descriptive Sociology of England*, which described the condition of women in this way: "Our laws are based on the all sufficiency of man's rights, and society exists today for woman only insofar as she is in the keeping of some man."[4]

Abigail Adams feared that English common law, which had recently (1765-69) been drawn together into Blackstone's Code, would be used as the foundation upon which the laws of the new United States would be based. Her fear was realized. Blackstone's code was used as the basis for family law as the states concretized their laws after the revolution. It marked a decided setback for women. Women's "very being or legal existence was upended during marriage, or at least, incorporated or consolidated into that of the husband, under whose wing, protection and cover, she performs everything," according to Blackstone. The two shall become one and the one is the man, the church proclaimed in canon law, and common law echoed the proclamation. According to women's rights advocates from Abigail Adams to her 19th century counterparts, marriage under common law was a legal institution that robbed women of their rights and created conditions that encouraged men to act tyrannically.

Under the European-inspired laws that were adopted by each state after the revolution, a single woman might be economically independent, owning property and earning her living; upon uttering the marriage vows, she lost control of her property and her earnings. She also gave away all rights to children she would bear. They became the "property" of the father who could give them away or grant custody to someone other than the mother, in the event of his death. With the words, "I do," a woman literally gave away her legal identity. The woman lost her name, her right to control her own body, and to live where she chose. A married woman could not make any contracts, sue or be sued; she was dead in the law. Wife-beating was not against the law, neither was marital rape.

Women's rights could not be easily incorporated into Eurocentric thought; rather, feminism challenged the very foundation of Western institutions.[5] Gage wrote:

> As I look backward through history I see the church everywhere stepping upon advancing civilization, hurling woman from the plane of "natural rights" where the fact of her humanity had placed her, and through itself, and its control over the state, in the doctrine of "revealed rights" everywhere teaching an inferiority of sex; a created subordination of woman to man; making her very existence a sin; holding her accountable to a diverse code of morals from man; declaring her possessed of fewer rights in church and in state; her very entrance into heaven made dependent upon some man to come as mediator between her and the Savior it has preached, thus crushing her personal, intellectual and spiritual freedom.[6]

Discontent came to a head for radical women's rights reformers in the late 1880s as their goal of equality in the church, state and family remained unmet. Women had been denied the right to vote by the United States Supreme Court, were still seen as the source of evil by the church because of Eve's "original sin," and were still expected to be the "great unpaid laborers of the world," the virtual slaves of the household. These reformers, who had worked for change with little success for forty years, began calling for a radical transformation of the social order.

It was not simply the absence of rights that was the problem, they came to believe. It was the fact that, as Stanton said:

> Society is based on this four-fold bondage of woman—
> Church, State, Capital and Society—making liberty
> and equality for her antagonistic to every organized
> institution.[7]

Gage expressed it this way:

> During the ages, no rebellion has been of like impor-
> tance with that of Woman against the tyranny of
> Church and State; none has had its far reaching
> effects. We note its beginning; its progress will over-
> throw every existing form of these institutions; its
> end will be a regenerated world.[8]

These two women, Gage and Stanton, the major theorists of the radical wing of the women's suffrage movement, became increasingly disenchanted with the inability/unwillingness of Western institutions to change and embrace the liberty of not just women, but all disfranchised groups. They looked elsewhere for their vision of the "regenerated world" which Gage predicted. Gage, and to a lesser extent Stanton, found it in Upstate New York. They became students of the Haudenosaunee—the Six Nations of the Iroquois Confederacy—and found a cosmological worldview which they believed to be far superior to the patriarchal one of the white nation in which they lived.

What were their sources, how did they know about the Iroquois? They read Lewis Henry Morgan, of course, but he was only one of many Gage cites. For example, in documenting the matrilineal system, Gage says:

> Although the principal chief of the confederacy was a
> man, descent ran through the female line, the sister
> of the chief possessing the power of nominating his
> successor.[9] ... The line of descent, feminine, was espe-
> cially notable in all tribal relations such as the elec-
> tion of Chiefs, and the Council of Matrons, to which
> all disputed questions were referred for final adjudi-
> cation.[10] ... Not alone the Iroquois but most Indians of

North America trace descent in the female line; among some tribes woman enjoys almost the whole legislative authority and in others a prominent share.[11] Lafitte and other Jesuit missionary writers are corroborated in this statement by Schoolcraft, Catlin, Clark, Hubert Bancroft of the Pacific coast, and many students of Indian life and customs.[12]

Clark, the regional historian that Gage mentioned, wrote that with both marriage and separation, among the Iroquois, there was "no special ceremony, no disgrace, and each keeps their property."[13]

Another local historian read by Gage was C. Smith, who quoted Ephriam Webster, who came as a trader in 1786, lived with the Onondaga and Oneidas for a quarter of a century, and was adopted into the Onondaga nation. Webster said,

> The Indians have no altercations, and that in ten years I have not heard any angry expression nor seen any degree of passion. They treated their women with respect, even tenderness. They used no ardent spirits. They settled differences amicably, raised wheat and corn in considerable quantities, and also apples.[14]

Gage also read Horatio Hale, who wrote:

> When a chief died or (as sometimes happened) was deposed for incapacity or misconduct, some member of the same family succeeded him. Rank followed the female line; and this successor might be any descendent of the late chief's mother or grandmother—his brother, his cousin or his nephew—but never his son. Among many persons who might thus be eligible, the selection was made in the first instance by a family council. In this council the "chief matron" of the family, a noble dame whose position and right were well defined, had the deciding voice.[15]

> Now there is another thing we say, we younger brothers. He who has worked for us has gone afar off; and he also will in time take with him all these the whole body of warriors and also the whole body of women-they will go with him. But it is still harder when the woman shall die, because with her the line is lost.

And also with the grandchildren and the little ones
who are running around—these he will take away;
and also those that are creeping on the ground, and
also those that are on the cradleboards; all these he
will take away with him.[16]

"Because with her the line is lost." The same sentiment prevailed among the Hurons. "For a Huron
killed by a Huron," writes Father Ragueneau in the
letter just quoted, "thirty gifts are commonly deemed
a sufficient satisfaction. For a woman forty are
required, because, as they say, the women are less
able to defend themselves; and moreover, they being
the source whence the land is peopled, their lives
should be deemed of more value to the commonwealth, and their weakness should have a stronger
support in public justice." Such was the reasoning of
these heathen barbarians. Enlightened Christendom
has hardly yet advanced to the mark of these opinions.[17]

Gage remarked:

So fully, to this day is descent reckoned through the
mother, that blue-eyed, fair-haired children of white
fathers are numbered in the tribe and receive both
from state and nation their portion of the yearly dole
paid to Indian tribes. The veriest pagan among the
Iroquois, the renowned and important Keeper of the
Wampum, and present sole interpreter of the Belts
which give the most ancient and secret history of this
confederation, is Ephriam Webster, descended from a
white man, who, a hundred or more years since,
became affiliated through marriage with an Indian
woman, as a member of the principal nation of the
Iroquois, the Onondagas.[18]

Gage read at least some of the many non-Indian women who studied and wrote about the Iroquois during her lifetime. There were pro-
fessional ethnologists like Alice Fletcher or Erminnie Smith, and
"amateur" ethnologists, women like her, who had developed an interest in, and friendships with, members of one of the six Iroquois
nations. These women, several dozen of them, wrote often with an

astonishing understanding, which would no doubt have been recognized and respected into this century had they been men.[19]

Laura M. Sheldon Wright, wife of a missionary at Cattaraugus, published a Dictionary of the Seneca Language around 1835. Harriet Maxwell Converse, the woman who arranged for Gage to be adopted into the Wolf clan of the Mohawk nation, wrote extensively for the New York papers. While her *Myths and Legends* has been criticized for being romanticized, her newspaper articles were straightforward and highly descriptive. They also document her extensive support and lobbying work for the Iroquois. Converse "has ready for the press a volume of lyrics, sonnets and Indian myth songs," Harriet Phillips Eaton wrote Gage in the 1890s. Eaton, who was Gage's cousin, wrote about the Iroquois.

Helen F. Troy, of Syracuse, then Auburn, was adopted by Thomas and Electa Thomas into the Snipe clan of the Onondaga nation in 1894. She was given the name Spirit Dipping into the Silent Waters (Gar-wen-nesho) . The *New York Herald* announced that "Mrs. Troy is at present at work on and is soon to have published an elaborate translation of the 'Book of the Sacred Wampum,' or the Iroquois Bible, also a dictionary for use in the colleges, of the Onondaga and Mohawk tongues with their equivalent meanings in English," the result of fifteen years of research. The book was to be illustrated by her husband, John H. Troy. The manuscript "is about to be submitted to printers for publication" the paper reported.[20]

In 1880, only six years before her death, Erminnie A. Smith became interested in the Six Nations and was appointed by the Smithsonian Institution to study them. She "lived among the Indians to study their habits and folklore and was so well-liked by the Tuscaroras that she was adopted into the White Bear clan" and given the name of Ka-tie-tio-sta-knost, meaning "Beautiful Flower." At the time of her death she was completing an Iroquois dictionary containing 15,000 classified words; 6,000 of the Tuscaroras, 3,000 of the Onondagas, and a thousand each of Oneidas and Senecas. She was just beginning her work with the Cayugas when she died.[21] J.N.B. Hewitt, of the Bureau of Ethnology, a Tuscarora who was her assistant, completed the dictionary, and called Smith "a superbly gifted scholar."[22] Horatio Hale said Smith "had pursued studies which in ethnology alone would make any man famous." The New York Academy of Sciences, in recognition of her work, elected Mrs. Smith a Fellow of their society, the first time this honor was conferred on a woman. A member of the Association for the Advancement of Science, the English Anthropological Society, and one of the leaders of Sorosis, she contributed largely to various scientific journals.[23] Smith's *Myths of the Iroquois*, originally published in 1883, has been reprinted by Iroquois Reprints.

Mary Elizabeth Beauchamp was the daughter of William M. Beauchamp, who *The Dictionary of American Biography* claims "became, among white men, the greatest authority on the history and institutions of the Iroquois. In a sense he was the successor of Lewis Morgan in this field." Mary Elizabeth was her father's secretary and also wrote on the Iroquois.

William Beauchamp wrote, in *Iroquois Folk Lore*, that he had an "interesting series of Seneca tales from Miss Myra E. Trippe of Salamanca, New York, which I procured for the State Library. Unfortunately they were destroyed, along with the Moravian journals I sent there at the same time." Whether or not any copies still exist, there is a good chance that Gage read them during her lifetime, as she was a friend of the Beauchamps. While Gage read Morgan, Lafitte, Schoolcraft, Catlin, and Clark on the Iroquois, she knew Beauchamp. There were strong family ties between the two. Beauchamp's father was editor of a local paper and Gage wrote for him. Beauchamp's daughter-in-law wrote a song, "The Battle Hymn of the Suffragists" for Gage.

Identifying how a Fayetteville, New York resident of 1890 knew about the Iroquois is an easy task. In fact, it was hard to pick up a newspaper or magazine in upstate New York in the nineteenth century without reading something about the Iroquois. The local paper Gage read, the *Onondaga (Syracuse) Standard*, reported everything from condolence ceremonies to the lacrosse scores when Onondaga played the Mohawks. When legislation was introduced to break up the Iroquois nations' lands into individual ownership, the protests that came from Onondaga were published in full by the paper, along with the names of all the signatures to the petitions. The level of sophistication of these newspaper stories indicates that the average non-Indian in upstate New York 100 years ago possessed a level of knowledge about the Iroquois that, in the white nation, is held only by a relatively small number of scholars today.[24] It comes as no surprise then, that when reformers like Matilda Joslyn Gage looked outside of their culture for a model upon which to base their vision of an egalitarian world, they quickly found their well-known Indian neighbors.

Rose Yawger wrote about lineage in her *Good Housekeeping* approved book which was published in Syracuse in 1893:

> The children always followed the totemship of the mother, and to this significant fact alone much of the existing confusion in regard to the tribe of certain prominent characters is, in a great measure, due. If a Seneca brave married a Cayuga squaw [sic], the children were not Senecas, as might be supposed, but Cayugas, and even though they were born and brought up among the Senecas, they were aliens to the tribe and had to be adopted in the same ceremonious manner that strangers sometimes were. The Cayuga nation could even call on them to take arms in case of war.[25]

Or Minnie Myrtle, who was published by the popular Appleton press in 1855:

> The children are of the tribe of the mother, as are the children's children to the latest generation, and they are also of the same nation. If the mother is a Cayuga, the children are Cayugas; and if a Mohawk, the children are Mohawks. If the marriage proves unhappy, the parties are allowed to separate, and each is at liberty to marry again. But the mother has the sole right to the disposal of the children. She keeps them all if she chooses, and to their father they are ever [mere] strangers.[26]

This issue of lineage had great bearing on the status of women, as these early feminists analyzed it.[27] Gage wrote about the absence of a woman's right to her children in the white nation:

> The slave code has always been that children shall follow the condition of the mother; hence, as the present law of marriage makes the wife the irresponsible slave of the husband—robbing her of her name, her earnings, her accountability—it consistently follows that she shall be robbed of her children. Blackstone, the chief exponent of common law, says: "A mother has no legal right or authority over her children; she is only entitled to respect and honor." The United

States, governing itself by English law, inherited this with other oppressions, and it to this day holds force in most of the thirty-seven States of the Union. One or two States have by statute law placed the mother on equal basis of legal right with the father ... men, calling themselves Christian men, have dared to defy God's law, and to give to the father alone the sole right to the child; have dared make laws which permit the dying father of an unborn child to will it away, and to give any person he pleases to select the right to wait the advent of that child, and when the mother, at the hazard of her own life, has brought it forth, to rob her of it and to do by it as the dead father directed. What an anomaly on justice is such a law![28]

Gage also wrote about the recognition of the primacy of the mother-child bond among the Haudenosaunee:

If for any cause the Iroquois husband and wife separated, the wife took with her all the property, she had brought into the wigwam; the children also accompanied the mother, whose right to them was recognized as supreme.[29]

Matilda Joslyn Gage's public connection with the Iroquois began in the 1870s when, as President of the National Woman Suffrage Association and an amateur ethnologist, she published a series of articles on the Iroquois which were featured prominently in the *New York Evening Post* and reprinted in several other papers in the state.[30] The introduction to the series recognized the significance of this suffrage/Indian connection, stating:

Mrs. Gage has given some attention to the traditions of the aboriginal inhabitants of this country, and we understand that she intends to write a book about them...Mrs. Gage, with an exhibition of ardent devotion to the cause of woman's rights which is very proper in the president of the National Woman Suffrage Association, gives prominence to the fact that in the old days when the glory of the famous confederation of savages was at its height, the power and importance of women were recognized by the allied tribes.[31]

In the ensuing series of articles, Gage contended that "division of power between the sexes in this Indian republic was nearly equal."[32] She noted that:

> The family relation among the Iroquois demonstrated woman's superiority in power. When an Indian husband brought the products of the chase to the wigwam, his control over it ceased. In the home, the wife was absolute; the sale of the skins was regulated by her, the price was paid to her.[33]

This information was in marked contrast to the cultural mythology of Indian women as beasts of burden. It was precisely this role in the home that gave a woman her status, Gage contended,

> ...the women being the chief agriculturists...their method of farming was entirely different from our own. In olden Iroquois tillage there was no turning the sod with a plough to which were harnessed a cow and a woman, as is seen today in Christian Germany, but the ground was literally "tickled with a hoe" and it "laughed with a harvest."[34]

> Three of the five ancient feasts of the Iroquois were agricultural feasts connected with this their great staple...Centuries ago was agriculture thus honored by this ancient people...To themselves the Five Nations were known as the Ongwe Honwe, that is, a people surpassing all others. In Christian Europe during the middle ages the agriculturist was despised; the warrior was the aristocrat of civilization. In publicly honoring agriculture as did the Ongwe Honwe three times a year, they surpassed in wisdom the men of Europe.[35]

> There are pretty stories of these Three Sisters, the corns, beans, and pumpkins, [squash] but it is noteworthy that the Indian Thanksgiving day antedated our own. It is more American than we have ever claimed.[36]

Women lost all rights to their property when they married in the white nation, and both Gage and Stanton pointed to the contrast between the property rights of white and Iroquois women.

Alice Fletcher, a noted suffragist, ethnographer, and government agent, described the opposite condition among the Indian women in the numerous tribes and nations she had observed. Gage had helped organize an International Council of Women in 1888; Stanton had sailed back from England to attend. Speaking before this audience, Fletcher touched a nerve sensitive to suffragists, their lack of property rights, as she recounted this personal experience with the Omaha:

> At the present time all property is personal; the man owns his own ponies and other belongings which he has personally acquired; the woman owns her horses, dogs, and all the lodge equipment, children own their own articles, and parents do not control the possessions of their children. There is really no family property, as we use the term. A wife is as independent in the use of her possessions as is the most independent man in our midst. If she chooses to give away or sell all of her property, there is no one to gainsay her...37

> When I was living with the Indians, my hostess...one day gave away a very fine horse. I was surprised, for I knew there had been no family talk on the subject, so I asked: "Will your husband like to have you give the horse away?" Her eyes danced, and, breaking into a peal of laughter, she hastened to tell the story to the other women gathered in the tent, and I became the target of many merry eyes. I tried to explain how a white woman would act, but laughter and contempt met my explanation of the white man's hold upon his wife's property.38

A similar story came from the pen of a Frenchwoman, Emma Borglum, who married the sculptor Solon Borglum, and spent her honeymoon among the Lakota on the Crow Creek reservation of South Dakota in 1891:

> One day I showed some astonishment at seeing a young Indian woman, in the absence of her husband, give two horses to a friend, she looked at me very coldly and said: "These horses are mine." I excused myself saying that in my country a woman would con-

sult her husband before giving such expensive presents. The woman answered proudly: "I would not be
a white woman!"[39]

Minnie Myrtle again:

> In regard to property, too, the wife retains whatever
> belonged to her before marriage, distinct from her
> husband, and can dispose of it as she pleases without
> his consent, and if she separates from him, takes it
> with her, and at her death, either before or after sep-
> aration, her children inherit all she possessed.[40]

It was far different for white women under common law which
denied property rights to non-Indian women, as suffragist attorney
Carrie S. Burnham described:

> By marriage, the husband and wife are one person in
> law; that is, the legal existence of the woman is
> "merged in that of her husband." He is her "baron," or
> "lord," bound to supply her with shelter, food, clothing
> and medicine and is entitled to her earnings—the use
> and custody of her person which he may seize wher-
> ever he may find it.[41]

In a speech before the National Council of Women in 1891,
Elizabeth Cady Stanton called on the memoirs of Ashur Wright, a
long-time missionary among the Seneca, whose wife Laura had published a dictionary of the Seneca language. Ashur Wright related:

> Usually the females ruled the house. The stores were
> in common; but woe to the luckless husband or lover
> who was too shiftless to do his share of the providing.
> No matter how many children, or whatever goods he
> might have in the house, he might at any time be
> ordered to pick up his blanket and budge; and after
> such an order it would not be healthful for him to
> attempt to disobey. The house would be too hot for
> him; and unless saved by the intercession of some
> aunt or grandmother he must retreat to his own clan,
> or go and start a new matrimonial alliance in some
> other.[42]

Stanton was especially sensitive to this issue of divorce. Among suffragists, she was uniquely courageous in publicly and consistently advocating that the laws be changed to allow women the right to leave disagreeable marriages. For this stand, she was labeled an infidel by organized Christian religion which generally held that marriage was a covenant with God which no woman had a right to break, even if her life was in danger from a violent husband. Again, the situation was very different for Indian women, as Alice Fletcher had explained:

> ...the wife never becomes entirely under the control of her husband. Her kindred have a prior right, and can use that right to separate her from him or to protect her from him, should he maltreat her. The brother who would not rally to the help of his sister would become a byword among his clan. Not only will he protect her at the risk of his life from insult and injury, but he will seek help for her when she is sick and suffering...

In the *Journal of American Folklore*, Beauchamp related an Iroquois story in which "a man who had beaten his wife cruelly upon earth, struck a red hot statue of woman. The sparks flew with every blow and burned him."[43]

Fletcher was concerned about what would happen to the Indian women when they became citizens and lost their rights, and were treated with the same legal disrespect as white women, as she explained to the International Council of Women in 1888:

> Not only does the woman under our [white nation] laws lose her independent hold on her property and herself, but there are offenses and injuries which can befall a woman which would be avenged and punished by the relatives under tribal law, but which have no penalty or recognition under our laws. If the Indian brother should, as of old, defend his sister, he would himself become liable to the law and suffer for his championship.[44]

She was referring, of course, to sexual and physical violence against women. Indian men's intolerance of rape was commented upon by many eighteenth and nineteenth century Indians and non-Indian reporters alike, many of whom contended that rape didn't exist among Indian nations previous to white contact.[45]

Hewitt, for example, quoted Gen. James Clinton, commanding the New York division of the Sullivan punitive expedition in 1779, with orders to disperse the hostile Iroquois and to destroy their homes, [who] paid his enemies the high tribute of a brave soldier by writing in April, 1779, to his lieutenant, Colonel Van Schaick, then leading his troops against the Onondaga and their villages, the following terse compliment: "Bad as these savages are, they never violate the chastity of any woman, their prisoner." And he added this significant admonition to his colonel, "It would be well to take measures to prevent a stain upon our army."[46]

Also Mary Elizabeth Beauchamp, daughter of the noted Iroquoianist, in a letter to the *Skaneateles Democrat*, dated 10 April 1883, wrote:

It shows the remarkable security of living on an Indian Reservation, that a solitary woman can walk about for miles, at any hour of the day or night, in perfect safety. Miss R.* often starts off, between eight and nine in the evening, lantern in one hand and alpenstock in the other, and a parcel of supplies strung from her shoulder, to walk for a mile or more up the hillsides. [*Miss Remington, "had long been in charge of the mission house." She was adopted into the Snipe clan of the Onondaga in 1886, and given the name "Ki-a-was-say," A new word.][47]

The reality of a culture in which rape was not allowed is difficult to comprehend by a European tradition which legalized both marital rape and wife battering, and in which one out of three women are raped, according to current FBI statistics. As Carrie S. Burnham, the legal genius of the National Woman Suffrage Association who worked with Gage and Stanton analyzed common law:

The husband being bound to provide for his wife the necessaries of life, and being responsible for "her morals" and the good order of the household, may choose and govern the domicile, choose her associates, separate her from her relatives, restrain her religious and personal freedom, compel her to cohabit with him, correct her faults by mild means and if necessary chastise her with the same moderation as [if] she was his apprentice or child.[48]

The vote was the tool that women could use in the white nation to gain their rights, and suffrage was a right which they believed to be inherently theirs in a republic. The white government believed otherwise. State laws denied women suffrage, and in 1874 the United States Supreme Court ruled that they had the constitutional right to do so. Women did not receive the constitutional right to vote in the United States of America until 1920. Iroquois women had always possessed suffrage, as these early feminists well knew. Stanton, for example, wrote:

> The women were the great power among the clan, as everywhere else. They did not hesitate, when occasion required, "to knock off the horns," as it was technically called, from the head of a chief and send him back to the ranks of the warriors. The original nomination of the chiefs also always rested with the women.[49]

Women suffrage papers regularly carried stories like this one which pointed out the contrast between the political position of women in the white nation and Indian nations:

> It is stated that an Indian Pueblo about fifty miles from the City of Mexico, is governed by a council of twelve, half of whom are elderly women who must have raised large families and proved devoted mothers and kind neighbors. "The venerable mothers," is the title by which they are known, which is certainly an improvement on the "old grannies" which we so often hear.[50]

Minnie Myrtle wrote in 1855:

> The legislative powers of the nation are vested in a Council of eighteen, chosen by the universal suffrages of the nation; but no treaty is to be binding, until it is ratified by three-fourths of all the voters, and three-fourths of all the mothers of the nation![51] So there was peace instead of war, as there would often be if the voice of woman could be heard! And though the

Senecas, in revising their laws and customs, have in a measure acceded to the civilized barbarism of treating the opinions of women with contempt, where their interest is equal, they still cannot sign a treaty without the consent of two thirds of the mothers![52]

The emblem of power worn by the Sachem [chief] was a deer's antlers, and if in any instance the women disapproved of the election or acts of a Sachem, they had the power to remove his horns and return him to private life. Their officers or runners from council to council were chosen by themselves and denominated women's men, and by these their interests were always fully represented. If at any time they wished any subject considered, by means of their runners, they called a council in their clan; if it was a matter of more general interest there was a council of the nation, and if the opinions of the women or Sachems of other nations were necessary, a grand council was called as readily to attend to them as to the interests of men. Thus a way was provided for them to have a voice in the affairs of the nation, without endangering their womanly reserve or subjecting them to the masculine reproach of publicity, or a desire to assume the offices and powers of men![53]

The purely democratic nature of Iroquois decisionmaking was described by Gage in this way:

The common interests of the confederacy were arranged in councils, each sex holding one of its own, although the women took the initiative in suggestion, orators of their own sex presenting their views to the council of men.[54]

One implication of the combination of female political power and female property rights was manifested in the making of treaties, according to Gage:

No sale of lands was valid without consent of the squaws[55] and among the State Archives at Albany, New York, treaties are preserved signed by the "Sachems and Principal Women of the Six Nations."[56]

Fletcher also described women's involvement in treaty negotiations:

> In olden times the women claimed the land. In the
> early treaties and negotiations for the sale of land,
> the women had their voice, and the famous Chief
> Cornplanter was obliged to retract one of his bargains
> because the women forbade, they being the land-hold-
> ers, and not the men. With the century, our custom of
> ignoring women in public transactions has had its
> reflex influence upon Indian custom.[57]

Iroquois women also influenced war decisions, according to Gage:

> Although it was a confederation of warriors, owing its
> permanence and its growth to prowess in arms, yet
> its women exercised controlling power in peace and
> war, forbidding at will its young braves to enter bat-
> tle, and often determining its terms of peace.[58]...Sir
> William Johnston mentions an instance of Mohawk
> squaws forbidding the war-path to young braves.[59]

Minnie Myrtle wrote:

> In the year 1791, when Washington wished to secure
> the neutrality of the Six Nations, a deputation was
> sent to treat with them, but was not favorably
> received, as many of the young Chiefs were for war
> and sided with the British. The women, as is usual,
> preferred peace, and argued that the land was theirs,
> for they cultivated and took care of it, and, therefore,
> had a right to speak concerning the use that should
> be made of its products. They demanded to be heard
> on this occasion, and addressed the deputation first
> themselves in the following words: "Brother:—The
> Great Ruler has spared us until a new day to talk
> together; for since you came here from General
> Washington, you and our uncles the Sachems have
> been counselling together. Moreover, your sisters, the
> women, have taken the same into great consideration,
> because you and our Sachems have said so much
> about it. Now, that is the reason we have come to say
> something to you, and to tell you that the Great Ruler
> hath preserved you, and that you ought to hear and

listen to what we, women, shall speak, as well as the Sachems; for we are the owners of this land, AND IT IS OURS! It is we that plan it for our and their use. Hear us, therefore, for we speak things that concern us and our children; and you must not think hard of us while our men shall say more to you, for we have told them."

They then designated Red Jacket as their speaker, and he took up the speech of his clients as follows:

"BROTHERS FROM PENNSYLVANIA:—You that are sent from General Washington, and by the thirteen fires; you have been sitting side by side with us every day, and the Great Ruler has appointed us another pleasant day to meet again.

"NOW LISTEN BROTHERS:—You know it has been the request of our head warriors, that we are left to answer for our women, who are to conclude what ought to be done by both Sachems and warriors. So hear what is their conclusion. The business you come on is very troublesome, and we have been a long time considering it; and now the elders of our women have said that our Sachems and warriors must help you, for the good of them and their children, and you tell us the Americans are strong for peace.[60]

William Stone in 1841 wrote:

It is one of the peculiar features of Indian polity that their lands belong to the warriors who defend, and the women who till them, and who, moreover, are the mothers of the warriors. And although the sachems, as civil magistrates, have ordinarily the power of negotiating treaties, yet whenever the question of a sale of land is the subject of a negotiation, if both the warriors and women become dissatisfied with the course the sachems are pursuing, they have the right to interpose and take the subject out of their hands.[61]

The Indian women with whom Fletcher had contact were well aware of their superior rights:

As I have tried to explain our statutes to Indian women, I have met with but one response. They have said: "As an Indian woman I was free. I owned my home, my person, the work of my own hands, and my children could never forget me. I was better as an Indian woman than under white law."[62]

She found a similar response among Indian men:

Men have said: "Your laws show how little your men care for their women. The wife is nothing of herself. She is worth little but to help a man to have one hundred and sixty acres." One day, sitting in the tent of an old chief, famous in war, he said to me: "My young men are to lay aside their weapons; they are to take up the work of the women; they will plow the field and raise the crops; for them I see a future, but my women, they to whom we owe everything, what is there for them to do? I see nothing! You are a woman; have pity on my women when everything is taken from them."[63]

Indian men were not unmindful of the unjust inferior political position of non-Indian women, and supported white suffragists in their struggle for political justice. Gage cited Dr. Peter Wilson, Seneca chief and maternal nephew of Red Jacket, who addressed the New York Historical Society in 1866, encouraging white men to use the occasion of Southern reconstruction to establish universal suffrage, "even of the women, as in his nation," according to newspaper reports.[64]

This support for women's suffrage from an Iroquois chief, came at a critical historic moment. The fifteenth amendment, which granted suffrage only to black men, was being ratified by the states. Women, black and white, were being told by abolitionists to wait for suffrage until after black men received it. Gage and Stanton's organization, the National Woman Suffrage Association, refused to take a back seat, and it comes as an amazing historical surprise that they received public support from a well-known and respected Iroquois who admonished white men to treat women as well as they were treated in his nation.

Arthur Parker also supported women's rights, writing at length:

Does the modern American woman [who] is a petitioner before man, pleading for her political rights, ever stop to consider that the red woman that lived in New York state five hundred years ago had far more political rights and enjoyed a much wider liberty than the twentieth century woman of civilization?

...The Iroquois woman was never the drudge that history has sought to picture her. She seldom worked as hard as the modern American woman of the middle class, and still the contrary opinion prevails. An instance comes to mind of a prosperous farmer who was arguing with a young man of Indian descent. Arrayed in his Sunday suit the farmer sat in his parlor. "I tell you," said he, "your poor Injun' women had to suffer while you men took it easy huntin', fishin', and killin' enemies. Them poor squaws had to lug water, dig potatoes, chop wood—aye, slaves they were! Now we white men—" There was a confusion of sounds outside, but the practiced ear of the Indian distinguished the sound of the axe, then the creak of the pump and the tread of feet. The outer door of the kitchen opened and a woman clad in a loose calico gown entered, holding in one arm a load of wood and bearing a pail of water in the other. "Your hired girl?" ventured the Indian. "Wall, no," said the farmer with a shamed faced look, "that's my wife."

This is no exaggeration but a true story of what actually happened and barring the Indian from the scene its like occurs daily everywhere in civilization. Women do men's work while men talk. Of course the reverse frequently happens also, but that's "Woman's Rights."

Parker then went on to talk about the taking of captives and related:

no man by word or deed ever offend[ed] the dignity of her sex...Civilized man and woman found in so-called savagery the acme of personal liberty. As late as 1826 several captive white women who had been carried by the Indians beyond Lake Superior were discovered by friends and offered every means of escape to home

and kindred, but one by one each rejected the over-
ture. They had shaken off the burdens of artificial life
and returned to nature. Never more did they wish to
resume the troubles of imperfect civilization.

Parker concludes:

Today as woman stands the advocate and petitioner
of her own cause, should she not offer an ablation of
gratitude to the memory of the Iroquois Indian, who
called the earth his "first mother" and through his
savage sense of justice gave to the mothers of his
race, their rights, maternal, civil, religious, social and
political.[65]

The political support went both ways. In her women's rights paper,
Gage editorialized:

That the Indians have been oppressed—are now, is
true, but the United States has treaties with them,
recognizing them as distinct political communities
and duty towards them demands not an enforced citizenship, but a faithful living up to its obligations on
the part of the government.[66]

While most early women's rights advocates found a similarity
between the treatment of slaves and married women, Gage made a
rare connection in the 1870s, comparing the government's treatment
of Indians with that of white men's treatment of wives. She introduced a resolution into the NWSA in 1879 which read: "That the policy of this government in appointing agents to educate and civilize the
Indians, to obtain calico dresses for squaws and aprons for papooses
and a comfortable salary for their own pockets out of money justly due
the Indian tribes, is in harmony with man's treatment of women in
appropriating her property, talents, time and labors, and using the
proceeds as he pleases in the name of protection."

Gage saw through the patriarchal posture of chivalry and benevo-
lence that kept women and Indians in economic subservience. And she
saw further. This was during a time when common wisdom agreed:

Pity the poor squaw
Beast of burden, slave;

chained under female law
from puberty to grave.

Gage, on the other hand, believed that "under [Iroquois] women the science of government reached the highest form known to the world."[67] "But the most notable fact connected with women's participation in governmental affairs among the Iroquois," she wrote, "is the statement of Hon. George Bancroft that the form of government of the United States, was borrowed from that of the Six Nations."[68]

This, according to Gage, was the most important conclusion she drew from her Iroquois study. Male-rule, or the Eurocentric social/government system she labeled the patriarchate, based its institutions on inequality of rights as exemplified in its long history of women's oppression. "Thus to the Matriarchate or Mother-rule," she concludes, "is the modern world indebted for its first conception of inherent rights, natural equality of condition, and the establishment of a civilized government upon this basis."[69]

While the Western theory of feminism came from dissidents who were chastised by the church and arrested by the state for their ideas, the Iroquois, on the other hand, practiced feminism. The idea of women's rights may have been refined in the unsuccessful centuries of struggle to gain it in the white nations. But the world-historic fact was that the behavior of equality was uniquely indigenous to Native people, these suffragists believed. Christianity and Western "civilization," they charged, had been the downfall of women.[70]

Knowledge of their lack of rights under English-inspired law was pervasive among these women, as was awareness of the prestigious position of Native women who lived in matrilineal/matrifocal systems.

For Matilda Joslyn Gage, the Haudenosaunee—the People of the Long House—were an example of the political/economic/gender/religious/social system of gynocracy she called The Matriarchate. "Never was justice more perfect, never civilization higher than under the Matriarchate."[71]

REFERENCES

1 Elizabeth Cady Stanton, "The Matriarchate," *The National Bulletin* I (February 1891) 3.
2 Matilda Joslyn Gage, Elizabeth Cady Stanton and Susan B. Anthony,

History of Woman Suffrage (Reprinted., Salem NH: Ayer Company, Publishers, Inc., 1985) I: 29. [Hereafter referreed to as *HWS*]

3 See Sally Roesch Wagner, *A Time of Protest: Suffragists Challenge the Republic, 1870-1887* (Carmichael, CA: Sky Carrier Press, 1988) Chapter 4.

4 Gage, Stanton and Anthony, *HWS* I: 26.

5 For an excellent theoretical analysis of the "Eurocentric notion," see José Barreiro, "Challenging the Eurocentric Notion" in *Indian Roots of American Democracy.* (Ithaca, NY: *Northeast Indian Quarterly,* 1988) xii-xvi.

6 Matilda Joslyn Gage, *Woman, Church and State.* (Chicago: Charles Kerr, 1893. Reprint Edition: Watertown, MA: Persephone Press, 1980) 245. [Hereafter referred to as *WCS.*]

7 Quoted in Lois Banner, *Elizabeth Cady Stanton: A Radical for Woman's Rights* (Boston: Little Brown and Co., 1980) 145.

8 Gage 246.

9 *New York Evening Post*, 24 September 1875.

10 Gage, 1893: 10.

11 Alexander, *History of Women,* quoted in WCS: 10.

12 Gage, 1893: 10.

13 Joshua V. H. Clark, *Onondaga, or Reminiscences of Earlier and Later Times* (Syracuse: N.P., 1848) 49-50.

14 R.P. Smith. *Historical and Statistical Gazetter of New York* (Syracuse: N.P., 1860) 69.

15 Horatio Hale, ed., *The Iroquois Book of Rights*, with an Introduction by William N. Fenton, (Philadelphia: D.G. Brinton, 1883; repr., Toronto: University of Toronto Press, 1963) 29.

16 *Ibid.,* 141,143.

17 *Ibid.,* 168.

18 Gage, 1893: 10.

19 These women will be the subject of another article.

20 *New York Herald*, 5 November 1905.

21 *Onondaga Standard*, 8 January 1946.

22 Marcellus Observer, 8 July 1949.

23 Unidentified newspaper clipping, 17 April 1893, Iroquois collection, Onondaga Historical Association, Syracuse, NY.

24 The Iroquois collection in the Onondaga Historical Association in Syracuse, NY, is an extraordinarily rich resource of 100 years of newspaper clippings.

25 Rose N. Yawger, *The Indian and the Pioneer: An Historical Study* 1 (Syracuse, New York: C.W. Bardeen, 1893) 39.

26 Minnie Myrtle, *The Iroquois; or, The Bright Side of Indian Character* (New York: D. Appleton and Company, 1855) 85-6.

27 I'm choosing here to look at status as Ann Eastlack Schafer did in her 1941 MA thesis in Anthropology for the University of Pennsylvania, "The

Status of Iroquois Women." Schafer defines status as simply, the "collection of rights and duties" of "all the positions which she occupies," as distinct from the Iroquois woman's role: "the dynamic aspect of a status."

28 Matilda Joslyn Gage, "The Mother of his Children," *San Francisco Pioneer*, 9 November 1871.

29 Gage, 1893: 10.

30 In 1893 she was adopted into the Wolf clan of the Mohawk nation and given the name Karonienhawi.

31 *The New York Evening Post*, 24 September 1875. Matilda Joslyn Gage scrapbook of writings, Gage collection, Schiesinger Library, Radcliffe College.

32 *Ibid.*

33 Gage, 1893: 10.

34 *The New York Evening Post*, 3 November 1875.

35 *Ibid.*

36 W.M. Beauchamp, "The New Religion of the Iroquois," *The Journal of American Folk-Lore*. 10 no. 38 (July-Sept. 1897) 177.

37 Alice Fletcher, *Report of the International Council of Women* (Washington, D.C.: Rufus H. Darby, Printer, 1888) 239-240.

38 Fletcher 238.

39 Emma Vignal Borglum, *The Experience at Crow Creek; A Sioux Indian Reservation at South Dakota*, Collection of the Manuscript Division, Library of Congress.

40 Minnie Myrtle, *The Iroquois or, The Bright Side of Indian Character* (New York: D. Appleton and Company, 1855) 85-6.

41 Carrie S. Burnham, *Tract No. 5: Common Law*, (N.P.: n.d.), Women's Rights Volume 2, Department of Rare Books, Olin Library, Cornell University. When Burnham applied to the University of Pennsylvania to study law, Spencer Miller, who was dean of the law department, said that if women or Negroes were admitted, he would resign. Ultimately she won and studied law there.

42 Stanton, 1891: 5.

43 Beauchamp 178.

44 Fletcher 238.

45 For a more complete account, see Sally Roesch Wagner, "The Iroquois Confederacy: a Native American Model for Non-sexist Men," *Changing Men* 19 (Spring/Summer 1988) 32-34.

46 Hewitt 482-3.

47 Gage is likely to have had this information. Beauchamp's daughter-in-law wrote a song, "The Battle Hymn of the Suffragists," dedicated to Matilda Joslyn Gage. Gage also wrote short stories for his father's paper, *The Skaneateles Democrat*, in the 1950s.

48 Burnham.

49 Stanton, "The Matriarchate."

50 *Woman's Tribune*, November 1887: 1.

51 Myrtle 303.
52 Myrtle 162.
53 Myrtle 42.
54 *The New York Evening Post*, 24 September 1875.
55 Gage, like most non-Indians of her day, was apparently unaware of the derogatory nature of this term.
56 *Documentary History of New York*, in Gage, 1893: 10.
57 Fletcher, 239.
58 *The New York Evening Post*, 24 September 1875.
59 Gage, 1893: 10
60 Myrtle 161.
61 William L. Stone, *The Life and Times of Red-Jacket or Sa-Go-Ye-Wat-Ha; Being the Sequel to the History of the Six Nations* (New York, Wiley and Putnam, 1841) 155-6.
62 Fletcher 238-239.
63 *Ibid.*
64 *Syracuse Journal*, 10 January 1866.
65 Unidentified newspaper clipping in the Harriet Maxwell Converse collection, State Museum, Albany, NY.
66 *National Citizen and Ballot Box*, May 1878.
67 Gage, 1893: 10.
68 *History of the United States*, volume 1, cited in Gage, 1893: 10.
69 Gage, 1893: 10.
70 Nineteenth-century Eurocentric language defined Indians as "savages," "pagans," etc. *Basic Call to Consciousness* (Mohawk Nation via Rooseveltown, NY: *Akwesasne Notes*, 1978) has a helpful analysis of the terminology
71 Gage, 1893: 9.

GONE TO PROPHETSTOWN
Rumor and History in the Story of Pan–Indian Resistance

Rachel Buff

A T THE TURN OF THE EIGHTEENTH CENTURY, THE United States, having won independence from Britain, shifted its political and military attention to westward expansion. Motion west, according to thinkers like Jefferson, solved European problems of economic scarcity and social hierarchy by ensuring that every man could own and farm a piece of land. But contrary to the mythology of manifest destiny, the land was not vacant and the period was not peaceful. By 1775, Indian nations west of the Appalachian Mountains had been engaged for almost a hundred years in what Bil Gilbert has called the "First American Civil War"[1]; the struggle to maintain their lands and ways of life against colonial encroachment.

What follows is a fragmented account of the mass popular movement that arose among Indians in this period. Beginning with the Shawnee and Delaware of the Ohio River Valley, this movement spread as far north as the Ojibwa, living in what is now called Minnesota, as far west as the Dakota on the western plains, and south among the Creek and Cherokee of Georgia and Alabama. Thousands of Indians left their homes and their people between 1780 and 1808 to move to the centers of this Indian movement, present day Ohio and Indiana. Together they built a military federation that attempted to combat British, French, and, after 1783, American incursions into Indian lands. In addition, the Pan-Indian settlements at Kekionga, Greenville, and Tippecanoe were religious and culturally oriented, one among many movements to arise among the Native peoples of this continent in their attempts to resist the destruction of their ways of life and to reshape and rearticulate their culture under siege.[2]

The story of Tecumseh and his brother Tenskwatawa, known as the Great Shawnee Prophet, is recounted in both popular and official mythologies of United States national formation. Among a handful of Indians whose stories were told in official accounts of American development and expansion west, Tecumseh is celebrated as one of the great patriot chiefs. These accounts speak of him as a unique orator, a brave warrior, and an exemplary Indian whose failed defense of his people's land west of the Ohio River constitutes a noble footnote in the forward march of national destiny. Historical accounts that are critical of emergent American nationalism and attempt to restore a narrative of Indian history and resistance recall Tecumseh's foresight, his promotion of unity among southern and midwestern Indian nations during the late eighteenth and early nineteenth centuries, and, less often, look to the role of the Pan-Indian religion spread by the Great Shawnee Prophet in fulfilling this vision of Indian solidarity.[3] In many Shawnee homes in Oklahoma, portraits of Tecumseh hang today, maintaining a popular memory of his story among members of the tribe.[4]

Various memories of Tecumseh and Tenskwatawa hinge on divergent concepts of patriotism and national formation. The image of Tecumseh carries the notion of the noble authenticity of the Native peoples of this continent, and conjures pictures of hand-to-hand combat and brave warfare. The patriotic conception of Indians as part of the American landscape usurps images of Indian nobility as part of national heritage. In this vision, the romantic individualism of Indian wars and frontier conflict mirrors a central component of American identity.

Alternatively, we can see this "early national period" as a time when ascendant official national consolidation displaced popular social and political formations. Tecumseh and Tenskwatawa represent, in this context, the patriotism of the national-popular[5]: the emancipatory, diverse imaginings of cultural politics that struggle for local sovereignty and heterogeneity against the rise of the official nation. Tecumseh understood colonial politics and insisted on Indian self-determination and racial unity at a time when traditional concepts of native identity were more tribally based. Tenskwatawa's preachings, that a return to tradition ensured the restoration of Indian land and peace, called on both the religious and the political in Indian life to resist colonization.

As what may now be called Gramsican "organic intellectuals", Tecumseh and Tenskwatawa understood the historic position of Indians with respect to European and American colonizers and attempted to articulate unified military and cultural resistance. This involved complex negotiations with Indian ideas about racial formation and identity, land tenure, and the ongoing syncretism of Native and Christian religions. In addition, both drew on pre-existing memories of connections among Indians of different tribes, dissenting Euro-Americans, and the network that brought escaped African slaves into contact with sympathetic Indians.[6] The settlement that the two brothers founded at Prophetstown represented a convergence of Indians from diverse tribes east of the Mississippi. These Indians left their traditional homes because they understood that the best hope of defending them lay in a broadly-conceived alliance. Tecumseh and Tenskwatawa became sources for counter-memory because they represented a mass popular uprising against consolidated, expansionist American nationalism.

Unfortunately, the available sources which I used to piece together the consciousness of this popular movement draw on the perspective of colonialists whose writing sought, by its nature, to obliterate the existence and the memory of such people. Historians need to understand the worldviews of people who completely changed their lives, moving thousands of miles away from their homes to join a risky new religious and political movement. At the same time, the lack of sources that explain events from an Indian perspective make understanding popular consciousness in this period elusive.

Resolution of this paradox is not to be found in some authentic, untainted voice existing beyond the ravages of colonial or neocolonial history. This does not mean, however, that the historian can reduce the differences between Indians and Euro-Americans, or ignore the deeply ingrained biases that accompany colonialist accounts of history. Negotiating these contradictions, Gayatri Spivak calls for an understanding of "strategic essentialism"[7] which means that categories of difference, like race or gender, are constructed at strategic moments by various groups to generate historical and political coherence. By responding to Euro-American categories of "Indian" and "White," creating a Pan-Indian movement where no notion of race or "Indianness" had existed before, Indians in this period adopted a strategic identity. The historian must both be able to see these strategic moves and be able to deploy essentialism herself in understanding the elusive appearance of popular consciousness in history, granting the difference between American Indian and Euro-American epistemologies while trying to understand the exchange between them.

By reading the existing colonialist sources, I attempt to recuperate the complexities of this Pan-Indian movement and its encounter with early United States expansionism from the available historical documents. For the most part, these sources offer official reactions to the Pan-Indian federation and the threat it was perceived to represent in relation to the triumph of the American republic. I then turn to consider some contemporary representations of this mass movement and the historical narratives that these stories create and uphold. Finally, I examine the implications of contemporary popular memory for the ways in which we understand history, culture, and politics.

BAD BIRDS AND BAD NEWS: RUMORS OF WAR

THE PRIMARY TEXTS OF COLONIAL PROSE—THE LETTERS, communiqués, and speeches of officers and governors—came out of direct contact with Native peoples.[8] How these writers portray Indians and, in particular, their dealings with Native leaders like Tecumseh and Tenskwatawa reveal a lot about what was ideologically at stake in the battle over cultural and political control in the Northwest Territories. Cracking these texts open, we can glimpse some of the discursive power wielded by the Indians during this period.

The letters of William Henry Harrison (federal governor and military commander of the western territories during the first two decades of the nineteenth century, best remembered as "Old Tippecanoe" for his destruction of Prophetstown at Tippecanoe in 1808) to officials like William Eustis (Secretary of War under Jefferson and Madison) express great concern over the integrity and rationality of Indian leaders and the volubility of the Indians as a people.[9] Besides seeing the Indians as a military and political threat to the expanding nation, his correspondence with Washington constructs a racialized discourse of distrust. Indians here are essentially unstable, warlike subjects, and Harrison indicates that no bargain of equals can ever be made with such people.

Harrison's correspondence with Tecumseh and Tenskwatawa reflects similar anxieties about trustworthiness and discursive stability, though obviously toned down for the benefit of his audience. In these letters Harrison constructs literary power through his association with United States' military power. He portrays himself not as a deputy with access to all of the ammunition possessed by the army of the "Seventeen Fires" (the term Harrison used to explain the idea of the United States to the Indians), but instead through his position as intermediary. Harrison here is trying to establish with Tecumseh and

Tenskwatawa the guidelines for the law and order required by United States colonial administration. In his correspondence with the two brothers, he talks a lot about the process and reception of reports and rumors and about how his word, as law, clears out confusion and is worthy of Indian trust. Tenskwatawa is repeatedly admonished to "shut his ears against bad talk" from the British, trusting instead the words of the "Seventeen Fires."

The Treaty of Paris, which ended the American Revolution in 1783, left the Native peoples of the Northwest Territories faced with a single enemy on the east instead of the diffusion of French, British, and American forces that they had previously been fighting against and playing off one another. Frederic Jameson has argued that such a change in the arrangement of colonial force generates a displacement in the "axis of otherness", shifting the focus of military and cultural tensions from intra-European competition to a more racialized division between Euro-American "civilization" and its opponents.[10] Where the previous efforts of official nationalism focused on fighting the British and the French, the racializing of discourse about Indians found in these letters constitutes a shift in the focus of political anxiety to the western frontier.

By establishing himself as the intermediary between the Indians and the military power of the United States, Harrison tried to order the associations involved in colonial communications. His letters to the Indians privilege certainty over rumor, and assurance and contract over seduction and affinity. In the letters from Tecumseh and Tenskwatawa to Harrison it is clear, however, that the Indians did not accept Harrison's vision of colonial order, and that they destabilized his system at every opportunity.

In 1806 Harrison spoke to a council of Delaware Indians, attempting to throw into question the religious powers of Tenskwatawa. He urged the Delawares to doubt the vision of the Prophet, who was quite popular among them, and to interrogate his presumptions to spiritual authority. But Tenskwatawa's authority only grew when he accurately predicted the solar eclipse that occurred that summer. Rumors of this powerful augury spread throughout tribes from the northern Great Lakes to the Cherokee nation, increasing support for Tecumseh and Tenskwatawa, and adding greatly to the numbers of Indians living with the two brothers at Greenville.

Spread through unofficial networks of communication, rumor functions to legitimize truths that are unaccompanied by official sanction, usurping the power that Harrison was attempting to claim by acting as intermediary for colonial communications. In contrast to the rule of statutes and ordinances that Harrison was trying to establish, rumor eludes the stable meaning necessary for the imposition of law on a colonized people, instead assuming varying interpretations as it is passed along.[11] In their correspondence with Harrison, both brothers refer obliquely to this power of rumor; rumors are the "bad birds" that impede the rational communications necessary to colonial hermeneutics. Tecumseh, in a long address to Harrison in 1810 in which he insisted that Harrison had not clearly understood him, says "I hope you will confess that you ought not to have listened to those bad birds who bring you bad news." The "bad birds" here unsettle colonial meaning, implying that Harrison is the one subject to untrustworthy influences. Tecumseh and Tenskwatawa both insist to Harrison that they are the ones conveying the real truth. At the same time, their constant reference to rumor mocks Harrison's demands for a stable truth among military enemies.

In one of his addresses to Harrison, Tecumseh goes so far as to invert the relationship Harrison is trying to impose between Indians and Euro-Americans, calling into question the most sacred text of the "Seventeen Fires." He asks: "How can we have confidence in the White people. When Jesus Christ came upon the earth you kill'd and nail'd him on a cross, you thought he was dead but you were mistaken."

This reading of the letters between Harrison, Tecumseh, and Tenskwatawa allows the historian to see some of the discursive negotiations between Americans and Indians during this early period of American expansion. Again, this reading does not put Tecumseh, Tenskwatawa, and their followers back together whole. What is more evident here is the force field within which Euro-Americans and Indians operated during this period. Indians tried to maintain self-determination. At the same time Euro-Americans sought to expand the new nation onto what were traditionally commonly held tribal lands. These military and territorial struggles were fought in the contexts of the colonial hermeneutics I have defined here, and both Indians and Euro-Americans sought to control the terms, as well as the outcome, of this encounter.

"A BIG BABY! A BIG BABY!"

MY ANALYSIS SO FAR BEARS HEAVILY ON THE SPEECHES AND writings of Tecumseh and Tenskwatawa, to the exclusion of the thousands of Indians from diverse tribes that followed them and made the Pan-Indian military and religious accomplishments of the period possible. Other than a few testimonies from Indian agents and witnesses to the enthusiastic religion spread by the Great Shawnee Prophet, there are no written sources that tell us this story. It enters the national history of school textbooks, public art, romantic literature, and political rhetoric as a footnote, that mentions only the military genius of Tecumseh.

The focus on Tecumseh to the exclusion, and often derision, of Tenskwatawa is common to almost all secondary sources on the two brothers and the period.[12] While Tecumseh is valorized in these sources almost from birth as exceptionally brave, strong, competent, and intelligent, Tenskwatawa, known as Lalewethika before his conversion experience in 1805, is described from birth as lazy, stupid, and worthless, a burden on the nobility of his older brother. Benjamin Drake, writing in 1841, was only the first biographer of Tecumseh to invoke republican hyperbole in describing him: "He loved hunting because it was a manly exercise, fit for a *brave*.[his pun]."[13] Another nineteenth century historian, E.G. Randall, said that Tecumseh, "though a savage of the forest, evidenced in his character a rare combination of Italian craft, Spanish revengefulness, German patience, and Anglo-Saxon fortitude"[14]; clearly, high commendation.

Tenskwatawa, on the other hand, gets no such praise from historians. Stories of his ineptitude abound in these sources. According to historiographical mythology, he lost his eye by accidentally shooting an arrow backwards when drunk, and had to be economically supported by his brother, and even (unlike a *brave*) by his wife. Lalewethika is the historiographical butt of jokes. Tenskwatawa is seen, somehow, as the victim of colonization, while Tecumseh, even in defeat, is portrayed as a powerful agent.

Like Harrison, Drake and most of the historians that follow him, assume Tenskwatawa's religious visions and leadership were a fraud designed to cover up his inadequacies as a warrior, an Indian, and a respectable person in general. Most histories of Tecumseh contain some psychologistic theorizing about Tenskwatawa as a sluggard or fanatic. Drake theorizes that Tenskwatawa included common ownership of property in his preaching because of his laziness, epitomizing the hyperbole deployed to castigate this religious leader and dismiss the movement he represented.

Why doesn't Tenskwatawa merit serious historical treatment? Like Wovoka, whose visions of a land rid of Euro-American colonization began the historic resistance of the Ghost Dance religion, Tenskwatawa was part of a long tradition on this continent of visionary leadership. What is ideologically at stake in reducing such a prophet to the figure of a sullen and incompetent child?

The historiographical treatment of the two brothers is not only hyperbolic and unequal, it neatly polarizes Tecumseh and Tenskwatawa into binary oppositions. Tecumseh is fetishized here. His image takes on the Euro-American projection of primitive sexuality that accompanies racialized discourse. At the same time he transcends his racial identity and appears in some respects European. In contrast, Tenskwatawa is feminized, sinking discursively into the irrational, victimized status that Harrison describes in his letters back to the Secretary of War. Where Tecumseh is historically associated with oratory and eloquence, the dominant mode of communication, Tenskwatawa is allied with rumors, whispers, and fanaticism.

As Debra Root has cogently pointed out,[15] this polarization installs a European vantage point which claims Tecumseh as part of American history at the same time it rejects Tenskwatawa as Indian, irrational and other. This perspective doubly subverts the cultural possibilities of understanding the mass, Pan-Indian movement led by the two brothers. Tecumseh can be celebrated in official narratives as a patriot only insofar as there are ample grounds to dismiss the collective resistance embodied in the Pan-Indian federation he and his brother organized. Tenskwatawa provides the shadow that underscores Tecumseh as an exception to his race, reminding the reader of the truly "cunning", irrational nature of the Indian mind and, by extension, racial collectivity.

In official nationalist narratives then, Tenskwatawa stands in for the collectivity of Pan-Indian consciousness during this period. Unlike Tecumseh, who rises, to quote Drake, "above the moral degredation in which [Indian civilization] is shrouded", Tenskwatawa remains with the people, a creature of rumors and strong emotions. The binary opposition between the two brothers takes apart the important dialectic between religious and political life that existed in Amerindian resistance during the nineteenth century, where alternative spiritual and cultural visions inflamed and informed political and military resistance.[16]

Traditionally, Indian nations had always associated religious and political cultures, and, with the expansive U.S. colonization that reached across the continent during the nineteenth century, Pan-

Indian religions like the Ghost Dance and the Great Shawnee Prophet religion became important for inter-tribal communications and unity. These syncretic religions combined the vision of leaders like Tenskwatawa or Wovoka with both the local cosmologies of the different tribes who embraced them and a century of Native experience with the messianic teachings of Christianity. Calling for the return to Indian ways, believers in these Pan-Indian religions foresaw a time when the land would be free of colonial domination. According to a Sioux ghost dancer: "We saw a land created across the ocean on which all the nations of Indians were coming home."

The political implications of such religious movements for anti-colonial stuggles are important; these Pan-Indian movements strategically constituted a resistant identity for the beseiged nations of North America. Tenskwatawa, Wovoka, and other prophetic figures invoked and created a popular religious identity that brought people together, infusing the struggle for liberation. The invention of Pan-Indian religions was a political intervention in the colonial process of defining membership in race and nation; insisting on defining identity from the bottom up rather than from the top down.

Tenskwatawa's preachings about Indian identity separate the origins of the Indians from those of the Americans. Part of his theology held that the Master of Life had created Europeans and Indians, though separately, but had not created the Americans at all. He preached against alcohol use, polygamy, and accumulation of capital. While these are, in part, fundamentalist teachings, they respond to the very real effects of European conquest on Native life. In this way, the "strategic essentialism" of the Great Shawnee Prophet religion drew on national-popular memory to suggest a political and cultural alternative to colonial domination.

The emphasis on Tecumseh in the dominant historiography found in grade school textbooks and public sculptures functions to elide a memory of struggle that drew on Indian and African popular culture: popular religious revivals like those led by Tenskwatawa, Wovoka, and the Delaware Prophet; voudon, santeria, and other Afro-American syncretic religions; popular music and dance like the Ghost Dance religion and the sundance; and the stories that circulate throughout the hemisphere, defying national boundaries and the autocratic dictates of empire. The alliance of popular culture and politics among Indians, from the portraits in Shawnee homes to the repeated references in American Indian Movement literature to

Tecumseh, is a powerful form of resistance. Such alliances are consistently attacked by the forces of official nationalism as attested to by the dangerous abridging of the Indian Religious Freedom Act during the summer of 1990. Tecumseh can be written about as a hero, at the expense of the movement he represented, because official policy seeks to erase the memory of powerful past coalitions with simple myths about military leaders.

In any case, it is impossible to understand the history of the Pan-Indian federation and its significance for the multiple histories of the national-popular, without considering both religious and political aspects and the dialectical relationships between them. The Shawnee, who had been largely relocated to Oklahoma by 1840, fought overwhelmingly on the side of the Union during the Civil War. This was in part due to the rearrangement of popular perceptions of race that took place during the Pan-Indian movement, where both Tecumseh and Tenskwatawa spoke about the parallels between Euro-American treatment of Indians and their enslavement of Africans.

In 1900 Big Jim, Tecumseh's grandson, led a band of Shawnee who were opposed to the United States government's policies of allotment and acculturation to Mexico to found a new land. He went in search of a lost Pan-Indian nation that persisted in Shawnee cultural mythology. This story, along with many others, attests to the strong persistence of imaginings of alternatively formulated communities, and to the ongoing desire of Indians, African-Americans, and Euro-Americans for another vision of America.

REFERENCES

1 Bil Gilbert, *God Gave Us This Country: Tekamthi and the First American Civil War*, New York: Atheneum, 1989.
2 For excellent discussions of the history of such Pan-Indian movements and their relationships to EuroAmerican settlements, see Gregory Evans Down, *A Spirited Resistance: The North American Indian Struggle for Unity, 1745-1815* (Baltimore: Johns Hopkins, 1991); Joel Martin, *Sacred Revolt: The Muskogees' Struggle for a New World* (Boston: Beacon, 1991); and Richard White, *The Middle Ground: Indians, Empires, and Republics in the Great Lakes Region, 1650-1815* (New York: Cambridge, 1991).
3 See particularly Roxanne Dunbar Ortiz, *Indians of the Americas*, Zed: London, 1984.
4 James Howard, *Shawnee! The Ceremonialism of a Native Indian Tribe and its Cultural Background*, Ohio Press: Athens, 1981, p. 197.
5 The term is Antonio Gramsci's, used to denote an "organic relationship

between Italian intellectuals and the broad national masses." See *An Antonio Gramsci Reader*, David Forgags, ed., New York: Schocken Books, 1988, p. 363.

6 See James Koehnline, "Legend of the Great Dismal Maroons," Panic Publishing: Skokie, 1989.

7 Gayatri Spivak, "Subaltern Studies: Deconstructing Historiography," in *Selected Subaltern Studies*, Ranajit Guha and Gayatri Spivak, eds., Oxford University Press: Oxford, 1988.

8 The taxonomy of primary, secondary, and tertiary sources here comes from Ranajit Guha, "The Prose of Counter-Insurgency,"in *Selected Subaltern Studies*, Guha and Spivak, eds., Oxford University Press: Oxford, 1988.

9 Harrison's letters are contained in Logan Esary, ed., *Messages and Letters of William Henry Harrison*, vols, I-II, Indiana Historical Commission: Indianapolis, 1922.

10 Frederic Jameson, "Modernism and Imperialism," in *Nationalism, Colonialism, and Literature*, University of Minnesota Press: Minneapolis, 1990.

11 See Spivak, 1988, for an excellent discussion of the power of rumors. Useful analysis of such strategies of gossip and rumor can also be found in James Scott, *Weapons of the Weak*, Yale University Press: New Haven, 1985.

12 See, for example, R.David Edmonds, *Tecumseh and the Quest for Indian Leadership*, Little, Brown, Inc.: Boston, 1984; Amanda Porterfield, "Tecumseh, Tenskwatawa, and the Complex Relationship between Religious and Political Power," in *Religion and the Life of the Nation*, Rowland Sherill, ed., Illinois University Press: Champaign-Urbana, 1990; Glenn Tucker, *Tecumseh: Vision of Glory*, Russell & Russell: New York, 1956; and William Van Hoose, *Tecumseh: An Indian Moses*, Daring Books: Canton, 1984.

13 Benjamin Drake, *Life of Tecumseh and His Brother the Prophet, with a historical sketch of the Shawnee Indians*, E. Morgan and Company: Cincinnati, 1841, p. 83.

14 Quoted in Carl Klinck, ed., *Tecumseh: Fact and Fiction in Early Records*, Prentice Hall: Englewood Cliffs, 1961, p. 161-2.

15 Debra Root, "The Imperial Signifier," *Cultural Critique* 9, Spring, 1988.

16 Jan Nedeveen Pieterse, "Amerindian resistance: the gathering of the fires," *Race and Class* 26:4, 1986.

African Seminoles

Doug Sivad

New Year's Eve, 1978

A DENSE FOG CRAWLS ALONG THE GROUND, ITS WET FIN-
gers reaching out, engulfing the bramble and cactus on the out-
skirts of a small west Texas town. The fog continues its way-
wardness and the community is surrounded, submerged in the cold
19° mist. Even the water tower at the old fort south of the highway is
swallowed by the chilly drizzle. A dreary day.

It's New Year's Eve, a day for basketball, football, liquid refreshment and food; a day of celebration for the Black Seminole Indians. At
six o'clock this evening, twelve hours of crying, laughing, singing,
dancing, drinking, praying and preaching will begin. Tons of beans,
osfkee, napolitos, and cabrito, prepared this early morning, will be
placed on tables so that people may eat whenever they are hungry.
Some fifty or sixty Black Seminole Indians, many intermarried with
Mexicans, have journeyed here from Nacimiento, Coahuila, Mexico to
be with cousins, aunts and uncles on this dank, icy day.

Demery's Bar sits quietly. Usually it bustles with the movement
and conversations of drinkers against the background of the blues
from the juke box. Today, Louis Demery's mountain lion trophy over
the barroom mirror has the place to itself.

Maggie's across town has but a few Mexicans, Kickapoos, and
whites who sit quietly as soul top forty tunes bellow from the juke
box. Maggie, born in Nacimiento to Black Creek and Black Seminole
Indian parents, is in the kitchen preparing her special enchiladas,
carne guisada, and tacos for the upcoming festivities.

"Ah lib' don' deah til ah wuz nin'te'n, and ah don' niva' go bock nuh
mo'. Too ho'd don' deah," she'll tell you in her Americanized Gullah

language. She, like her ancestors, speaks at least three languages: English, Gullah, and Spanish.

But the mood of the people is depressingly like the weather. The day is not the usual one of jubilation: one of the "old people" (the third in a month) has died and will be buried today. Unca' Ned Factor, a descendant of Congressional Medal of Honor winner Pompey Factor, Black Seminole Indian scout, won't see the new year. He, and many of the "old people" of Black Seminole Indian ancestry are dying rapidly, and stories of America's past and the language of the American Black, called Gullah or Plantation English, die with them. Their epic story, two centuries older than the United States, has been passed down in African and Indian oral tradition through the centuries by their culture-conscious ancestors.

Recollections tell of battles with the "buckra" (American people; any outsider) through Africa, Florida, Indian Territory, Mexico, and Texas. Memories retrace the joining of forces between Seminole Indians (refugees from the Creek nation), *maroons* (free Africans residing in early America's hinterlands), *cimarones* (freed Spanish African slaves), and the *estelusti* (slaves escaped or stolen from plantations) in fighting against the ruthlessly expanding English American colonies. In the United States these free Blacks' lives have been a rebellion against enslavement. Seminole, a Creek word meaning runaways or rebels, identifies not a nation but rather a composite made up of many nations: Black and Red peoples who united in rebellion to preserve their cultures and maintain their freedom. The alliance that was feared most by the European colonists and their descendants.

BEGINNINGS, 1497–1760

WHEN AMERIGO VESPUCCI, LIKE COLUMBUS, AN ITALIAN navigator sailing under the Spanish flag, left Spain in 1497 and arrived in present-day South Carolina, he found there Native Americans whom he hoped to enslave. He took many "Indians" back to Spain, but Red Men proved to be a poor choice, for they chose to die rather than work as slaves. Indian mothers even killed their babies rather than have them grow up in bondage.

Lucas Vasquez de Allyon followed the ocean route of Amerigo Vespucci in the summer of 1526 and landed at the mouth of the Peedee River in present-day South Carolina with five hundred

Spaniards and one hundred African slaves brought out of Haiti. The settlement was short lived for malaria took the lives of half the Spaniards, including de Allyon himself. Indian raids, and ultimately a slave revolt, forced the remaining colonists to flee America's east coast and return to Haiti leaving their Black slaves to become the first permanent settlers from the Eastern Hemisphere within the confines of the present-day United States. African *maroons* remained and prospered in the new land, friendly to some Indian tribes and formidable foes to others. Since no African women were brought during early African slaving, these blacks intermarried with Indians and the Afro-Indian evolved in North America.

In 1630, King Charles I of England awarded land grants to Sir Robert Heath for the territory between the 31st and 36th degree parallels, later to be named Carolina (Latin for Charles) in his honor. African *maroons* and Indian warriors raided the small colony, slaves revolted, and Sir Robert's lack of intestinal fortitude caused the colony's demise. Thirty years later, King Charles II reissued the same land grant to eight "Lord proprietors." Agriculturally Carolina prospered from the production of rice and indigo. Soon the colonists expanded southward into Oconee Creek country, closing fast on Spanish Florida. To combat English encroachment from the north, Spain, in 1692, made notice in Virginia and the Carolinas that any Black slave reaching Spanish territory would find freedom. In turn, the Spanish freed their enslaved Africans and settled them thirty miles west of St. Augustine at Mbasa Village.

Slave revolts and escapes increased in the Carolinas with the Spanish announcement. African villages multiplied in Spanish Florida. Fifty years later, Ahaya the Cowkeeper, a Lower Creek chief, broke away from the Creek Confederacy and relocated his tribe of Red and Black Indians at Alachua in northern Florida, the Creeks' winter hunting grounds. Together, the Indian and African factions became known as Seminoles—outlaws, rebels.

THE SEMINOLES, 1760–1837

THE SEMINOLES WERE A COLORFUL PEOPLE, FROM THEIR brightly hued turbans and Florida fowl feathers, to the eye-catching shirt which was thigh or knee-length, and the tight fitting blue English pants, or buckskins. Ears, arms, neck, waist and sometimes knees were adorned with rings, bracelets, necklaces, and ribbons. A

Pensacola
Mulatto King
Blountstown
Toihulga
Choconickla
Negro Fort

CREEK
Alligator Hole
Apalachee
Tallahassee
Ochuceulga
King Heijuhas Town
Cuscowilla
Eufalla
John Hicks Town
Chukuchatta
Hitchapuesussee
Big Hammock
Thonotossassa

Cowetas
Suwannee

Alachua
Okihumki

King Philips Town
Mulatto Girls Town
Peas Creek
Pelaclekaha
Oclawahaw
Kissimmee
Bucker Womans Town
Okeechobee
Pahokee
Calusa

**NATIVE AMERICAN &
AFRICAN VILLAGES
EAST & WEST FLORIDA**

Seminole chief always dressed in an ankle-length turkey feather cloak for ceremonies. During trips to Washington, D.C., Seminoles always drew the envy of male officials because their wives and lovers chose to spend their time in the company of these light-hearted, eloquent "savages."

As a result of contact with British colonists, slavery was introduced to "The Five Civilized Nations" (Cherokee, Chickasaw, Choctaw, Creek, and Seminole) as a divide and conquer tactic to turn Indians and Africans against one another and prevent runaway slaves from finding refuge among the Indians. Except among the Choctaw, and particularly the Chickasaw, Indian slave owners treated their slaves very differently than the Europeans. While no system of bondage is without fault, the Indian system of slavery was typically milder and more lenient, and, when practiced among the Seminoles, it was in name only. Among the Creek, the Indian master allowed his slaves to live on their own land, requiring that they contribute a portion of their harvests in a system more like feudalism than chattel slavery. Africans were not considered an inferior race, slavery was not hereditary, intermarriage was acceptable, and slaves could not be sold.

Slaves even mustered for battle under their own captains. Contrary to European expectations, any *estelusti* that entered an Indian village, by whatever means, was quickly incorporated into the community. Among the Seminole, the device of claiming to own slaves was often used to shelter escaped slaves, and so the Seminoles subverted the English motives for introducing slavery to the Indians in the first place.

The Black factions (*maroons* and *estelusti*) were valuable allies of the Indian Seminoles, and, although many Blacks preferred to marry Blacks and live in their own towns, racial mixing continued between Africans and Indians. Juan Caballo was born to an Indian father and a Black Indian mother, c. 1810. The Indians and Blacks considered him an "Indyen" but because of his ginger colored skin, whites classified him as Black. This posed problems for slave holders in reclaiming an escaped slave. Seminole Indians always claimed Blacks as slaves, or family members, consequently slave catchers would capture *any* Black and claim he was a runaway. The capture of a Black Seminole Indian drew the wrath of the tribe to which the *estelusti* or *maroon* had pledged alliance.

Concern for these Black Seminoles increased when slave importation was prohibited in 1806. Slave prices rose drastically. The Creek War of 1812-14, with the U.S. Army under Major General Andrew Jackson aided by the Lower Creeks, forced more *estelusti* and *estecata* (Red people) from other southeastern tribes into Florida. The Seminole population tripled, and the threat of an all out war increased. The inevitable happened in 1816 when whaleboats carrying supplies up the Apilachicola River in Florida, destined for Georgia troops, was attacked by Blacks and Indians just north of Fort Nichols, the "Negro Fort" where many Blacks and Indians resided. The boats' crews were killed instantly from ambush along the river banks.

In retaliation under General Jackson's orders, a massive land force invaded Florida and the U.S. Navy, under the command of Sailing-master Jarius Loomis, ordered a continuous barrage of the fort. For nine days the bombardment had no effect. On the tenth day, Loomis instructed that the cannonballs be heated red hot and fired over the walls of the fortress. Luck was with them: the first battery of heated balls hit the ammo dump inside the fort and set off a chain reaction of explosions and fires inside. Hundreds were killed or maimed. General Duncan Clinch and his troops swept in from the north and took the fort with little resistance. Garcon, the Black leader who had stood on the walls and laughed as the cannonballs struck the sides of his impregnable walls, was executed by a firing squad. The Florida Seminoles, enraged by the fort's destruction, struck back in what is known as the First Seminole War (1817-1818). Comparing it to his recent war with the Creek, General Jackson stated, "This is not an Indian war, it is a Negro and savage war. I would rather fight 500 white men than do battle with 50 Black Seminole."

The Spanish were embroiled in the war when Jackson attempted an assault on Tampa Bay invading across the international boundary line. Eventually Jackson convinced Congress that the only way to shut off slave escapes into Florida was to purchase the territory from Spain just as they had done with the French in Louisiana. Secretary of State John Adams met with Luis de Onis in 1819 and purchased Florida effective in 1821 after Jackson had captured Pensacola. This was the first step in Jackson's plan to move the Indian Seminoles west of the Mississippi and enslave the Black Seminoles. Jackson became the new territory's governor, and Americans began to encroach on Seminole land in north Florida, but were met with fierce opposition from King Phillip in the St. Johns River region, and Chief Micanopy in central north Florida, both headmen of the Muskoghee Seminoles. The Seminoles countered with raids on nearby plantations, shouting to the slaves, "Com' ot', Este Fasta [the God of Breath] sen' we fuh yunnah [you; ya'll]," freeing them and gaining more allies.

The initial step towards Seminole removal was the Treaty of Moultrie Creek in 1823. No major chiefs were present, however, so all signatures on the treaty were useless and besides, no chief had the power to sign away land that did not belong to him. Americans were enraged when the Seminoles ignored the timetable set forth in the treaty. Again, the white populace screamed to the government, because "no one was safe with the Seminoles in the country."

The second attempt by the United States to obtain a treaty from the Seminoles came at Payne's Landing Florida, May 9, 1832. All of the Seminole leaders in Florida were present, some having traveled for days and hundreds of miles with their families and escorts for this all important meeting. Micanopy, chief of chiefs, was present with his head counselor and interpreter, Abraham. The treaty required that the Seminoles sell all properties to the U.S. and remove to the west as all of the south and southeastern tribes had previously done, and that Blacks be returned to their "rightful" owners. The Seminoles balked at the terms of the agreement. Osceola, a former leader of the Red

Stick movement, who continued to resist after the Creek War from guerrilla bases in the tropical Florida swamps, leapt to his feet, withdrew his huge hunting knife and embedded it into the treaty papers. Negro Abraham, renown for his cool and unchanging continence, spoke for Micanopy, stating:

> "Duh tarm we gib you a' dese; you lay down arm and stop de war; you sojas go back an' stay in der fo'ts; we Indyen cross ober duh Ouitaloochie [River]; an from dis time fort' for ebber affer, we make de Grand Ribber duh line o'boundary 'atween de two. We promise lib' in peace an good tarm wi'all white neighbor. Dat all got say."

The Seminole's proposal was ridiculed and Abraham again answered:

> "An wuh fuh we submit? We not conquered! We whup you people one, two, tree time. We whup you, damn, we keel you well too. Mek so [Why] we submit? We com' heah gib' conditions, not askum."

In another attempt at persuasion, U.S. authorities invited a number of leading Seminole chiefs to Washington, D.C. and on a tour of Indian Territory where the Cherokee, Chickasaw, Choctaw, and some Creek had already relocated. When the touring Seminoles returned to Florida they were faced with the information that Chief Charlie Emathla, a Seminole friendly to the whites, had agreed to removal and had already sold his properties and ordered his followers to prepare for relocation. Osceola, infuriated, attacked Charlie Emathla and killed him. The legendary chief was on the warpath. He proceeded to Fort King seeking revenge for an earlier insult, where he found his target, Seminole Agent Wiley Thompson dining with nine other men at the sutlers' house, a half mile outside the fort's walls. The rebel warriors riddled the house with ball shot killing everyone inside except for one soldier escort who was badly wounded but survived to tell the story. Not far away, Major Francis Dade was marching to Fort King with two companies of men when they were ambushed by a large contingent of Seminoles dressed for war, naked and painted half black and half red. Sniper fire killed the officers first, followed by bloodcurdling Seminole whoops that frightened the surprised infantrymen into a frenzy, scattering them into the swamps. These incidents were the beginning of the Second Seminole War.

However, by 1837, Osceola had been captured and, after constant warfare without victory, Commander-in-Chief of Florida operations, General Thomas Jesup had reluctantly agreed that the Black Seminoles could migrate with freedom from slave traders. It was determined that a slave once free made a poor slave, and usually caused rebellions. The Seminoles agreed to remove and began their trek to Tampa Bay. To Jesup's dismay, the majority of those coming in were slaves who had just escaped from plantations during the last war. Faced with this situation, Jesup reneged. In the dark of the night, Juan Caballo, Coacoochie (Wildcat), and their close friend, Halpatta Tustenuggee (Alligator) sneaked into the compound at Tampa Bay and delivered the bad news that Jesup had retracted his offer to allow all Blacks to remove. Slaves recently escaped would have to surrender to the proper authorities. The three warriors aided over two hundred Seminoles in fleeing back into the swamps to continue their battles against the American government.

The Seminoles defeated the United States Army and Navy but attrition took its toll on the once prosperous rebels who were forced to live in lean-tos and survive on stray cattle, alligator, snake, tallow, and prematurely harvested corn and beans grown in hidden villages in the swamps. Still refusing to be enslaved, or removed, many Blacks sailed long boats to the Andros Islands of the Bahamas, or to Guanabacoa, Cuba, where slavery had been abolished. The English and Spanish merchant ships also helped the Seminoles by taking them aboard and sailing them to these locations. Others were chained and claimed by slave catchers upon their arrival on the other side of the Gulf in New Orleans. Aside from those stolen in this way, between mid-1837 and 1843, most Black and Indian Seminoles had migrated west of the Mississippi River to Indian Territory under the leadership of Wildcat and John Horse.

THE LOS' PLA'NS, ARKANSAS TERRITORY, 1837–1849

IN THE TERRITORY, OR "LOS PLA'NS" AS IT WAS CALLED BY the Seminoles, problems arose. The United States located the Seminoles amongst their arch-rivals, the Creeks, in an effort to rejoin the warring factions. The Creeks had taken the best land leaving only the barren prairies for the newcomers. The Cherokees and Upper

Creeks offered to share their lands with the now destitute Seminoles, who had not been paid for their properties left in Florida, but they were required to live with the Lower Creeks, whom they skirmished with regularly, to receive promised rations. Besides, the Lower Creeks and slave-catchers raided Black farms for slaves and sent their captives back down the Mississippi River to be sold on the auction block, or south into Texas. Since *maroons, estelustis*, and Black Indians were lumped into one category, "freedmen," some Seminole Indians sought to segregate themselves from Black Seminole Indian families. To the slave catchers, African physical features determined who was categorized as a "freedman", and subject to be captured as a slave. Consequently, Black Indians whose ancestors never knew enslavement were confused with Africans who had only recently escaped from plantations before removal.

Dissension between Blacks and Indians, encouraged by Southern propaganda put forth by emissaries from the slave states, caused a separation within the Seminoles. Some Seminole Indians and Upper Creeks sided with the Blacks (now called freedmen), but non-payment of monies owed to the Seminoles by the United States was the seed of distrust sown between Indians and Blacks. The blame was placed on the Black Seminole interpreters who negotiated the agreements. They were the only ones whom the Federal Government had seen fit to pay for their services and estates in Florida. Some interpreters were killed and others had attempts made on their lives. When Blacks fled to Fort Gibson for protection, this angered some Indians, who said that the United States cared more for the Blacks than for the Indians.

After months at Fort Gibson, barely scraping survival from the land around the fort, Chief Juan Caballo asked for land for his people as a refuge. The land was granted and the Black Indian chief named the village Wewoka. Banded together, the Black Seminole Indians were better prepared to protect themselves, but all Blacks were prohibited from carrying guns. Without firearms, slaving increased. Black Indians and freedmen were now being sold within the Five Civilized Tribes among those who were indifferent to the Seminole Indian and Black relationship.

Matters worsened when Micanopy, a true and trusted friend to the Blacks, died in 1848. Wildcat (Coacoochie) had been his head counselor since Abraham had retired to his farms on choice lands specially awarded to him by the Federal Government: no one harmed any of Abraham's people for fear of retribution from the United States Army.

Wildcat was the choice of the Seminoles by birthright to succeed Micanopy, but the Indian Agent Marcellus DuVal opposed it because Wildcat continued to side with the Blacks and DuVal shared in the profits of Lower Creek slaving activities. The Indian Agency appointed Chief Jim Jumper as head Seminole chief since he had sided with the Lower Creeks and whites so that his people could receive tools and rations for their survival.

Jumper's appointment upset many Seminoles and Upper Creeks. Making matters worse, in 1849, Black Seminoles were legally declared to still be slaves under U.S. law. Wildcat was outraged. He and John Horse (Juan Caballo) began to plan the unification of all Indian tribes in Texas and Mexico into a confederation that would drive all whites from Texas and the Indian Territory, resist slave-hunters, both Creek and white, and provide a haven for Indians and Blacks as had been attempted previously in Florida. Word went out to the Texas Rangers each time the two Seminoles journeyed into Texas for pow-wows with the Caddo, Waco, Kitchee, Tonkawa, Comanche, and Lipan Apache south of the Red River. Spies were sent amongst the two chiefs' bands and Wildcat narrowly escaped assassination. He and John Horse decided that escape from the Indian Territory was the only solution for them and their people.

The Trail to Coahuila

JOHN HORSE (JUAN CABALLO) AND WILDCAT (COACOOCHIE) led some five hundred Indians and Blacks out of the Los' Pla'ns for Mexico in the late fall of 1849. The thought of these "blood thirsty savages" crossing Texas caused much excitement. Texas Governor P.H. Bell alerted the Texas Rangers. After a major skirmish with pursuing Indian Agency troops, the refugees reached the Brazos River at a fording point in Falls County. Here they established temporary homes with the Caddo and Waco for the oncoming winter.

Negotiations with the Texas tribes continued until Comanche Chief Buffalo Hump brought an end to Wildcat's plan of a great confederation. Buffalo Hump was positive that once across the Rio Grande, the Seminoles would act as "border patrollers" and would fight for Mexico against Comanche and Apache raiders just as the Cherokees and *maroons* already there were doing. The Indian/African/Mexican federation failed. Buffalo Hump agreed to safe passage through his nation for the group now on its way, but would allow no others to follow.

Before the first signs of tree sap and plant buddings, the Seminoles planted an early crop of beans and corn. The warriors were allowed to hunt the Caddo and Waco hunting grounds. But their village at Cow Bayou (between Waco and Marlin, Texas) was attacked several times by the Texas Rangers and Texas slavers. The attacks were little more than a nuisance for the battle-hardened Seminoles, but they increased their resolve to reach Mexico. As soon as the beans and corn were harvested, the Seminoles, joined by 200 Kickapoos also living near Cow Bayou, continued their trek.

In July, 1850, the Seminoles reached the Rio Grande just below present-day Eagle Pass. Though slavery had been abolished in Mexico twenty years earlier, they were unsure of their welcome there, so they waited for dark before crossing. Mothers muffled their babies' cries in their bosoms as they crossed aboard the unsteady, makeshift rafts. Mounted horsemen drove the horses and cattle. All Black Seminoles crossed safely: the Paynes, Griners, Bruners, Perrymans, Bowlegs, Fais, Julys, Factors, Kibbetts, Coffees, Warriors and Wilsons, and the Cherokee Thompsons; seeking a new home and freedom.

Head chiefs Wildcat, John Horse, and Papicua, with two hundred heavily armed warriors, met with Colonel Juan Manual Maldonado, sub-inspector for the Colonais de Coahuila at San Fernando de Rosas, on July 12, 1850. Not looking for a fight, the colonel provided tools, seed, livestock, and ammunition to the immigrants. In return, the newcomers were to guard the northern Mexico border against marauding Texas filibusters and "los Indios barbaros" who raided Mexican settlements and retreated to the Texas side of the river. The Blacks settled mostly at Moral, a few miles up river from Piedras Negras. The Indian Seminoles settled at La Navaja, and the Kickapoos at Guerrero. All settlements were located in northern Coahuila, with Moral, on the southern banks of the Rio Bravo del Norte, the most vulnerable.

GUARDS OF THE BORDER FOR MEXICO, 1850–1870

THE SEMINOLES ALLIED WITH THREE THOUSAND BLACKS living in the Sierra Madre Mountains (mostly escaped slaves and free Blacks from Texas) under the leadership of *cimarone* chiefs Felipe Alvarez and Felipe Sanchez, and secured northern Coahuila for Mexican settlers. In 1854, one observer, Gerard Guajardo, stated that the Seminoles and the Blacks refused to give up their native customs, had no military discipline, but were always victorious in battle. The Blacks preferred planting and cattle raising to fighting but fought in repayment to the Mexican government for aiding them in their new homeland. Juan Caballo wouldn't allow the children to fight with the Mexican children because the Mexicans had given them a home when no one else would. The Black chief also refused to involve the Seminoles in Mexican civil conflicts: "The Seminole would never fight with one bunch of Mexicans against another. Here we are all living in one house. How can I take up a gun and kill you, who are my brothers, or how can I take up a gun for you and kill that other man, who is also my brother?"

Texas slavers, led by Captain Warren Adams, made continual attempts to capture Black Seminoles and break the strength of the community. At a dance in Piedras Negras, Gopher John, as Juan Caballo was sometimes called, was shot in a fight. Adams and his men rushed to the border town to capture the Black man who had killed so many whites and provided a refuge for Texas slaves, and took him to Eagle Pass on the United States side of the Rio Grande. Word of the capture reached Wildcat who immediately set out, with warriors, for Eagle Pass. The Seminole leader paid a ransom of five hundred dollars in gold and promised to return some slaves recently escaped from Texas ranches. After John was freed, Captain Adams inspected the gold and discovered it was stained with blood. The Texas slavers got the message and left without waiting for the slaves.

In retaliation, the Seminoles raided farms and ranches in Texas until they felt compensated for the five hundred dollar loss. Knowing of the Seminole's prowess in battle, south and west Texas shivered with the fear that the vicious Floridians would surely kill them in their sleep. The revenging warriors returned to Mexico with their booty—mostly cattle—to the approval of General Cardona of Coahuila, and the relief of surviving Texans. From that point on, every Indian raid along the Rio Grande was labeled as a Seminole massacre. If a Black was present, it had to be the notorious Gopher John, although other Indian tribes had many Blacks living amongst them. The Seminoles were well armed and could raise 500 warriors in an emergency, although their usual fighting force numbered about 100 or 120.

Adams' slaving raids continued into Coahuila, however, capturing an occasional Black from outlying farms. The Seminoles complained to the Mexican authorities about their land grants along the Rio Bravo. Presidente Antonio Lopez de Santa Anna heard the Seminole's plea and awarded land to them never to be taken away. Wildcat and Coyo[te] removed their people from La Navaja, to four *sitios* of *ganado mayor* (pastureland measuring 6.6 miles square) at Alto, and other *sitios* in the *hacienda* of Nacimiento in the Santa Rosa Mountains, northwest of Musquiz. Nacimiento Mountain provided additional protection for the Seminole Indians living on the mountaintop at the mouth of the Sabinas River, and the Seminole Blacks situated in the mountain's valley. Now the families could better protect themselves while the warriors were away on expeditions.

Juan Caballo de la Mascogos and Wildcat were awarded the ranks of Colonel in the Mexican Army. Their sub-chiefs, John Kibbitts (Siteetastanachi), Cuffee, and Felipe Sanchez of Colonel Caballo's band; Coyote, Nokosimala, Leon and Juan Flores of Wildcat's band, were ranked as Captains. The warriors fought valiantly and made Coahuila the safest Mexican border state. Yet a scourge greater than any army hit the Seminoles in January, 1857. Wildcat and Coyote returned from battle with the Comanches and found that their adversaries had been infected with smallpox. The disease swept through the Indian bands like wildfire, taking the lives of Wildcat, Coyote, twenty-eight women, twenty-five men, and nineteen warriors by March, even though the panic-stricken Indians fled in all directions to avoid infection.

Nevertheless, the industry of the Black Seminoles who survived the epidemic turned Nacimiento into choice farm and pastureland. Governor Santiago Vidaurri wanted to move the Seminoles to less productive land and sell Nacimiento to land barons. Soon the seed of animosity was planted between the Indians and Blacks. Leon, rather than Nokosimala, Wildcat's kinsman, was placed as chief of the Indian Seminoles. Indian Seminoles complained that the Blacks owned more cattle and possessed more land than they did because the Blacks spent more time farming and ranching than fighting. Some Indians were upset with the fact that Juan Caballo outranked them, and remembering the internal conflict in Indian Territory, refused to follow the orders of a Black man. Seminole Chief Jim Jumper in the Territory had ordered the Seminoles back to the reservation since the U.S. government had finally acknowledged them as separate from the Creek Nation and given them their own land. When Indian complaints of the Blacks' water consumption, greater than theirs because of the Blacks' greater numbers, were not acted upon by the Mexican government, many decided to return to Indian Territory. In February, 1859, with urgings from emissaries of Napoleon III now taking advantage of the unstable conditions in Mexico, Tiger, Pasaqui, Leon, Juan Flores and their families, fifty-one women, men, and children left for Indian Territory. They left behind twenty-two Indian fighting men and sixty women and children under the command of Nokosimala. No Black Seminoles returned.

The land barons were now ruthless in their greed to take the land at Nacimiento. The diminished numbers of Seminoles encouraged more slaving raids, so John Horse, with the Sierra Madre *maroons*, and some Seminole Blacks removed to the area of Laguna de Parras in southwestern Coahuila. They continued in service to the Mexican Army, operating from the lakeside jungles against French troops during Maximillian's brief Mexican presidency. Chief Jim Jumper had again ordered that all Seminoles should return to the Territory to increase their forces for the Confederacy, as the Civil War had begun. At this point, all but six Indian Seminoles journeyed to Texas, leaving only the Black Seminole Indians in Mexico. Then, with the abolition of slavery in the United States after the war, many who had been reluctant to go back to the land of bondage began to reconsider.

TEXAS, 1870 AND AFTER

IN 1870, PLAINS INDIANS WERE WREAKING HAVOC ON American settlements in west Texas. The cavalry, mostly Civil War veterans, could not control the Comanches and Apaches across the vast western plains. After the war's end, some Seminoles and *maroons* began to make their way into Texas for work. The calvary was well aware of the Seminoles and their fighting abilities, so Captain Franklin W. Perry was sent by Major Zenas R. Bliss to Nacimiento to recruit the Seminoles. Meeting the headman, Chief John Kibbetts (John Horse was still in the Laguna), an agreement was reached by which the United States Cavalry would enlist every able bodied Seminole man for six month terms as scouts only. They would be paid regular cavalrymen's salaries and receive land for their families. John Kibbetts' band reported to Fort Duncan at Eagle Pass on July 4, 1870, for enlistment and clothing issue, ready for their first duties which, initially, were recruiting other Seminoles.

In the summer of 1871, twenty Black Creeks from the Elijah

Daniels band, and a number of Seminoles who had relocated in Matamoras, were signed up. The scouts used their personal horses and were compensated for such, issued Spencer rifles, ammo, and full cavalry wool clothing of which most wore only the shirt and pants mixed with their Indian attire. They were not well dressed soldiers and, as in Mexico, they did not respond to military discipline. While they distinguished themselves as scouts and fighters, after three years they had not received the land that had been promised to them.

On a major expedition to Palo Dura Canyon in the Texas Panhandle, Private Adam Payne was cited for gallantry and great courage during the battle on September 20, 1874, that broke the will of the Kiowa, Comanche, and Cheyenne. The battle was ferocious, with the cavalry having to retreat twice, and the Indians once. When the Indians were scattered, the Black soldiers killed their horses. Rarely was an Indian killed, rather his horse was killed because a Plains Indian on foot was of little danger. For his efforts in the battle, Adam Payne was the first Black to receive the Congressional Medal of Honor, given to him in Seminole County, Texas.

The Seminoles were accustomed to full freedom and this some-

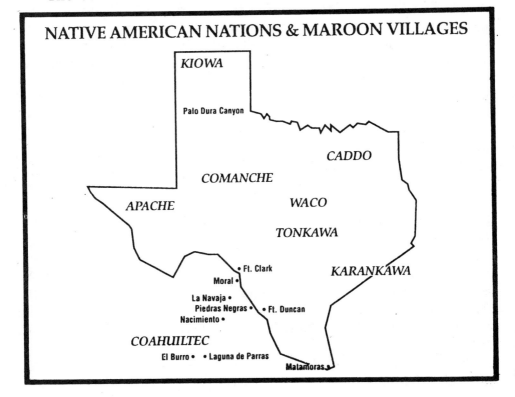

NATIVE AMERICAN NATIONS & MAROON VILLAGES

KIOWA

Palo Dura Canyon

CADDO

COMANCHE

APACHE   *WACO*

TONKAWA

• Ft. Clark   *KARANKAWA*
Moral •

La Navaja •
Piedras Negras • • Ft. Duncan
Nacimiento •

COAHUILTEC

El Burro • • Laguna de Parras

Matamoras •

times drew complaints from the Black soldiers and the surrounding white townsmen. The whites never were particularly happy with the Seminoles' cockiness about having killed so many whites in previous wars, and the American Blacks felt they were odd because they continued to hang onto their African and Indian heritage in language and customs. The Black Indians were often ridiculed for their speech by the Blacks; consequently, Gullah became a "closed language." Lies were told that they stole cattle and anything else they could, but though poor, honesty was one of the Seminoles' greatest attributes next to being mighty warriors. The lies they could withstand, but on Christmas 1874, Corporal George Washington, nephew to John Horse by marriage, and Scout Dan Johnson were fatally shot in a gunfight by the notorious outlaw King Fisher and his gang. Fisher was also wounded. This incident forced all of the Seminole scouts and their families to be moved to Fort Clark in Brackettville.

There the Seminoles lived in makeshift shelters on the fort lands. Seminole architecture was of the "chink house" type using materials from their surroundings. Originally, interwoven mesquite limbs supported the walls; later, slats of wood replaced the mesquite. Two pallets, one for the inside, the other for the outside, were tied to the supports with the space between "chinked" with rocks, then mud (adobe) was used to cover and seal the walls. After a rain, children enjoyed throwing mudballs against the house to strengthen and thicken the house walls. The roof, in the African manner, was constructed of thatched grass. They preferred sleeping and eating on blankets covering the dirt floor. The cooking rooms were built separate from the sleeping area and were merely a grass thatched roof supported by four poles.

Finally, the answer from Washington came: it was no land. According to the bureaucrats, the Seminole rolls had been closed and those registered were in Indian Territory. As for the Black Seminoles, no compensation was due them because they were Negroes, not Indians. Since the Comanche threat was reduced, thanks to the Seminole scouts, the Black Seminole Indians' services were no longer needed. The United States not only reneged on its promises of land, but greatly reduced the number of scouts and restricted allowances to active scouts only. Many of the families that followed the scouts north of the border who had been gainfully employed at Fort Clark were now destitute.

Again, locals hired King Fisher, this time to do his dirty work on the grounds of Fort Clark. Head Seminole Chief John Horse and Titus Payne, two dear friends from as far back as the Florida swamps, were walking in front of the dispensary when shots rang out. Titus was killed outright but John, shot four times, was saved by his horse, American—named because it was white and blue-eyed. The situation for Black Seminoles once more had become desperate.

As if the attempted assassination of the Seminole head chief was not enough, discharged Seminole scout and Medal of Honor recipient Adam Payne was in a fight in a Brownsville, Texas saloon where he knifed a Black soldier to death. With a local sheriff in hot pursuit, Adam arrived at Fort Clark as New Year's Eve (1877) celebrations were in progress inside the church. Without calling his name or giving any kind of warning, the sheriff killed Adam with a shotgun fired at such close range that it set his clothes afire (no lawman was fool enough to try and take the short, stockily built warrior alone and definitely not face to face). This was the last straw: John Horse, despite his weak condition, led the majority of his people across the Rio Grande to Mexico, never again to place their faith in the North American people.

NEW YEAR'S EVE, 1978

THE REUNION OF TEXAS AND MEXICAN BLACK SEMINOLES prompts observations about the changes time has brought.

"Duh youngun' dem nuh lika' we way," Dub Warrior, an officer in the Seminole Cemetery Association, and Del Rio lawman, groans.

"Dem nuh lika' we duh talk lika' dis," the highly literate Brackettville, Texas school teacher, Miss Charles Wilson explains. "When I speak Seminole to my friends, the young folk say it's just bad English, but I beg to differ with them."

Brother Joe Dixon has been feeling low lately. "Chicken" had a heart attack the other day. Unca' John July, ninety-seven years old, is losing some of his spryness. Miss Bess is confined to a wheel chair and is losing her hearing. The "old people" continue to die away, taking with them stories of history that books can never tell.

REFERENCES

Aptheker, H. *American Negro Slave Revolts—1526-1860*, International Publishers, 1952.

Campbell's Abstract of Seminole Indian Census Cards & Index, 1925.

Carroll, J.M., ed. *The Black Military Experience In The American West* , Liveright Pub., 1971.

Cline, H.F., "Colonial Indians in Florida, 1700–1823," Manuscript is owned by the estate of Wm. C. Sturtevant, copies found in major libraries.

Coe, C.H., *Red Patriots: The Story of the Seminoles*, The Editors Pub., Cincinnatti, Oh, 1898.

Covington, J.W., "An Episode In The Third Seminole War," *The Florida Historical Journal*, 45(1):45–59, 1966.

Dillard, J.L., *Black English: Its History and Usage in the United States*," (a book review) *Florida Reporter*, (Spring/Fall), 1972. p. 21.

Foreman, G., *The Five Civilized Tribes*, University of Oklahoma Press, Norman, Ok., 1934.

————, "The Texas Comanche Treaty of 1846," *Southwest Historical Quarterly*, LI, No. 4, April, 1948, pp. 313–332.

Gifford, J.L., *Billy Bowlegs and the Seminole War*, Triangle Co., Coconut Grove, Fl, 1925.

Goggins, J.M., "The Seminole Negroes of Andros Island, Bahamas," *Florida Historical Quarterly* 24(3):201-206, 1946.

Hancock, Ian F., "Gullah and Barbadian Origins and Relationships," *American Speech*, 55, 1980.

————, "Texan Gullah—The Creole English of the Brackettville Afro-Seminole," *Perspectives On American English*, edited by J.L. Dillar, The Hague, Mouton, 1980, pp. 305-333.

————, *Lexical Expansion Within A Closed System, Sociocultural Dimensions of Language Change*. Academic Press, Inc. 1977.

————, *Krio*, (manuscript), 1976.

Holt, R.D., "John Horse—Scouting Seminole Chief," *Heap Many Texas Chiefs*, Naylor Press, San Antonio, Tx, 1966.

Jones, J.C., "Old Seminole Scouts Still Thrive On Border," *Frontier Times Magazine*, May, 1934, pp. 327–332.

Katz, William Loren, *Black Indians: A Hidden Heritage*. Macmillan Publishing Company, 1986.

Littlefield, D.F., *Africans and Seminoles—Removal to Emancipation*, Greenwood Press, 1977.

————, *Africans and Creeks*, Greenwood Press, 1979.

Mahon, J.K., *History of the Second Seminole War: 1835–1842*, Gainsville: University of Florida Press, 1967.

Mathurin-Mair, L., "Erotic Expediency: The Early Growth of the Mulatto Group in West Africa, *Caribbean Journal of African Studies Association of the West Indies*, 1978.

McReynolds, E.C., *The Seminoles*, University of Oklahome Press, Norman, 1957.

Porter, K.W., "Relations Between Negroes and Indians Within the Present Limits of the United States," *Journal of Negro History*, 17(3):287–367, 1932.

—————, "Florida Slaves and Free Negroes in the Seminole War, 1835–1842," *Journal of Negro History*, 28(4):390–421, 1943.

—————, "A Legend of the Bilozi," (A letter to John R. Swanton), Smithsonian Institute, 1944.

—————, "The Hawkins Negroes Go To Mexico," *Chronicles of Oklahoma*, 1944, pp. 55-59.

—————, "Notes on Seminole Negroes In The Bahamas," *Florida Historical Quarterly* 2(1):56–6, 1945.

—————, "The Last Ride of John Horse," Collected in *No Rain From These Clouds*, John Day, 1946.

—————, "The Founder of the Seminole Nation: Secoffee or Cowkeeper," *Florida Historical Quarterly* 27(4):362–384, 1949.

—————, "The Seminole In Mexico, 1850–1861", *The Hispanic American Historical Review*, Vol. XXXI No. 1, Feb., 1951, pp. 1–36.

—————, "The Seminole Negro-Indian Scouts, 1870–1881," *The Southwestern Historical Quarterly*, Vol. LV No. 3, 1952, pp. 358–377.

(Along with various letters of correspondence and telephone calls with the author before Mr. Porter's untimely death in 1981.)

Pratt, T., *Seminole*, University of Florida Press, Gainsville, Fl, 1953.

Price, R., ed. *Maroon Societies—Rebel Slave Communities in the Americas*, John Hopkins University Press, Baltimore and London, 1979.

Teall, K.M., *Black History of Oklahoma—A Resource Book*, Oklahoma City Schools, 1971.

Mètis Camp, circa 1865, Minnesota

The carts, called charettes, were the primary form of overland transport for the Mètis and Canadien people. The small tipi reflects Plains Indian influence on Mètis culture.

A NEW NATION IN THEIR HEARTS
The Historical Evolution of the Mètis People

Richard Kees

"It is true that our... origin is humble, but it is meet
that we honor our mothers as well as our fathers.
Why should we concern ourselves about what degree
of mixture we possess of European or Indian blood? If
we have ever so little of either gratitude or filial love,
should we not be proud to say we are Mètis."[1]

IN THIS 1869 QUOTE, THE *MÈTIS* LEADER LOUIS RIEL SOUGHT
to define a people embarking on a mission to save their native land
from foreign conquest. While his battles were lost, the struggle of
his people continues on.

The *Mètis* people, and their name, have ancient roots in North
American history. The words by which they named themselves, their
collective actions over the centuries, and the sweeping tide of
European colonization came to define them as a nation. The word,
Mètis, is French for "mixed", and the French-Catholic priests of early
Canada and the U.S. used it as a descriptive term for French-
Canadians (in this chapter referred to as *Canadiens*) of Native-
American background. The early American Colonists had a similar
word, *mustee,* by which to call local English and Dutch "mixed bloods,"
but the English colonists soon replaced this with the derisive "breed."

Louis Riel popularized the word *Mètis* partially as a swipe at the
derogatory attitudes of the English speaking colonists by emphasizing
that which the racists among them most feared, mixture. The word
Mètis came to be both a national appellation and a concept of who
they were. It said that *Mètisage,* the action of mixture, was cultural
and economic as well as genealogical, that they had reason to be
proud of who they were; and that they had become the New Nation.
The people of this New Nation were the cultural descendants of those

Canadiens who had moved into the Great Lakes, Mississippi Valley, and Great Plains areas, (the whole region being called the *Pays d'en Haut*) as well as all the Native-American nations they had established kinship ties among. Their nation was not one of taxation, prisons, or governmental dominance and coercion. Their nation was not a physical thing, but something in the hearts and minds of its people.

NEW FRANCE AND THE COLONIAL ORIGINS OF THE NEW NATION

MÈTIS HISTORY CAN TRACE ITS EARLIEST ORIGINS TO THE half-hearted French colonization of modern Canada. In the year 1600, a Frenchman named Pierre Chauvin established a tiny trading post at the coastal Montagnais Indian town of Tadoussac, entering the Indian nations of the area into nearly four centuries of colonial, economic, and cultural contact. By 1634 about one hundred Frenchmen, and a very few Frenchwomen, had settled along the St. Lawrence in the colony of Canada. In fact, during the first 140 years of European colonization in Canada only some 6,500 French had emigrated, a percentage of whom returned to their homeland. Most of the males among these colonists were from the lower classes of France, many of whom had been convicted of petty crimes and were coerced into leaving their country. French society in the Canadian colony was stratified into classes with the merchants, colonial administrators, and the Catholic clergy forming the ruling class, relegating the mass of the colonists into a type of servitude. Christianized Indians in the colony were assumed to be a part of the lower class, while the local tribes became political and economic vassals of the colony.

New France, which had existed between the years 1600 and 1760, consisted of two colonies, *Acadie* and Canada. Acadie was formed by modern Canada's Maritime provinces, and was the ancestral home of the French speaking *Acadiens* and their southern cousins the Cajuns. The colony of Canada consisted of, roughly, modern Québec and the eastern part of Ontario province. Neither colony received large numbers of French colonists, leaving most of the country open to the Native-Americans and drawing a large proportion of the French population into the only real economic activity available to them, the fur trade. With growing channels of economic, cultural, and political interchange the colonists came into intimate contact with the Native tribes forming a mutual ground between the peoples. With the establishment of kinship ties, and the adaption of many Native cultural

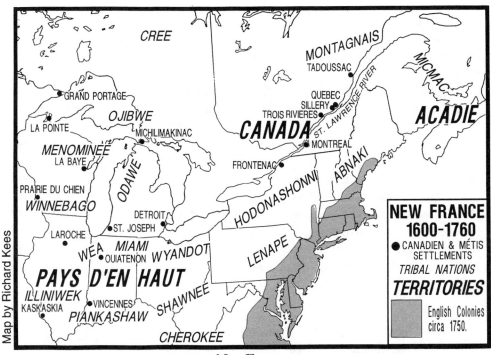

New France

traits, the colonists of New France began the process of Mètisage, becoming *Canadiens* and *Acadiens* rather than French.

The primary importance of marriages between the Indians and the French was not genetic but cultural. In early *Canadien* society the women, overwhelmingly, bore the brunt of child rearing and the passing on of the culture, beliefs, and manner of speaking. Native-American women, their *Mètisse* daughters and women arriving from France all contributed to the makeup of the emerging *Canadien* society. Historians, many of whom were overly influenced by medieval European concepts of "race" and "racial purity", have vehemently argued about the degree of Indian "blood" flowing in the veins of the *Canadiens*. The more outwardly racist ones claimed that no intermarriages occurred, while apologists identified *Mètisage* as a class phenomenon, stating "that hardly any family in the lower ranks of original settlers in Canada is without some Indian blood."[2] Regardless of the specific number of marriages between colonists and Natives, they formed only a part of the *Mètisage* of the *Canadien* people. The many elements of Native herbology and curing practices in *Canadien* folk medicine, as well as the use of Algonquian and Iroquoian words in their language, all reflect the influence the Indian wives and husbands and neighbors had among the French Colonists.

Economic and social ties were primary conduits of culture between the peoples. Within the first decade of French colonization, the French had developed as great a need for Native technologies as the Indians had developed for European ones. To meet this demand for Native products the Abnaki, Micmacs, Huron and other nations, developed a trade in canoes, snowshoes, baskets, footwear, and other manufactured goods. The *Canadiens* along the St. Lawrence River, likewise, adopted elements of Native dress, this being particularly evident in their winter and travelling clothes. In the Great Lakes and Illinois areas the adoption of Native clothing became even more pronounced. By the mid 1800s *Canadien* fashions, especially in the West, had become rather distinctive, incorporating elements of French, Native-American and American styles. Commenting on the appearance of the *Mètis* in St. Paul, Minnesota, an American observer noted in 1859:

> One hardly knew whether to be most surprised at the odd uniformity of their costume of coarse blue cloth, richly ornate with brass buttons, their showy belts of red flannel, and their small jaunty caps, or at the remarkable diversity of their figures and complexions, including as it did, the fair skin and light brown curls of the Saxon, and the swarthy hue and straight black hair of the Indian, with every intermediate shade that amalgamation could produce."[3]

In the realm of food production the French were likewise dependent upon Native skills and crops. Varieties of squash, corn, beans, and other plants were adopted and gardened along their river lots. Hunting and gathering skills learned from the tribal people are still practiced, with modern tools, by *Mètis* and *Québecois* people. By the mid 1600s Native fishing practices were also adopted, with *Canadiens* and Montagnais Indians from the towns of Québec and Sillery jointly exploiting the eel fishery upriver from Québec. At Trois Rivieres the *Canadiens* learned the local ways to take harvests of pike. Along with foodstuffs, the colonists adopted Native ways to process food, such as smoking meat, the preparation of hominy and sagamite, and the production of maple syrup.

While most of the *Canadien* and *Acadien* people were meeting their Indian neighbors on mutual ground, they had no more control of the colony than did the tribes. France had created a three-headed monster to oversee its exploitation of New France—the colonial administration, the merchants, and the Church. A number of Catholic Orders came to compete with each other for the souls of Canada. Members of the Recollet Order had taken to browbeating Montagnais villagers as early as 1615, and within a decade the Jesuits joined in the melee, many of their missionaries living as destructive parasites in the Indian nations. Within their own cultural contexts they must have thought they were fulfilling some sort of mission here, but they usually only produced dissent and division among the tribes. For the *Canadiens* and neighboring Natives, there was an escape from the Church and the colonial officials by joining the Fur Trade and moving to the west or north of the core of the colony along the St. Lawrence River. Those people who permanently left the French colony became the first generation of the New Nation. The *Mètisage* of their *Canadien* roots smoothed the way for their economic, social, and genealogical acceptance among the Native nations of the west.

THE FUR TRADE & ECONOMIC INTERCHANGE BETWEEN THE PEOPLES

THE FUR TRADE WAS A MEGALITHIC STRUCTURE IN THE *Canadien* economy, with the French and colonial merchants having a political and social influence as great as the Church. The Fur Trade was originally administered from France, but after 1710 merchants in Trois Rivieres and Montrèal increasingly began to take over its local control. The *Canadien* merchants could not hope to become rich in continental French terms, having to fork over most of their profits to the monarchy and its local officials. For the rest of the *Canadiens* the Fur Trade was a constant source of low-paid employment, and in many areas was the only way of earning hard currency. On the local level most of the residents of the core colonies, Indian and *Canadien* alike, had some involvement in the interchange of goods between the peoples. However, they were really only "middlemen." Throughout the colonial period most of the profits continued to flow into Europe.

The primary product the European colonial powers sought in the northern half of our continent were the processed pelts of the beaver. These were shipped to Europe and manufactured into stylish clothing for the upper classes. For the Native-Americans the acquisition of iron tools and utensils from the Europeans maintained their interests in further developing the trade. In the early years, when beaver were still abundant, both parties to the trade thought they were getting the better of the other. The acquisition of iron goods produced something of a revolution in the cultures of both the agricultural and hunting tribes. The durability and portability of metal kettles allowed the hunting tribes greater mobility, and sewing needles, knives, axes, and saws sharply reduced the labor time needed to manufacture their basic needs. Nicholas Denys, writing of the tribes around the Gulf of the St. Lawrence, in 1672 stated,

> They have abandoned all their own utensils, whether
> because of the trouble they had as well to make as to
> use them, or because of the facility of obtaining from
> us, in exchange for skins which cost them almost
> nothing, the things which seemed to them invaluable,
> not so much for their novelty as for the convenience
> they derived therefrom.[4]

To increase their profits the merchants established trading posts throughout the *Pays d'en Haut*, a region consisting of all the Native held lands to the west and southwest of the *Canadien* settlements along the St. Lawrence. To protect these profits they established trading monopolies and tried to prevent *Canadiens* and colonized Indians from entering the trade on their own. These independents in the Trade called themselves *les gens libres*, translated here as "Free-Traders." They became a dominant force in the shaping of *Mètis* history. The *Coureur du Bois* and *Voyageurs*, who formed the backbone of the merchants labor force in the *Pays d'en Haut*, often were in collusion with the Free-Traders, and many eventually left the employ of the merchants to join the independents. The Free-Traders, often termed smugglers by colonial officials, operated independently of the monopolies but still traded with the *Canadien* merchants. Whenever colonial officials attempted to prevent this trade, these independents would simply turn to English merchants in the American colonies. These *Canadiens* living in the west were becoming an independent lot, they conceptualized themselves as the *Gens Libres*, the "Free People," and free trade and personal liberty became a recurrent theme in their history.

In the modern state of Michigan, the Trading companies had established posts at Michilimakinac and Sault Ste. Marie by the 1670s, both being centrally located along the trade routes. A major advantage to these sites was the ready access to food to feed the thousands coming to trade and to supply canoe brigades leaving for the St.

Lawrence settlements. As early as 1688 the *Canadiens* had formed a settlement at Michilimakinac, the town becoming both a depot for traders moving farther into the hinterland and a major marketplace for the French and the Native Nations. The Odawe and other nations that traded here were no strangers to the trade, nor to the manufacture of goods to be sold in that marketplace. Michilimakinac was

> the general meeting place for all the French who go to trade with the stranger tribes; it is the landing place and refuge of all the savages who trade their peltries...they make canoes, which they sell two at three hundred livres each. They get a shirt for two sheets of bark...The sale of their...strawberries and other fruits produces means for procuring their ornaments....They make a profit on everything.[5]

THE RISE OF THE *PAYS D'EN HAUT*

THE PROCESS OF *MÈTISAGE* THAT HAD BEGUN IN CANADA became more dominant in the *Pays d'en Haut*, where small French settlements were intermingled among Native villages. Among the *Canadiens* of the west, kinship ties to one or more Native nations were vitally important to their economic and social survival. These western *Canadiens* quickly became culturally and politically distinct from their eastern relatives. While they continued to define themselves ethnically as *Canadiens* their primary loyalties were to the western lands and their Native-American relatives.

The Illinois villages, in modern Illinois and Missouri, were among the first large focal points of settlement for the western *Canadiens* and their *Mètis* descendants. Having their origins in the 1680s, their history was similar to many of the other *Mètis* settlements springing up throughout the *Pays d'en Haut*. In the cultural tradition of the *Mètis* the history of families or villages are often traced to a distant common ancestor, and thus the founding of "French" Illinois can be prosaically attributed to Michel and Marie Accault.

Michel was typical of the *Canadiens* living in the west, arriving into the area as a *coureur du bois* in the employ of the Fur Trader Rene de LaSalle in the early 1680s. Accault, reputedly, could speak at least five of the Native languages and he was used by the colonial officials and traders as an interpreter and agent among the tribes. Accault, like most of his compatriots in the west, had little use for the

Church, but he managed a rapprochement with the missionaries when he attempted to wed Marie Aramipinchicoue, a Catholic convert and daughter of an influential chief of the Illiniwek Indian nation. Accault's marriage to Marie connected the French to the powerful Rouensa family and to the Illiniwek as a whole. Other daughters of Rouensa had probably married *Canadiens*, as had several daughters of Papappe Chicagou, another important Illiniwek chief. Life in the west was a hazardous one for those early *Canadiens* and French, and most women, like Marie, would go through a number of husbands in their lifetimes.

Marie Aramipinchicoue was representative of the women who mothered the Illinois, French, and *Mètis* people elsewhere. Her people, the Illiniwek, had shrunk in population to less than 12,000 by the time of her marriage to Accault due to devastating epidemics of European and Asian origins. Marie's second son, Michel Jr., was born in Rouensa's village, then located at the site of modern St. Louis, in February, 1702. In that same year her first husband died, and the following spring she and her family, along with their Illiniwek and *Mètis* followers, moved to the present site of Kaskaskia, Illinois. Soon after the death of Michel Sr. she married Antoine Baillargeon, a resident *voyageur*. Marie and Antoine did not get along so they had the marriage annulled. Antoine then married Domitilde Cheoupinoua, another Illiniwek, and founded a *Mètis* family dynasty that spread through the Illinois and Wabash territories. In 1703 Marie married a third and final time, to Michel Philippe, a *Canadien*, with whom she bore an additional six children. By the time of her death in 1725, she had seen her branch of the Rouensa family spread through the "French" villages of the Illinois country. Of her known children only Michel Accault Jr. was not living in the *Mètis* settlements, having established himself in the Illiniwek villages. Her other children all married local *Canadiens* and *Mètis*, further increasing the influence of her family.

Her last husband, Michel Philippe, was a lieutenant in the Kaskaskia *Mètis* militia, a locally led and maintained armed force that was nominally under the control of the colonial administrators. The village militias, in the *Pays d'en Haut*, were intended to protect the local settlements and to serve as a source of soldiers in the French struggle to prevent English incursions. To maintain and develop colonial control over the area the French established a line of forts across an arc of North America, from the St. Lawrence settlements to New Orleans. They sought an active alliance among the Native nations and slowly and somewhat clumsily entered into a mediator role among the often feuding tribes. With the exception of several policy crises in the early 1700s, the French filled the role adequately. They attempted to forge an already existent Native alliance into a unified force that would fight in the interests of France, and to negotiate a peace between the various nations so that trade could be pursued more efficiently. This *Pax Français* only succeeded to the degree that France's goals were similar to that of many of the tribes. The trade routes and the traders were much safer, but intertribal conflict continued to undermine unified action.

This French and Indian military alliance became involved in a series of colonial actions known to history as the French and Indian Wars. As early as the 1690s the *Canadiens* and their Algonquian allies had become embroiled in the long struggle between France and England over the colonial control of Canada, *Acadie,* and the *Pays d'en Haut.* The fall of New France had begun. The English armies first gobbled up *Acadie,* and in 1760 forced the capitulation of Canada. To deal with the *"Acadien* problem" in newly conquered *Acadie,* the British rounded up the French-speaking inhabitants, locking them up in stockades until they could be deported or sold into slavery in the American colonies or the West Indies. Some of these deportees escaped to Louisiana, being the ancestors of the modern Cajuns, while others fled into the woods, surviving for decades under the protection of their relatives in the tribal nations.

Five years later Montrèal and Quèbec had fallen to the English, and with the active collusion of the Church, the colony was soon pacified. The *Canadiens* were forced to sign an oath of loyalty to the English, as well as to turn in their arms. Only the *Canadiens, Mètis* and Indians of the west remained distant from effective English rule. While French colonial rule had collapsed, the *Mètis* and Indians, with the material help of French and *Canadien* merchants, continued to fight the French and Indian Wars for another fifty-four years. The fall of Canada to the English changed the *Canadiens.* The newly arriving English colonists in Canada coopted its name, becoming Canadians, while the conquered *Canadiens* along the St. Lawrence were renamed *Quèbeçois,* for the capital of their district. The *Canadiens* of the *Pays d'en Haut,* after the year 1760, had lost their ties to France as well as to the word Canada. As they reformulated their identity, the French of the west, whatever their specific genealogical background, became the people known to history as the *Mètis. Mètis* identity and nationalism

The *Pays d'en Haut* in the nineteenth century, with Mètis villages shown.

were tied to common cultural dynamics, language, and mutual interests, not to a specified territory or "race."

With France no longer on the scene, and most of its military posts
in the west delivered to the British, the leadership of the Native
alliance fell to Pontiac, an Odawe Indian from the Detroit area.
Pontiac and his Indian allies initially chose to remain at peace,
despite the failure of the British to understand Native protocol or to
serve as an effective mediator between the tribes. While the colonial
officials slowly tried to come into an accommodation with the tribes,

the movement of Anglo-American colonists onto Indian land led to war. The tribes and the British had agreed that the Appalachian Mountains would form the border between the Indians and the British colonists of America. The Native people understood that the maintenance of this frontier was necessary for their continued prosperity. The Native nations and the *Mètis* were developing a regional nationalism that sought economic independence, and the removal of the Anglo-American colonists and their military protectors from the Native lands. Francis Parkman, an American historian of the last century, wrote of the *Mètis* of this period:

> The discontent of the Indians gave great satisfaction to the French, who saw in it a... vengeance on their conquerors... fearing the English...they would have gladly seen them driven out of the country...and all classes of this...population, accordingly dispersed themselves among the villages...or held councils with them....They told their excited hearers that the English had formed a deliberate scheme to root out the whole Indian race, and, with that design, had already begun to hem them in with settlements on the one hand, and a chain of forts on the other.[6]

These *Mètis* partisans were not telling the Native nations anything new, for Indian refugees from the areas already conquered by the Anglo-Americans had been telling the same story for years. The situation was clear to the Native alliance. The options were evaluated and a course of action was chosen.

Soon *Canadien* and *Mètis* merchants were providing the alliance warriors with arms, clothing, and provisions. Within weeks of receiving news that France had given control of all the lands east of the Mississippi River to the English, the tribes were ready to strike. Warriors of a dozen tribes started working out a strategy to take some thirteen British military posts, and to push the Anglo-American colonists back east of the Appalachian mountains. To Pontiac was given the honor of the first strike. On May 9, 1763, he led 400 warriors in an abortive attack against the British troops holed up in their fort at Detroit. Failing to take the fort they laid siege to it, holding its defenders as virtual prisoners for nearly six months. Within eleven weeks of the initial attack at Detroit, nine English posts had been taken and destroyed and three others had come under siege by the Native forces.

In June, 1763, Pontiac summoned the local *Mètis* leaders to meet with him at the Odawe village near Detroit. In his meeting with the patriarchs of the Detroit French he sought to gain their active assistance in the struggle against English colonialism. He told the assembly that if they were to be French they must join the tribes, but should they acquiesce to the English, then they would be the enemies of the warriors. An elder of the *Mètis* answered Pontiac, declaring that the French capitulation at Montrèal had tied their hands. He stated that Pontiac's warriors must defeat the British before the *Mètis* could be free to join them. In other words, the cautious French speaking elders wished to be able to play the game both ways. They wished for the elimination of the British, but fearing that this could not be accomplished, they tried to convince the English garrison that their neutrality was due to their fear of, not sympathy with, Pontiac's assembled warriors.

Many of the younger *Mètis* at the Detroit council, however, wished to join the Native forces. They

> were seated with the council, or stood looking on, variously attired in...Indian leggins, and red woolen caps. Not a few among them, however, had thought proper to adopt the style of dress and ornament peculiar to the red man, who were their usual associates... Indeed, they aimed to identify themselves with the Indians....It was one of these that now took up the war belt, and declared that he and his comrades were ready to rise the hatchet for Pontiac.[7]

Most of the *Mètis* could move fairly fluidly between Indian and "French" society and on the following day Pontiac's new recruits joined in another assault on the British held fort, but again the Native forces were unsuccessful. The warriors then settled in for a protracted siege, and set their attention to directing the war against the Anglo-American colonists to the east. Small bands of warriors searched out the Americans squatting on Indian lands and evicted them or burned them out. Thousands of Americans fled the frontier regions of Pennsylvania and Virginia, and hundreds of others lost their lives attempting to fight the warriors.

With autumn upon them, large numbers of warriors began returning to their villages to prepare for the coming winter. In October, the British forces managed to lift the siege on Detroit, and in the following year large British armies entered the *Pays d'en Haut* and began peace negotiations with the Nations of the west. Over the next few years the English pursued a policy of negotiation and accommodation with the tribes, but Pontiac and many of the *Mètis* remained hostile. Fearing English retribution, many Native-Americans and *Mètis* left their homes in the Great Lakes and Ohio regions and moved to Illinois, which had not yet been occupied by the British forces.

By the Treaty of Paris, in 1763, that part of the Illinois country that was east of the Mississippi River was turned over to the British, but they would not occupy it for another two years. In this interlude the Native warriors and the *Mètis* looked to the former French military commander of Illinois for aid in their war against the British. He would greet the Native embassies cordially, but he was unable to aid them or encourage them about the prospects of France reentering the war. Even so, Pontiac moved his headquarters to Illinois, encamping his people outside the French fort at Chartres. He still led a powerful alliance of Native villages, and he sent embassies enlisting the aid of other Native nations, as well as delegations of Indians and *Mètis*, to confer with the French colonial officials in New Orleans. By fall of 1765 the Native alliance had become convinced that the Ohio tribes had made peace with the British and that the east bank of the Illinois country was soon to be turned over to them. All hopes of French help were dashed asunder when France turned Louisiana and the west bank of Illinois over to the Spanish. Late in 1765 British forces relieved the French garrison at Ft. du Chartres, the French soldiers and administrators moving to the newly established *Mètis* village of St. Louis, Missouri. In 1766 Pontiac and the remaining hostile warriors made peace with the British, allowing them occupation of the western forts, but stating that all immigration of Americans into the Indian territories must end. A tenuous peace took hold, but the warriors remained on their guard.

The *Mètis* of Illinois remained hostile to the British and were bewildered by the Spanish takeover of the west bank of the Mississippi River. For five years after the French capitulation at Montreal St. Ange, the French commander held the Illinois country. Four more years would pass before Spanish administrators would reach St. Louis. During these nine years the 6,000 Indian and *Mètis* residents lived in a colonial limbo, approaching a state of independence. Being unhappy with the British rule of the east bank and apprehensive of the Spanish on the west, they set course to establish a sovereign government. *Mètis* meeting in Kaskaskia, in 1770, selected Daniel Blouin to carry their demands for autonomy to the head of the British occupation forces, General Gage, in New York. Despite ill treatment from the General, Blouin set forth the *Mètis'* demands only to have them rejected without consideration. Blouin was told that the military, not the *Mètis* or Indians, would dictate policy in the west.

That the British held the *Mètis* and Indians of Illinois in low esteem is illustrated by this 1765 quote by the English Lieutenant, Alexander Fraser:

> The Illinois Indians are about 650 able to bear arms. Nothing can equal their passion for drunkenness, but that of the French inhabitants who for the greatest part are drunk every day, while they can get drink to buy in the Colony...anyone who has had dealings with them must plainly see they are for the most part transported convicts, or people who have fled for such crimes; those who have not done it themselves are the offspring of those I just mentioned.[8]

The English Lieutenant-Governor, Hamilton, called the Illinois *Mètis* to council in 1772 to present the imperial plan for the Illinois country. The *Mètis* told Hamilton that they fully expected to be able to elect their own governors and all civil magistrates. After this council, one of the Illinois *patriotes* distributed a pamphlet urging the *Mètis* to hold fast to their demands for autonomy. The *Mètis* would keep up the struggle for another five years. Many became discouraged and moved into the growing number of *Mètis* villages on the Spanish held west bank, but an ill wind was blowing from the east. The Anglo-American colonists on the Atlantic coast wanted possession of the western lands and they were willing to fight both the Native and the British forces to get them.

AMERICANS AND IMPERIALISM IN THE *PAYS D'EN HAUT*

WITH THE BEGINNING OF THE AMERICAN REVOLUTION A virtual flood of Anglo-American colonists poured over the Appalachians, proceeded by merchants and land speculators seeking to gain an easy fortune. Initially the Native alliance attempted to hold a neutral stance, but even before the signing of the Declaration of Independence in 1776, most of the allies had made common cause with the British. From Virginia the Anglo-Americans sent soldiers to conquer the Wabash and Illinois areas, which they did, and held them under military control. The Native alliance rose up under the leadership of the Miami, Shawnee, and Wyandot nations in a war against the Americans that would last for 38 years.

The American revolutionists consolidated their hold on the east bank of the Illinois country, keeping the local Indians and *Mètis* under military rule for more than a decade. American rule was marked by the lawlessness of the soldiers and newly arrived Anglo-American colonists, by the loss of *Mètis* and Indian lands to the speculators, and by the general tone of oppression leveled at the Native inhabitants of the country. The anti-British Illinois *Mètis* had held high hopes for the American Revolution, but now, under its rule, many fled to the Spanish held west bank. Those remaining on the east bank sought to maintain an isolation from the new American colonists.

In the expanding American colonial empire even those *Mètis* and Indians on the west bank were not safe, for the Americans saw a quick and easy profit on the horizon, and it was France's Napoleon that gave it to them. In 1795 the Americans had made peace with the British gaining, on paper, all the country south of the Great Lakes. In 1800 Spain had turned over all claim to the country between the Mississippi River and the Rocky Mountains to France. Then in 1803, Napoleon sold the entire territory to the Americans for a paltry fifteen million dollars. The Native nations and the *Mètis* had now been sold out by every European power with which they had come into contact. Only alliance with the British in Canada offered the Indians and *Mètis* any hope for the future.

From the late 1790s until the War of 1812, the Americans nibbled off bits of the tribal lands; being somewhat careful to check their greed so as to avoid an all out Indian war. During this period the Native alliance was being reformulated by the Shawnee brothers, Tecumseh and Tenskwatawa. Joining the *Mètis* to this alliance were among others, Billy Caldwell of Chicago and Michel Brisbois of Prairie du Chien, Wisconsin. This expanding alliance sought to check the loss of Indian lands, preferably through negotiation, but through arms if necessary. The Americans, however, did not seek negotiation. They sought land and conquest, and in the long term they sought the elimination of the Native peoples. Without any hope of negotiation or compromise with the Americans, the Native forces joined the British in the War of 1812.

In an extension of the Napoleonic wars in Europe, the United States declared war on England on June 18, 1812. Soon the British sent forces from Canada to take and hold the Great Lakes, and the tribal nations and *Mètis* under the leadership of Tecumseh joined them in the coming battles. In the Great Lakes area the war lasted until mid 1815, having ultimately been lost for the Native alliance by the bungling British generals sent to the region. For the Americans, the War of 1812 was something of the finale to the War of Independence against Britain. They now held undisputed colonial claim to nearly all the land between Canada, Texas, and the eastern face of the Rocky Mountains.

The Americans had fought the war against the Native nations and the *Mètis* by pursuing a scorched earth policy. American forces would scour the country, attacking and burning Native villages and crops at will. Miamis, Weas, and Potawatamis took the brunt of this policy, but Anglo-American militias also burned the *Mètis* town of Peoria, taking its male inhabitants away in chains and leaving its women and children to perish in the woods. The Americans had harassed and pursued Tecumseh and his warriors; finally killing him in a pitched battle near Moroviantown, Ontario, on October 5, 1813. By 1816 the American forces had reoccupied the western forts taken by Native and British armies, and had begun to consolidate their control of the west.

In the post war period the Americans increased the flow of colonists pouring across the Ohio, into the southern halves of the Ohio, Indiana, and Illinois territories. When these territories had acquired a sufficiently large number of Anglo-American citizens they would gain entrance to the American Union as a state. The Indian and *Mètis*, however, were not consulted about their forced entrance into the United States. The American conquerors did not see the Natives as equals, arguing that they had no more rights under American law than the massive number of people held as slaves by United States citizens. The Americans tried to legitimize the stealing of Native lands and sovereignty through a long series of sham treaties. The treaties gave the Indians a means to negotiate with the Americans, but they soon discovered that if the Americans did not get exactly what they wanted, they would always declare war. Indian leaders found that the best they could hope for from this new government and legal system was to be able to negotiate the cost of the rape of their nations.

The violent prejudice held by the English and the Anglo-

Americans against people with a different hue of skin from their own, and the assumption of superiority which they lorded over others, permeated their relations with the Native people. The American settlers, after fifty five years of war, had developed a hatred and fear of the Indian people, sentiments viciously exploited by land speculators and other profiteers. The bigotry of most of these Americans was also suffered by the *Mètis*, whose history, culture, and often skin color, were shared with the Native-Americans. It is probable that only the colonial origins of the *Mètis* people saved them from sharing the effects of the genocidal policies the Americans unleashed upon the Indian Nations.

The government attempts to separate the Native peoples from their land had, by the late 1820s, evolved into a policy of physically removing the Indians and dumping them beyond the frontier. Despite the best efforts of many Indian and *Mètis* leaders, the Removal policy was sternly enforced. Some tribes managed to hold on to the last of their lands into the 1840s, but eventually the American military rounded up the holdouts. Through the 1830s and 1840s this policy reigned, and soon all of Ohio, Indiana, Illinois, Missouri and the entire southern United States were officially "free" of Indians. In the Great Lakes region many Odawes, Ojibwes, Potawatamis, and others fled to Canada, preferring to live as refugees than to live in militarily supervised Removal camps on the distant western frontier. Many of the Indian people managed to escape Removal, hiding in the woods for generations or living under the protection of *Mètis* kindred. In the American government's convoluted way of thinking, the "mixed-bloods" had a right to remain in their homes because of their European ancestry, but Indians, who owned the land in question, did not share those rights. In this new world order it became easy for Indians to pass as French, and *Mètis* and Indian alike learned to hide their ancestry from the English speaking settlers.

Though *Mètis* were exempted from Removal, many, particularly those connected with the Potawatami, chose to follow their relatives to the western frontier. While most remained in their old villages, others also chose to move to Michigan, Wisconsin, Minnesota, and other places where Native people still remained the dominant population. The Indians and *Mètis* who remained in the lower Great Lakes states were thrown into social isolation, not being readily accepted into Anglo-American society, but still being expected to meld into the lower classes as workers for their conquerors. The *Mètis* of the Detroit region, in the 1820s, sought to alleviate American rule by annexing themselves to neighboring Canada. Failing that, many chose to move across the Detroit River into the province of Ontario. Others moved to Saginaw or the Grand River area, away from the expanding American settlements.

By the late 1700s small *Mètis* settlements had begun to spring up in Minnesota, North Dakota, and Manitoba province. These areas, along with northern Michigan and Wisconsin, remained distant from American settlements into the 1860s. In this vast region the *Mètis* tried to reestablish their political identity within the context of the new colonial conquest. As Americans established local units of government in the territories, *Mètis* took to the ballot box and elected their own officials. The ability to vote in local elections encouraged *Mètis*, who had not yet done so, to become naturalized citizens of the United States. Indians, unlike the *Mètis*, were not allowed citizenship nor the vote, negating the numerical superiority of the Native peoples in the areas still under their control. In other words, the resident Indians, and those *Mètis* who had not yet become citizens, were not to be allowed the constitutional right of representation within any unit of the new government.

In the northern and western territories of the United States and Great Britain the fur trade had continued its own expansion, reaching from the Arctic circle to California. Spurred on by the fur companies, and the *Mètis* Free-Traders, new settlements were established throughout the area. The ethnic composition of the *Mètis* was changing from its original *Canadien* core. While their dominant language remained a distinct *patois* of French, many English and Scots "mixed-bloods," likewise children of the fur trade, joined their communities. In the subarctic, the Great Plains and the western mountains many families followed a hunting and trapping tradition, living a semi-nomadic lifestyle, and often preferring a Native-American language to French or English. A percentage of the fur trade, at least in the United States, came to be controlled by local *Mètis* interests. The Chouteaus, a major French family of St. Louis with extensive Native and *Mètis* connections, dominated the fur trade on the Missouri River, while families such as the Rolettes, Renvilles, and Faribaults traded extensively throughout Wisconsin, Minnesota, and the Dakotas.

By the closing decades of the eighteenth century a substantial *Mètis* population had grown up in southern Manitoba, in an area collectively known as the Red River Settlement. This area, until its annexation by Canada in 1870, became the core of the *Mètis* Nation in a world newly shaped by the American conquest. Red River, all of western Canada for that matter, was considered as British territory, though all civil authority was still held by the Indian nations and local *Mètis* communities. Two rival fur trade companies vied for economic control of this vast territory, the English Hudson's Bay Company and the "French" Northwest Company; the former being controlled by *Mètis*, *Canadien*, and Anglo-Canadian interests. The *Mètis* of the area saw their economic and political interests as being best served by the Northwest Company and became partisans in its struggle to eject the English competitors from their lands.

In 1812 shocked *Mètis* residents learned that the British government had given the Red River Settlement, which they considered to be theirs, to Hudson's Bay Company as a colony for immigrants from Scotland. With a trade war already in progress, the *Mètis* were prepared to defend their rights. Along with the colonists came colonial administrators, neither being welcome additions to the landscape. Over the next two years the colonial Governor, and his oppressive laws, pushed the *Mètis* to war. Under the leadership of Cuthbert Grant, who was of Scots and Cree Indian background, the *Mètis* organized their military strength, coercing many of the colonists to leave the area and forcing the Governor to sign a treaty in which the remaining settlers would vacate the area and free trade would be allowed throughout the country. However, in 1815, the settlers returned, under a new Governor, abrogating the treaty and reestablishing colonial rule. In June of 1819 Grant and his little *Mètis* army marched on the colony to reopen free trade, as well as to again evict the settlers. The Governor, with 24 armed settlers, attempted to prevent the advance of the *Mètis* force. In the ensuing battle the Governor and all but four of his men were killed. The settlers surrendered to Grant and within weeks they vacated the colony.

The Northwest Company merged with the Hudson's Bay Company in 1821, ending the decade long trade war between them and leaving the Bay Company with an absolute trading monopoly over the country. With peace now prevailing in the territory, the Red River Settlement grew and prospered. Retired employees of the Fur Trade and *Mètis* fleeing from troubles in the U.S. swelled its population. French speaking *Mètis* remained the dominant population though English "mixed-bloods" grew into a significant minority. After 1836 the Hudson's Bay Company sought to enforce its monopoly over the west by declaring the *Mètis*, English and French speaking alike, to be merely tenants on the land, and by suppressing the rights of the Free-Traders and *Mètis*. The *Mètis* resisted the Company rule over the territory, continuing their trade south of the border and among the western Indian nations. After the Company started to censor the mail in 1844, the *Mètis* demanded that their rights be recognized. Alexander Christie, then the appointed governor of the district, replied that the *Mètis* essentially had no rights, being subjects of the all powerful Company.

Three years later, flexing their monopolistic powers, the Company put on a show trial, prosecuting three Free Traders suspected of smuggling furs. Armed *Mètis* arrived, en masse, at the trial of the first defendant, saving him from punishment at the hands of the court. In this action they defeated the monopoly and rule of the Company. The *Mètis* had left the courthouse crying *le commerce est libre!* (the trade is free!). The *gens libres* (the free people) had marked another page in their history.

Back across the border, in the United States, the *Mètis* continued to be treated as a subject people by the American government. Though unwilling to negotiate with them as a group, the Americans did feel an obligation to recognize some of their rights and land claims by a 1787 treaty with England. Within the first 30 years of American rule in Southern Illinois and Indiana, however, the vast majority of *Mètis* lands had been taken by speculators and military officials. A government commission to investigate *Mètis* claims was not created until 1807 and it merely rubberstamped the claims of the new settlers. In this way a son of General Clark, who commanded the American military rule of Illinois, managed to gain some 12,000 acres of prime farm land. While selected Americans became wealthier, most of the *Mètis* became tenants on their former lands. Remaining *Mètis* holdings in the region, and throughout all the areas colonized by the Americans, were in danger of being lost through the American legal system. Under American law land could be taken for non-payment of taxes, the amount of taxes due being based on the market value of the land and its improvements. Poor *Mètis* often lost their property by this form of taxation. Others lost it through their inability to speak the language of the judicial system, English.

Leaders of many of the Native-American nations tried to provide for their *Mètis* relatives in the treaties they signed with the United States. Most of the earlier treaties stipulated that the *Mètis* should be provided with land from within the cession areas, and, in some cases, they would continue to have hunting and fishing rights as well. By the late 1820s thousands of people of Potawatami, Odawe, and other tribal descent had benefitted from such treaties. Since the U.S. has always traced tribal rights by governmentally defined rules of inheritance, (i.e., rights and race are based upon a person's genealogy rather than upon their culture or ethnicity), the government construed that *Mètis* receiving lands or other concessions from the treaties had been paid in full for their share of the tribal inheritance. Henceforth these "mixed-bloods" became legally, at least on paper, white. Into the 1860s the tribes continued to attempt to provide for their *Mètis* kindred, but American policy soon allowed only for cash payments or the issuance of negotiable certificates (scrip) for land.

Land certificates were issued to thousands of Ojibwe *Mètis* under several treaties ranging from 1854 to 1866. The certificates were issued to all heads of households and single persons over the age of twenty-one, and would entitle their bearers to select up to 80 acres of land within areas taken from their tribal relatives. American land speculators and lumber interests devised ways to subvert the intentions of the treaties. They sent their own attorneys into the *Mètis* settlements, collecting applications for scrip, and paying the often illiterate people a few dollars for the right to represent them before the government. The attorneys would then pack up their bundles of applications, get them approved by the federal authorities, and use them for their own purposes. In subsequent hearings on the matter it became evident that most of the attorneys never told their *Mètis* clients that their applications had been approved. Other lawyers paid their clients a small sum for their certificates. Lumber interests would use these certificates to locate themselves on a section of forest land and strip cut it. Then they would move on to the next section and "float'"the title to the land from place to place. This "floating script," as it came to be called, made fortunes for many Americans but only created poverty for the Indians, *Mètis*, and other people living in the northern forest lands that had thus been stripped.

THE MÉTIS AT MID-CENTURY

THE HISTORY OF THE *MÈTIS* IN MINNESOTA IS FAIRLY REPRESENTATIVE of the upper Great Lakes portion of the U.S. after the Removal period. Since at least the 1790s, small *Mètis* settlements had

Illustration by Richard Kees

The *Mètis* National flag, c. 1815.

been developing throughout the territory. Their villages usually consisted of a few connected extended families whose members were closely allied with either the Ojibwe in the north or the Dakota in the south. Most of the earlier settlements were centered around trading posts, or along major transportation routes, and their economic structure was deeply rooted in the Fur Trade. With the close of the War of 1812, large numbers of *Mètis* from Illinois, Michigan, and Wisconsin started moving into the region joined by a century long migration of others from the Red River Settlement and Canada. *Mètis* villages became concentrated along the Mississippi River in the area now occupied by the Minneapolis-St. Paul metro region, which, for the purposes of this article, will be called the St. Peters district. In the northwest corner of the state, south of the international border from the Red River Settlement, another large center of population developed around Pembina and St. Vincent. The St. Peters district was particularly well suited to the *Mètis*, being centrally located to many still sovereign tribal nations as well as to *Mètis* settlements from Wisconsin to the Dakotas. The economic foundation of the district was built on its accessibility to the western frontiers of the American fur trade as well as to the Free-Traders of Pembina and the Red River Settlement.

The Americans established a military presence in the district in 1819 with the establishment of Ft. Snelling, at the confluence of the Minnesota and Mississippi rivers. Initially the military, with its small complement of soldiers, played something of a peace-making role between the Ojibwe and Dakota nations. Later, in the 1830s, the Americans began coercing the tribes into giving up lands in the St. Peter district, raising fears among the *Mètis* and Indians of a massive immigration of American settlers into their territory. Paving the way for the future settlers, in 1838, the military decided to evict all *Mètis* settlements, except Mendota, from the modern limits of St. Paul and Minneapolis. These *Mètis*, some residing in the area for four or five decades, were called squatters, and were hated by the Americans for their many-hued skins, their French language, and their overwhelming support for the British in the War of 1812. The people of the St. Peter district, however, were not going to lose their lands without some kind of battle. Accordingly, residents met on November 16, 1839, publicly adopting a series of resolutions condemning the American officers and declaring the evictions as contrary to the principles of justice and honesty. This *Mètis* council attempted to establish their rights to the lands they occupied by sending their resolutions and petitions to the United States Senate and the Wisconsin Territorial Legislature, which at that time administered Minnesota. The Americans remained unmoved and the Secretary of War ordered the eviction to be carried out. The soldiers and officers carried out their orders with dispatch, leveling the residents' homes and farms, abusing the people, and chasing them down river to seek shelter in *Mètis* communities near the Wisconsin border.

Over the next decade most of the evicted people were able to reestablish themselves in the area, occupying about a dozen communities varying in size from a dozen to several hundred people. In 1848 the United States Government "opened" the St. Peter district for American settlement, the land to be sold at public auction in the town of Stillwater. An American, sympathetic to the *Mètis*, informed them that they would need to go to the auction in order to buy title to the lands upon which they lived. To protect their holdings, and realizing that further petitions to the government would be fruitless, they went to bid on their lands. To increase their bargaining power they came equipped with sticks and clubs insuring that the land speculators and others would not bid against them. The success of this tactic allowed them to gain legal American title to their land, much of it remaining in the possession of their descendants into the twentieth century.

The 1849 and 1850 Minnesota censuses, together with other sources, indicate a territorial population of around 19,000 people, 66 percent of whom were members of one of the three tribal nations then resident, the Ojibwe, Dakota, and Winnebago. About 18 percent of the population was affiliated with the *Mètis*, while the remaining 16 percent was composed of the newly arrived American settlers. By 1850 the Americans were already dominating the politics of the territory, and by 1855 they controlled more than three-quarters of the seats in the Minnesota Territorial Legislature. The 1850 census is interesting in that three of the census takers, who enumerated four of the nine existing counties, were *Mètis*. The American census takers often identified *Mètis* with an "H," indicating "Half-breed," but William Warren and Alexis Bailley, who were both *Mètis*, would not indicate people by their "race." Joseph Rolette, who enumerated Pembina county, went a step further. While he didn't identify *Mètis*, as such, he wryly indicated Americans with a big "W," for white. Rolette, whose father was a prominent Prairie du Chien trader, was proud of his origins and *Mètis* culture. Prior to Minnesota's statehood in 1858, he served the interests of the *Mètis* in the Minnesota Territorial Legislature as well as in his home district of Pembina County.

THE PROVISIONAL GOVERNMENT

BY 1865 THE *MÈTIS* POPULATION HAD GROWN DRAMATICALLY with as many as 60,000 living within the area of the United States and another 20,000-30,000 across the border in what now is western and northern Canada. The flood of American settlers was sweeping across the Mississippi River to the edge of the Great Plains. There the United States military was bloodily attempting to subjugate the Native-American nations of the west and force them to cede large portions of their lands. Yet, the militant resistance of such nations as the Lakota, Cheyenne, and Arapaho continued to prevent any significant

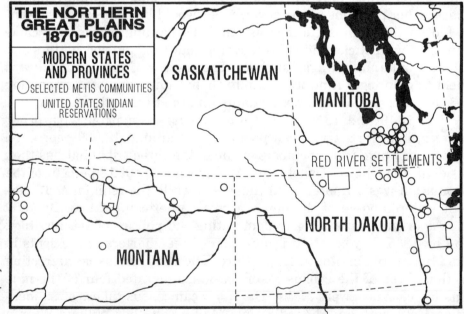

Minnesota, The Dakotas, Manitoba and Saskatchewan.

number of settlers from entering the Great Plains. In the old towns of the *Pays d'en Haut, Mètis* and *Canadien* immigrants continued on with their lives and cultures, even if at a disadvantage to their American neighbors. News and politics were dissemenated throughout the *Mètis* world by French language newspapers that were being published in places like St. Louis, Missouri, the Red River Settlement, and St. Paul, Minnesota. Only in western Canada, still under the feeble administration of the Hudson's Bay Company, did the *Mètis* retain their sovereignty. By the end of the decade the eyes of the autonomous New Nation were focused upon the Red River.

The history of the Red River Settlement came to a turning point when the Anglo-Canadian government began negotiating with England for the purchase of the entire west. While the *Mètis* were informed about the negotiations, neither they nor the Indian nations were consulted about their wishes in the matter. In 1869, prior to the Canadians successful bid for the land, the government in Ottawa sent surveyors and agents to scout out the territory. As the surveyors started mapping out lands in the Red River Settlement they were confronted by a band of men, led by Louis Riel, and ordered to stop surveying *Mètis* lands. *Mètis* people, with their long history behind them, were not willing to allow themselves to be conquered or purchased by another foreign power. If the political independence of the country was not feasible, then Riel and his followers were willing to negotiate, as a free people, for their entry into Canada as equals. The Anglo-Canadian government, in power through this period, was unwilling to negotiate with the citizens of the west, taking the colonial position that the *Mètis* and Indians were people without rights.

The Red River *Mètis* quickly formed *Le Comite National des Mètis* to act in defense of their rights, with John Bruce as their president and Louis Riel their secretary. In October of 1869 the *Comite* sent a message ordering Canada's Territorial Governor-select not to enter the region without their express permission. The Governor-select, McDougall by name, full of bluff and bluster, soon attempted to enter the territory, but was met by an armed force of *Mètis* and escorted back across the border into the United States. Riel and other leaders undertook to organize the 12,000 French and English speaking *Mètis* residents of Red River to be able to speak with one voice. This unity, Riel felt, would strengthen their negotiating position as well as preserve harmony between the various segments of the population. To further their cause, the *Comite National* garrisoned a small army in

Fort Garry, the headquarters of the Hudson's Bay Company, and the settlements were kept policed to maintain order.

With their control of the colony established, the *Mètis* set up the Provisional Government of Red River on December 10, 1869, Riel being named President on the 27th. Outmaneuvering Canadian emissaries sent to the district, the *Mètis* forced the Canadians to negotiate with delegates of the Provisional Government, who had been sent to the capital in Ottawa for that purpose. The *Mètis* demanded a set of rights to be recognized, including the right to a popularly elected legislature, bilingualism, popular control of all aspects of local government, legal recognition of all existing *Mètis* "privileges, customs, and usages", and entrance into the Canadian Dominion under equal and full Provincial status. Concluding negotiations in May of 1870, the *Mètis* agreed to union with Canada as the Province of Manitoba. The

Members of the Provisional Government of Red River, c. 1869.
Louis Riel is in the lower row, second from left.

Mètis of the province were promised about half of the three million acres they wished set aside for their use, but the demand that any Army forces in the area be composed of local residents was rejected outright.

On paper the Provisional Government had done well for the *Mètis*, but its members soon discovered that politicians are rarely to be trusted. Even as the Canadians were concluding the negotiations,

Illustration by Richard Kees

Michel Dumas, circa 1884, Western Canada
Dumas joined with other Mètis leaders to invite
Louis Riel to come to Saskatchewan to continue the
struggle for Mètis rights.

they assembled an army to invade Red River and establish military control. On August 21, 1870 the Canadian forces entered the territory, taking Ft. Garry and driving many of the *Mètis* leaders into exile. The military arrested numbers of people, while soldiers attacked and injured others. Among the people who were outright assassinated was Elzear Goulet, who was stoned to death while attempting to swim across the Red River away from his attackers. The Canadians sentenced Riel and Ambroise Lepine (another member of the Provisional Government) to death for the their role in demanding *Mètis* rights, but the pair had fled to the United States seeking the protection of *Mètis* and *Québecois* sympathizers there. With the establishment of Canadian authority, the *Mètis* of Manitoba became, and remain to this day, second-class citizens. Many of the Red River *Mètis*, particularly those who had lost their lands, moved further west, joining *Mètis* communities in Saskatchewan and Alberta; beyond the limit of effective Canadian control. Others followed Riel and Lepine to the United States, settling in Minnesota, the Dakotas, and Montana.

Even while under sentence of death Riel continued the struggle for *Mètis* rights and aspirations. In 1872 Joseph Royal, editor of *Le Mètis*, a prominent Manitoba newspaper, urged Riel to return from exile and run for election to the Canadian Parliament representing the primarily *Mètis* district of Provencher. At the time Riel was living in the St. Paul home of Louis Demeules, the Red River born editor of another

French language newspaper, *L'Echo de L'Ouest*. Riel returned to Manitoba to begin campaigning, but bowed out of the election on a promise from representatives of the Prime Minister that an amnesty would be granted to Lepine and himself.

The amnesty, of course, never materialized, and in a new election held the next year Riel was elected by acclamation. His ability to carry out his duties as a member of parliament was hampered by the continuing death sentence that was likely to be imposed if he attempted to take his rightful place in the halls of government. With help of *Québecois* politicians he managed to sign in and take the oath for entry to the House of Commons, but was rushed away by his cohorts who feared he would soon be recognized. The election of Riel was a message of dissatisfaction with the *Canadiens*, a message thrown in the face of the government by electing him in two subsequent campaigns.

THE END OF THE OLD WORLD

THE FOCUS OF THE NEW NATION HAD SHIFTED TO THE WEST in the decades following the fall of the Provisional Government. By 1884 Gabriel Dumont, Will Jackson, and other Saskatchewan *Mètis* had organized their people to resist the westward expansion of the Canadian Government. Again the Canadians failed to come into meaningful negotiation with the *Mètis* about their rights and property. A council of English and French speaking *Mètis* requested Louis Riel, then living among the Montana *Mètis*, to come north to help them in their struggle. Over the next nine months Riel and the other *Mètis* leaders worked tirelessly, trying to weld the *Mètis* and Indians into a cohesive political force, and attempting by all available means to negotiate with the government. It wasn't that the Canadians opposed all the *Mètis* demands. It was that they were not willing to negotiate with a people they felt were inferior to themselves. The government's attitude inevitably led to war. The Army was sent in overwhelming numbers into the Native lands, defeating the *Mètis* and Indian forces in a drawn out and hotly contested war.

In the aftermath, many of the *Mètis* and Indians fled the oppressive Canadian rule in Saskatchewan, becoming refugees in the American territories of North Dakota and Montana. Riel was caught, imprisoned, and tried for treason. In a aham trial the all English jury convicted him and the government judge sentenced him to hang.

Despite the intervention of prominent lawyers on Riel's behalf, and the loud protests of *Mètis, Québecois,* and sympathetic Americans, the government was determined to see Riel die. In response to riots in Québec the government declared that Riel would die even if "every dog in Québec barks in his favor." On November 16, 1885 Louis Riel was hung and the hopes of the people of the New Nation shattered.

The half century that followed Riel's death was a bleak time for the *Mètis* of Canada and the United States. It was a time of poverty, increasing social isolation, and continued degradation of what little land base they had managed to retain. Neither Canada nor the United States recognized them as a distinct ethnic or national group, both countries writing them out of the history books and transforming them into a people without a past. During these years the *Mètis* reformulated the meaning of their identity and the nature of their long term struggle to protect their rights.

Their ethnic identity was obscured by the fact that in many communities they did not call themselves *Mètis.* Often they called themselves French or Creoles, but most still identified themselves simply as *Canadiens.* They still maintained the New Nation in that they continued to identify with their common history and language. The greatest challenge to their national survival, though, was not conquest, but the extreme racism that permeated American and Canadian society. The process, begun in the 1830s, of *Mètis* hiding or denying their Native-American past became a dominant feature of their culture throughout the lands they inhabited.

In the 1920s a Catholic priest in Wisconsin attempted to ask various members of his French-Canadian parish about their "Indian appearance." His informants would declare that they had no Native background, but their neighbors, or the folks down the street, were of Indian ancestry. Into the 1970s Indians and *Mètis* alike sought to confuse a racist society by passing as French-Canadians, elevating themselves on the social ladder by denying their ancestors and history. In the growing urban areas this pattern of denial eased their assimilation into the dominant white English speaking cultures, but in rural areas and smaller towns the people retained and even fostered their feelings of ethnic distinctiveness.

The governments of both Canada and the United States held to the position that any rights or claims the *Mètis* might have had due to their Indian background had been relinquished in the 1800s by Indian treaties and the acceptance of grants of land. Not all *Mètis*, however, were willing to see their New Nation fade from existence. With the founding of *L'Union Mètis* of Manitoba in 1887, an organization still in existence, the New Nation began to rebuild itself in the new political and social environment that had been forced upon it.

From the 1930s to present day, *Mètis* social and political organizations have sprung up across Canada and the United States. Many of these organizations, particularly in the U.S., seek the preservation of their "French" culture. The more politicized groups, such as the Manitoba *Mètis* Federation and the *L'Alliance* in Québec, tend to emphasize the Native-American background, organizing among both the English and French *Mètis*. In Canada the success of these organizations over the last twenty years have turned the *Mètis* into a political force with which to be reckoned. In recent years, while Canada was trying to reformulate its constitution, *Mètis* delegates were there. This constituted the first time in history that an English speaking country had allowed the *Mètis* people representation in deciding their political and social future.

It has been a long road for the *Mètis* people. Their New Nation remains rooted in their history, a history of continuity and adaptation in a constantly changing social and political environment. While their mixed Indian and European background continues to define them as a people, it is still in their hearts, not in their genealogies or in state boundaries, that the New Nation continues to live and develop.

NOTES

1 Louis Riel, 1869. Quoted in *Notrez/Our Heritage* (frontpiece, the Union Mètis, St. Paul, Minnesota, 1979.

2 John Reade, *Transactions of the Royal Society of Canada*, 1886.

3 Collections of the Minnesota Historical Society, Volume 7, p 343.

4 Nicholas Denys, *Description of the Coasts of North America*. William L. Ganong, Toronto: Champlain Society, 1908. Quoted in the *Fur Trade in Canada*, Harold A. Innis, University of Toronto Press, 1970, p. 18.

5 La Potherie, quoted in Harold A. Inis, *The Fur Trade in Canada*, p. 60.

6 Francis Parkman, *The Conspiracy of Pontiac, 1851*. Reprinted by Collier books, New York, 1966, pp. 149-150.

7 *Ibid.*, pp. 225-226.

8 *Ibid.*, p. 440, note 4.

BIBLIOGRAPHY
Bergeron, Leandre. *The History of Québec, A Patriot's Handbook*, 1975, New Canada Publications, Toronto.

Charette, Guillaume. *L'Eppace De Louis Goulet*, 1976, Editions Bois-Brules, Winnipeg.

Innis, Harold A. *The Fur Trade in Canada*, 1970, University of Toronto Press, Toronto.

Lussier, Antoine S., and D. Bruce Sealey. *The Mètis, Canada's Forgotten People*, 1975, Manitoba *Mètis* Federation Press, Winnipeg.

Pelletier, Emile. *Le Vecu Des Mètis*, 1980, Editions Bois-Brules, Winnipeg.

Sawchuk, Joe. *The Mètis* of Manitoba, Reformulation of an Ethnic Identity, 1978, Peter Martin Associates, Ltd., Toronto.

Stanley, George F. *G. Louis Riel*, 1963, The Ryerson Press, Toronto.

Tanner, Helen Hornbeck. *Atlas of Great Lakes Indian History*, 1987, University of Oklahoma Press, Norman.

White, Richard. *The Middle Ground: Indians, Empires and Republics in the Great Lakes Region 1650-1815*, 1991, Cambridge University Press, Cambridge, England, and New York.

Williams, J. Fletcher. *A History of the City of St. Paul to 1875*, 1983, Minnesota Historical Society, St. Paul, Minnesota.

Louis Riel

RETURN FROM WITHOUT
Louis Riel and Liminal Space

Darren S. Wershler-Henry

> outside in the rain louis was dying
> its always these damn white boys
> writing my story these same stupid fuckers
> that put me down to try to make a myth out of
> me
> they sit at counters scribbling their plays on
> napkins
> their poems on their sleeves & never see me
> hell said george
> its the perfect image the perfect metaphor he's a
> symbol
> said johnny
> but he's dead thot billie but didn't say it out loud
> theyre crazy these white boys said louis riel
> — bp Nichol's "The Long Weekend of Louis Riel"[1]

"LOUIS RIEL" (THE SIGNIFIER, THE ONLY REMAINING trace of the historical man) is a contested site. Written and rewritten—*over*written—by "these damn white boys" (bp Nichol and myself included, for any essay on "Louis Riel" can only ever be another rewriting); the signifier, "Louis Riel," has been reconstituted "in a seemingly infinite number of ways,"[2] filled and refilled with countless ideologies and mythologies. These (re)writings are inevitably part of a political and ideological struggle to (re)locate "Louis Riel" on a given side of one or more of a number of binary oppositions: White/Red, Hero/Villain, Political Leader/Religious Leader, Canadian/U.S. American, Sane/Mad.

In "Sorties: Out and Out: Attacks/Ways Out/Forays," Hélène Cixous claims that binary oppositions such as these have been the determining metaphor of Western thought: "If we read or speak, the same thread or double braid is leading us throughout literature, philosophy, criticism, centuries of representation and reflection."[3] Further, she points out that a binary opposition is inevitably hierarchical; one term asserts its superiority by effacing the other. "[T]he movement whereby each opposition is set up to make sense is the movement through which the couple is destroyed. A universal battlefield. Each time, a war is let loose. Death is always at work."[4] This operation can be seen already at work in the list of binaries given above. One term constitutes itself as positive, as presence. The other, as its negative, as absence, becomes a pejorative instead of a valid alternative (which term is constituted as negative depends on the agenda of the writer). As Laurie Anderson says at the beginning of *Home of the Brave*, everybody wants to be Number One; nobody wants to be a Zero.

What Cixous calls for is "another way of knowing,"[5] a relational rather than hierarchical logic; a logic of "both:and" rather than "either/or." To speak from/with/in such a logic is to situate oneself between discourses, on margins and borderlines, in gaps and crevices, in the blank spots on the page and on the map. In "The Laugh of the Medusa," (a major piece of poetic terrorism), Cixous links revolutionary writing with a "return from afar, from always: from 'without,' from the heath where witches are kept alive, from below, from beyond 'culture'."[6] These are *liminal spaces*—"limen" meaning threshold, the space in the doorway that both separates and fuses two worlds.

In *The Sacred and the Profane*, Mircea Eliade explains the nature of this space through the example of a church doorway:

> The door that opens on the interior of the church actually signifies a solution of continuity. The threshold that separates the two spaces also indicates the distance between two modes of being, the profane and religious. The thresold is the limit, the boundary, the frontier that distinguishes and opposes two worlds— and at the same time the paradoxical space where those worlds communicate, where passage from the profane to the sacred world becomes possible.[7]

Arnold van Gennep elaborates on this idea in *Rites of Passage*, broadening the definition of liminal space to include streets, roadways and village squares. For van Gennep, these are not "places" as such, but the spaces *between* places.[8] By extension, then, liminal space becomes the space of carnival: a place where inversions and parodies occur, where hierarchies are abandoned in favor of true relationality...a space of revolution.[9] Liminal space—the space of communication and revolution—is the space in which Hakim Bey's *T.A.Z.* ("Temporary Autonomous Zone") manifests itself: it is "precisely *within* this margin of error [that] the TAZ can come into existence."[10]

The thesis of this article is that whether or not Louis Riel (the man) and the other Mètis of his time either had created or were on the brink of creating a T.A.Z., "Louis Riel" (the signifier) must be (re)written in a contra-diction, as both white and red, both hero and villain, Canadian and American, politician and prophet, sane and mad. Having "mixed feelings" about Riel is not only natural, but necessary for an effective textual politics. To (re)write "Louis Riel" into a liminal textual space (this essay, this book, and others like them) is to (re)situate "Louis Riel" as an irritant between the warring dialectical discourses on either side, in order to point out that they are constructions based on exclusion—constructions that can be changed.

Before doing so, however, a question must be posed: is this the "real" Louis Riel?

The following passage appears in *The Diaries of Louis Riel*:

> I have seen the first-minister. He adressed [sic] me saying: "Mr. Riel," and pronouncing my name as if written "Reel." And he said: "Is your name Reel or Riel?" I told him that it was Riel. "But you may pronounce it in English as the languish [sic; a pun?] wants you to do."
>
> And when I pronounced my name, as it is pronounced in French, it struck the attention of those who were present, that it was a brillant [sic] name. I did, even I self, realize that it was a glorious name to tell. My name rang somewhat as a silver bell.[11]

Unlike the bulk of the entries in Riel's diaries, this passage is written in English. Riel emphasizes the importance of the bi-lingual pun on his name ("Riel" pronounced as "Reel" not only sounds like the English "Real" but bears the same meaning in French) because it suggests that there is a certain irreducibility to himself and to his goals. Frank Davey picks up on this pun in his long poem, *The Louis Riel Organ and Piano Company*:

....The nice thing about Louis
was my mother always called him 'real'.

And later, on the same page:

The 'real' rebellion she called it.
I believed her. It hadn't happened in Mexico.
You couldn't play
cowboys & Riels, you couldn't play
Riels & Indians. There was no way
you could imagine it & therefore
it had to be a real rebellion.[12]

By emphasizing the connection between "Riel" and "Real," I am not suggesting that this (or any) writing can directly touch that reality, but rather that there may be something about Riel that is in excess of writing, that escapes any attempt to pin him down—"There was no way you could imagine it." Following the logic of both: and, this is both what Diana Fuss calls a strategic deployment of essence[13] and an attempt to avoid a homegrown version of the phenomenon Edward Said has dubbed "Orientalism": the constitution of "Orientals" (here read "Indians" or "Mètis") as the essence of Otherness, in order to examine, understand, and expose it.[14] To the extent that I am deploying essence here, I do not intend to "expose" it in Said's sense. The "Louis Riel" in this essay is not "Real," but it may be a more politically satisfactory (i.e. subversive) "Riel" than many that have gone before.

What textual grounds are there for (re)situating "Louis Riel" within a liminal space, the space of "both:and?" In his introduction to his edition of Riel's diaries, Thomas Flanagan writes that "It is virtually impossible to apply any descriptive adjective to [Riel] without also simultaneously affirming the opposite....in Riel's case internal ambiguity is so dominant that it characterizes his whole being."[15] The name of his people—the Mètis—suggests a similar ambiguity; "Mètis" is best translated into English as "mixed."[16]

As a nation, the Mètis have historically lived out the experience of liminality. Until the passage of the Manitoba Act in 1870, which brought the province of Manitoba into confederation, the bulk of Canada (Manitoba, Saskatchewan, Alberta, the Yukon and Northwest Territories, and most of northern Ontario and Quebec) was known as Rupert's Land, and was under the control of the Hudson's Bay Company. Technically, portions of this land were for sale to prospective citizens of the Red River Settlement (now Winnipeg), but the Mètis preferred to squat without title (even under the Manitoba Act of 1870, which brought the province into Confederation, the rights of squatters holding the land "in peaceable possession" were protected).[17] The company tolerated them because: (a) they were dependent on the Mètis to act as *coureurs de bois* ("runners of the woods"— guides for fur-traders and explorers along the rivers and trails of the Northwest); (b) because Rupert's Land was too large a territory for them to police; and (c) because many of the Mètis never stayed in one place for any length of time, preferring to follow the bison herds with the Plains Cree and the Wood Cree. Thus, a symbiotic relationship developed between what was in theory an omnipresent, all-powerful Company, and those who populated its cracks and vacancies—the (largely) nomadic Mètis.

There are strong resemblances between the popular (and highly romanticized) conception of the origin of the Mètis and that of the "grey-eyed" Croatan Indians as presented by Bey in *T.A.Z.* "They dropped out," he writes. "They became 'Indians,' 'went native,' opted for chaos over the appalling miseries of serfing for the plutocrats and intellectuals of London."[18] Consider the following passage from an article in the May 12, 1885 edition of the Belleville *Daily Intelligencer*, entitled "The North-West Half-Breeds":

> Why the French found no difficulty in penetrating the depths of the western forests while the English carried their lives in their hands whenever they passed the populous settlements was due to the different methods of dealing with the savages. The English went on the principle, which is still recognized by their American descendants as orthodox, that the right kind of Indian was a dead Indian, a conclusion to which the noble red man violently objected. The French pursued an exactly opposite course: their fur-hunters went among the Indians, hunted with them, lived with them, fought the Mohawks with them, and took up many aboriginal customs, giving in return to the tribe some slight veneer of civilization....[T]he coureur de bois looked on the Indian as his equal, and did not scruple about taking to himself a dusky maiden of the forest as his wife.[19]

The French succeeded where the English failed because they had, in a very real sense, "Gone to Croatan." Yet that success was a mixed one: for those French explorers who had "gone Indian," there was no longer any real incentive to act as colonizers for the French monarchy. In the process of entering the blank space on the map, they had become something else. Today, the Canadian prairies are dotted with small French-speaking communities, but none maintain the same legal and cultural ties to France that the province of Québec does.

One of the most startling things about the description of the Mètis in the aforementioned article is that it makes explicit an implicit link between two concepts in *T.A.Z.*: miscegenation and nomadism. "The offspring of such a union [*coureur de bois* and Indian] could not be other than a nomad; and thus there gradually grew up a hybrid race, who became universally recognized as the best hunters, the best boatmen, the most daring explorers," reads one passage. Later in the same article, the idea is reiterated: "The half-breed is, however, by nature, a Bohemian, and always feels like an oyster out of his shell when wed to a farm."[20] In the "Treatise on Nomadology" in *A Thousand Plateaus*, Gilles Deleuze and Félix Guattari state that it is the nomad, moving along his/her (liminal) trajectory, that creates the "smooth" space which challenges the "striated" space of civilization.[21]

"Smooth" space is one of a number of theoretical models that Bey gathers together under the sign of the T.A.Z.;[22] thus, a three-stage process emerges to link what initially seemed to be diverse concepts: miscegenation—nomadism—T.A.Z.

If the Mètis of Rupert's Land were living in an actual or potential T.A.Z. before 1870, that situation was soon to change. Elsewhere in the "Treatise on Nomadology," Deleuze and Guattari write the following:

> One of the fundamental tasks of the State is to striate the space over which it reigns, or to utilize smooth spaces as a means of communication in the service of striated space. It is a vital concern of every state not only to vanquish nomadism but to control migrations and, more generally, to establish a zone or rights over an entire "exterior," over all of the flows transversing the ecumenon.[23]

By 1869, the Canadian government was hell-bent on taking possession of Rupert's Land from the Hudson's Bay Company (which they had obtained for 300,000 pounds that year), and their attempt to literally "striate" that space was the incident that sparked the first resistance from within the Red River Settlement to assimilation into Confederation.

Traditionally, when the Mètis did decide to farm, they did so on long narrow lots (about 3 km long and varying in width) stretching back from a short piece of riverfront property.[24] The Canadian government, on the other hand, had instructed their surveyors to divide the land on a grid system (which is still in use today). The French-speaking Mètis petitioned the government to conduct their survey in a manner that would allow them to keep their traditional farms; this request was denied, although the English-speaking Mètis ("half-breeds") had successfully obtained that same right.[25] On October 11, 1869, a crew of government surveyors began to run a survey line across the hay privilege (a pasture area adjacent to the end of a farm lot furthest from the river) of a certain André Nault—a cousin of Louis Riel. Since Nault spoke no English, he went to fetch help in the form of Riel and eighteen others. Riel forced the surveyors to leave on the grounds that Canada had not officially taken control of the territory yet; this was the incident that established him as the *ex officio* leader of the Mètis resistance.[26]

Riel's status as leader was consolidated on December 27, when he was elected President of the Provisional Government of Red River; this was simultaneously the end of a possible T.A.Z. and the beginning of the "Louis Riel" myth. When Riel renamed the Red River Settlement "Manitoba" and began to negotiate for its entry into Confederation, its potential as a T.A.Z. vanished immediately. "As soon as the TAZ is named (represented, mediated), it must vanish, it *will* vanish, leaving behind it an empty husk, only to spring up again somewhere else, once again invisible because undefinable in terms of the Spectacle."[27] Yet something remains other than that "husk"—the dreamed Mètis promised land, always just beyond reach. It was what turned Louis Riel (the man) into a prophet.

After he became associated with the execution of a troublemaker named Thomas Scott[28] in 1870, Riel was forced to flee to the United States, where he spent the majority of the next five years (even though he held a seat in Parliament at the time). Riel had always been a deeply religious man, but on a visit to Washington in 1874, a drastic change occurred:

> The same spirit who had showed himself to Moses, in
> the midst of the burning cloud, appeared to me in the
> same manner....The voice said to me: "Rise up, Louis

> David Riel. You have a mission to perform." I received
> this heavenly message with open arms and bowed
> head.[29]

Riel had not been given a middle name at birth. The addition of
"David" signified that he was to take on the role of the Biblical David,
and create a new nation for his people. By the same logic, the enemy,
as characterized in his diaries, became David's Biblical enemy: "I have
seen the giant coming, he is hideous. It is Goliath."[30] Louis Riel had
become Lou Israel.

This was not just a convenient metaphor either. For Riel, it was a
literal truth. In his 1885 diaries, he stated it plainly: "The Indians of
the northern part of this continent are of Jewish origin." Riel believed
that an Egyptian merchant ship with some Hebrew slaves on board
had wandered off course and actually discovered the Americas. The
Egyptians moved into what is now South America, and, having lost
control over their slaves, gave them their freedom on the condition
that they settle in the north.[31] Accordingly, Riel referred to his second
Provisional Government as the Exovedate (Latin *ex* = "from" and *ovile*
= "flock"),[32] and planned to reinstate portions of the Mosaic law,
including married clergy, polygamy, a Saturday Sabbath and male cir-
cumcision.[33]

At the time, Riel's convictions seemed bizarre enough that his
uncle, John Lee, had Riel committed to the asylum of St. Jean-de-
Dieu on March 6, 1876. (He was later transferred to the Beauport
mental hospital, and remained there until January of 1878.)[34]
However, as Thomas Flanagan points out, his beliefs (that Providence
had given him a special mission and that God had spoken to him
directly) may have been presumptuous, but were in fact completely
within the possibilities dictated by conventional Roman Catholicism.
Flanagan also mentions that the idea of the Hebrew ancestry of the
Indians and of polygamy (in the case of the Mormons) were widely
accepted in that era.[35] In this light, the labeling of Riel as mad starts
to look more and more like a desperate bid by the State to control
him. Riel, then, was not mad, because his opinions were not idiosyncratic. "Madness is a sort of residual category used to describe those
who make individual aberrations from a common opinion, as opposed
to those who espouse beliefs supported by a group."[36]

After Manitoba passed into Confederation in 1870, it was flooded
with settlers, and the Mètis began to lose their land and influence to
the new influx of settlers, despite the provisions made in the

Manitoba Act to prevent exactly that from happening. Many of them moved westward, into the unsettled land along the Saskatchewan River. For a while, they resumed the lifestyle that they had lived before 1870, but history was repeating itself by 1884. Gabriel Dumont rode south to the Territory of Montana, where Riel had been living and working as a schoolteacher (and an American citizen), and brought him back to Saskatchewan. This time, however, he came not as a politician, but as a prophet.

Within the logic of nomadism and liminality, Riel's reconstitution of himself as a prophet can be seen as a necessary and effective strategy. His success as a politician had been mixed, because it demanded that he attempt to consolidate his T.A.Z. as a province; which, of course, killed it. But as a prophet, Riel moved beyond the strictures of political parties and fixed territories, back into a liminal space: "a prophet is supra-institutional."[37]

Like all good prophets, Riel was sometimes eerily accurate:

> God revealed to me that the United States are destined one day to inherit all the power and prosperity which Great Britain now possesses.
>
> God revealed to me that the government of the United States is going to become extraordinarily powerful. Providence will use it to chastise the countries of Latin America, after their continual wars render them guilty of great sins. Then the armies of the United States will return victorious from the distant lands of the equator, loaded with wealth, a colossal glory marching with them, the wind of heaven hardly sufficing to deploy the majesty of their banners.[38]

Of course, much of the time, his prophecies left much to be desired. In one vision God tells Riel that He wants to rename the heavenly bodies after Riel's family and friends ("God wants the Big Dipper to be called the 'Fabien Barnabé' "; "God wants the North Star to be called 'Henrietta'," etc.). God also insists on particular pronunciations for certain words:

> God wants the sun to bear the name of "Jean"....But in order to give the pronunciation of this name a greatness equal to its glory, God inspires me to put an acute accent on the letter "e" in the word "Jéan." God wants "Jéan," pronounced "Jean," to be the name of

the most glorious of the stars....Instead of saying "the
sun rises," etc., one should say, "the Jéan rises,"
etc.)39

Yet, Riel, as the prophet, managed to galvanize the Mètis and
Indian resistance against the new encroachment of settlers, launching
the Rebellion of 1885. Deleuze and Guattari define the role of the
prophet in a nomadic society in exactly those terms: "The *prophet*, as
opposed to the state personality of the king and the religious personality of the priest, directs the movement by which a religion becomes a
war machine or passes over to the side of such a machine."40

The Rebellion of 1885 was short-lived. Although the Mètis and
Indian forces had a decisive victory in under 40 minutes at Duck Lake
on March 26, 1885, where they were 300 strong against 120 soldiers
under the command of a Major Crozier,41 and another victory at Fish
Creek on April 24; a third group of 300 Mètis was no match for
General Middleton's forces at Batoche (May 9-13). In addition to 724
men, he also had the services of a United States army officer,
Lieutenant Howard by name, who brought a Gatling gun with him.42
Superior firepower won out, and Riel surrendered. He was charged
with treason on July 6, 1885, and hanged on that charge on November
16. Gabriel Dumont, on the other hand, escaped to the United States,
sending back the following message: "Tell Middleton I still have nine-
ty cartridges to use on his men."43

Since Riel's death, the Mètis have remained in a liminal space in
Canada, but this has rarely worked to their advantage. Because they
do not qualify as (full-blooded) "status" Indians, they are not entitled
to live on reserves (a dubious privilege at best) or to receive tax
exemptions. So, they remain as a major segment of the Canadian
urban poor.44 In the early 1900s, an exceptionally unlucky group were
referred to as "Gopher Mètis," because they "liv[ed] off gophers where
they'd squatted on narrow strips of road allowances set aside between
farms in the early years of white settlement."45

Even the images of Riel himself that were ostensibly created to
honor him have been the source of much controversy. The monument
to Riel on the grounds of the Manitoba legislature, which Riel founded, is particularly troublesome. The work of architect Etienne J.
Gaboury and sculptor Marcien Lemay, it consists of a grotesque
impressionistic statue of Riel that makes him look as if he were suffering from some horrible bone disease, surrounded (hidden) by two
nine-meter high concrete half-cylinders. The statue of Riel himself can

only be seen from directly in front of or behind the monument. Instead of being in front of the building, with the statues of Queen Victoria *et al.;* Riel is hidden around back, on an infrequently used street— except at night, when the area becomes the major gathering place for another marginalized group, Winnipeg's male prostitutes (many of whom are Indian or Mètis themselves). The overall effect is similar to the first line of the passage quoted from bp Nichol at the opening of this essay: "outside in the rain louis was dying." Recently (ca. 20 October 1991) vandals chiseled the penis off the statue. Opinion is split as to whether this act was perpetrated by the Mètis themselves (who disapprove strongly of the statue, and have entered negotiations with the artist to have it replaced), or by vandals motivated by racism.

If it accomplishes nothing else, the relation of the plight of Mètis past and present highlights the fact that a nostalgic longing for a physical return to an imaginary space entirely outside culture is not a desirable thing, or even a possible thing, since to be labeled "without" is to be in a position of total lacking and powerlessness. On the other hand, what a liminal textual practice desires is not another name for Apartheid, but the illustration, through its own writing, of the fact of its exclusion. As long as "Louis Riel" and the Mètis are either "out-side" (neglected) or "inside" (assimilated, effaced) "white" society, the score remains the same: Society 1, Mètis 0. However, situating a term such as "Louis Riel" on the imagined borderline between society and its others, by pointing out its contradictory and contested uses, disorganizes the exclusionary either/or logic through which society constitutes itself. It suggests that society is not a monolithic unity outside of which there is nothing, but a loose collection of differences, all simultaneously "within" and "without," and that each of those differences (many of which are excluded from dialogue) may have something to say.

The Mètis flag—a white infinity symbol (the circle of life) on a dark blue background—is testimony to the hope that rethinkings of "within" and "without" can offer. In the current round of Canadian Constitutional talks, the inherent right of Native Canadians (Mètis included) to self-government is a major issue, and Mètis leaders look back to Riel for inspiration. Gerald Morin of the Saskatchewan Mètis Society says, "The significance of the 90s is that we will see things reminiscent of Louis Riel, who acted on our pre-existing rights."[46] The future of Canada as a nation may depend on the recognition of rights of Canadian Natives to self-government and to their outstanding land claims, since the absence of a discussion of those issues was precisely what killed the last round of talks. Society, then (not just Canadian society), has reached a point where the notion of "wholeness" as we understand it is no longer viable. The voices of its excluded parts must be recognized, and, consequently, the entire notion of "wholeness" must be rethought.

The return of "Louis Riel" from banishment as both white and red, prophet and politician, hero and villain, mad and sane, will inevitably spark argument and controversy, dialogue and debate. Yet precisely as long as it remains on the borderlines is "Louis Riel" one of the signifers that makes a (crucial) difference.

REFERENCES

1 bp Nichol, "The Long Weekend of Louis Riel," in *No Feather, No Ink: After Riel*, ed. George Amabile and Kim Dales (Saskatoon: Thistledown Press, 1985), 117–18.

2 Donald Swainson, "Rielania and the Structure of Canadian History," *Journal of Popular Culture* 14.2 (Fall 1980), 286–97.

3 Hélène Cixous and Catherine Clément, *The Newly Born Woman* [1975], trans. Betsy Wing, Theory and History of Literature v. 24 (Minneapolis: University of Minnesota Press, 1987), 63.

4 *Ibid.*, 64.

5 *Ibid.*, 96.

6 Hélène Cixous, "The Laugh of the Medusa," trans. Keith and Paula Cohen, in *New French Feminisms: An Anthology*, ed. Elaine Marks and Isabelle de Courtivron (New York: Schocken Books, 1980).

7 Mircea Eliade, *The Sacred and the Profane: The Nature of Religion*, (New York: Harvest Books, 1957), 25.

8 Arnold van Gennep, *The Rites of Passage*, trans. Monika B. Vizedom and Gabrielle L. Caffee, (London: Routledge and Kegan Paul, 1960), 19.

9 The most detailed examination of carnival and carnivalization (the transposition of carnival into a literary signifying practice) can be found in the work of the Russian Formalist critic Mikhail Bakhtin: Mikhail Bakhtin, *Problems of Dostoevsky's Poetics* [1963], ed. and trans. Caryl Emerson (Minneapolis: University of Minnesota Press, 1984).

——-, *Rabelais and His World* [1965], trans. Helen Iwolsky (Bloomington: Indiana UP, 1984). There is a considerable amount of overlap in the treatment of carnival in the two texts, but on the whole, the version presented in *Problems* seems to be the more complete.

10 Hakim Bey, *T.A.Z.: The Temporary Autonomous Zone, Ontological Anarchy, Poetic Terrorism* (Brooklyn: Autonomedia, 1991), 101. Bey goes into considerable detail about "The TAZ as *festival*" (105); the sense in

which he uses "festival" seems completely synonymous with Bakhtin, yet his definition appears to have been derived from other sources.

11 Thomas Flanagan, ed., *The Diaries of Louis Riel* (Edmonton, Hurtig Publishers, 1976), 152.

12 Frank Davey, *The Louis Riel Organ and Piano Company*, (Winnipeg: Turnstone Press, 1985), 49.

13 Fuss's argument in *Essentially Speaking: Feminism, Nature & Difference* (New York: Routledge, 1989) is that there are historical moments when "essentialism may have some strategic or interventionary value," and that "the radicality or conservatism of essentialism depends on *who* is utilizing it, *how* it is deployed, and *where* its effects are concentrated" (20). As non-Mètis, perhaps my "right" to write on Riel is questionable at this particular historical moment, when North American Indian identity politics are so important, but I have tried to emphasize that my interest is not so much in recovering "the Real Riel" as in displacing the discourses that have already been written on him. If there is an "essential" Riel, it is up to others to articulate it.

14 Edward Said, *Orientalism* (New York: Vinatge Books, 1978), 38.

15 Flanagan, *op cit.*, 17.

16 As a people, the Mètis are not an homogenous whole; there are internal divisions and ambiguities here as well. Originally the term "Mètis" applied only to those of French and Indian descent, but now is taken to also refer to those of British or Scottish and Indian descent as well (a group originally dubbed "halfbreeds").

17 Hartwell Bowsfield, ed., "Introduction," *Louis Riel: Selected Readings*, (Toronto: Copp Clark Pitman, 1988), 5.

18 Bey, *op cit.*, 117.

19 Nick and Helma Mika, eds., *The Riel Rebellion 1885* (Mika Silk Screening, Belleville, 1972), 112.

20 Mika, op cit., 112–113.

21 Gilles Deleuze and Félix Guattari, *A Thousand Plateaus: Capitalism and Schizophrenia* [1980], trans. Brian Massumi (Minneapolis: University of Minnesota Press, 1987), 380–81.

22 Bey, *op. cit.,* 106.

23 Deleuze and Guattari, *op cit.,* 385.

24 Don McLean, *1885: Mètis Rebellion or Government Conspiracy?* (Winnipeg: Pemmican Publications, 1985), 49.

25 McLean, *op cit.,* 58.

26 Colin Davies, *Louis Riel and the New Nation* (Agincourt: The Book Society of Canada, 1980), 19–20.

27 Bey, *op cit.,* 101.

28 This was perhaps Riel's most controversial action, not because Scott was innocent of blame (he had escaped from imprisonment in Fort Garry at least once, and was a confirmed bully and bigot), but because Scott was an Orangeman. One possible argument is that Riel made a scapegoat out of

Scott, who stood for everything that threatened Mètis society. In any event, Scott's murder/execution was definitely one of the factors in Riel's execution, for the Orange Lodge in Ontario continually lobbied the government to have no mercy on Riel when and if he was apprehended (see the resolution passed by the Royal Orange Lodge No. 300 in the Friday, Oct. 9 edition of *the Daily Intelligencer*, in Mika, *op cit.*, 267.).

29 Louis Riel, quoted in Bowsfield, *op cit.*, 3.

30 Flanagan, *op cit.*, 3.

31 *Ibid.*, 165.

32 *Ibid.*, 61.

33 Thomas Flanagan, "Louis Riel: Insanity and Prophecy." In Bowsfield, 208–26, 210.

34 Olive Knox, "The Question of Louis Riel's Sanity." In Bowsfield, 181–98, 182.

35 Flanagan, "Louis Riel: Insanity," *op cit.*, 211.

36 *Ibid.*, 209.

37 *Ibid.*, 212.

38 Flanagan, *op cit.*, 169.

39 *Ibid.*, 164.

40 Deleuze and Guattari, *op cit.*, 388.

41 McLean, *op cit.*, 111.

42 *Ibid.*, 117.

43 Davies, *op cit.*, 68.

44 The exception to this rule is a group of 500 Mètis in Alberta, who communally own 1875 square miles of land ("'Survival as a people' at stake, Metis say," *Toronto Star*, Tues. Sept. 17, 1991). Elsewhere, hundreds of thousands of acres have been claimed by both the Mètis and other Native Canadians, including large pieces of the downtowns of major Canadian cities.

45 Wayne Roberts, "Remaking the Mètis Nation," *Now* 10.48 (August 8–14, 1991), 10–11, 16, 10.

46 Roberts, *op cit.*, 11.

BENEATH THE TUNDRA, THE PERMAFROST
(A Few Thoughts on Barrenness)

J. Zinovich

> **Axiom 1:** Humans see existence the way they see themselves; the way they organize is the way they grasp the world.

ON THE MORNING OF NOVEMBER 6, 1769 A TWENTY-THREE year old Englishman named Sam Hearne sets off from the shores of Hudson's Bay, travelling northwest through the snow. Hearne is bound for the arctic coast at the mouth of the Coppermine River. His Hudson's Bay Company superiors, whose royal charter gives them monopoly control of all economic activity in the Hudson Bay watershed, are responding to native reports of a rich lode of copper ore located near the Coppermine. Hearne is their agent-of-contact and designated explorer. He'll find a good anchorage near the deposits, say the Indians, and the mine is so rich that the English can ballast their ships with lumps of pure copper from the hillsides. The second great era of the European imperialist project is ramping full.

Recalcitrance and autocephaly have earned Hearne this dubious opportunity. He has openly despised Moses Norton—his immediate Hudson's Bay Company superior—as an autocratic nabob; and "one of the most debauched wretches under the sun." He has demanded more personal responsibility, so Norton has obligingly appointed him autonomous ambassador to the wintery landscape.

Hearne makes three attempts to find the native copper mines. Though his guides rob and abandon him during the first and second tries, by July of 1772, Matonabbee, the greatest of the Chipewyan trading chiefs, has taken him to the arctic coast and safely returned him to Prince of Wales Fort. Hearne traverses and maps a winding corridor more than 5,000 miles long, becoming the first European to travel across northern North America.

He doesn't get the truth about the copper until near the end of his odyssey. A woman first discovered the ore. His native guides tell him that for several years she led bands of men to the deposit of pure chunk copper. But, when after learning the way to the treasure, one

Matonabbee's Map

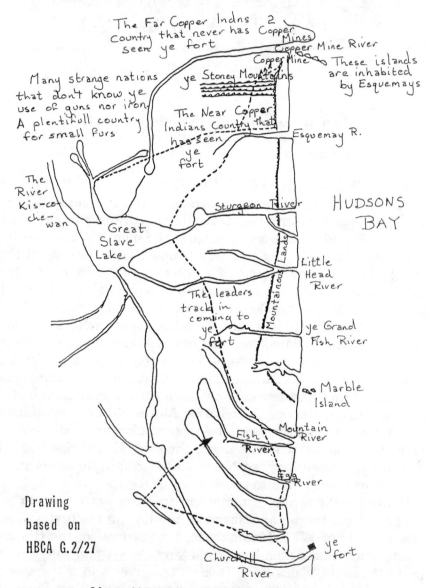

The Far Copper Indns 2 Country that never has Copper seen ye fort Mines

Copper Mine River

Copper Mine

These islands are inhabited by Esquemays

ye Stoney Mountains

Many strange nations that don't know ye use of guns nor iron. A plentifull country for small furs

The Near Copper Indians Country that has seen ye fort

Esquemay R.

The River Kis-co-che-wan

Great Slave Lake

Sturgeon River

HUDSONS BAY

Little Head River

The leaders track in coming to ye fort

Mountainous Lands

ye Grand Fish River

Marble Island

Mountain River

Fish River

Egg River

Drawing based on HBCA G.2/27

Churchill River

ye fort

Matonabbee's Map of the Barren Lands

group brutalized her, she pledged revenge. She was a powerful shaman and vowed to sit on the ore until she sank into the ground, taking it with her. When the men returned the following year they found her sunk to the waist. By the next year she had vanished, and only a few pieces of the copper remained scattered near where she had been.

> **Proposition 1:** "Maps" are abstract grids. However, under the restrictions of Power, mapping becomes a giant con, a carrot and stick imposition of Cartographies of Control, an endless assertion that conventional maps are the world.

During his first encounter with the arctic prairies they are snow covered and wind blasted and very nearly kill him, so Hearne christens them the "Barren Grounds." Toponymy constitutes metaphor. Hearne's sobriquet illustrates his own impression of a hostile environment. But it also speaks (I think unconsciously) the rhetoric of the imperialist moment in which he was traveling. It hints at the unearthly cultural oblivion the north country can impose on non-native travellers. These are part of the "Grounds", the lands of the imperial estate, says Hearne; but they are barren: sterile, destitute, unproductive and jejune; unsatisfying to intellect or spirit, dull, flat, and bald; devoid of all potential for progress, unsuitable for evolution. In one stroke he has designated more than half a million square miles of North America as a forbidden zone. He has *barrenized* the north.

There was, of course, an alternative opinion. When asked by a nineteenth century European priest if he aspired to heaven, at least one autochthonous northerner said [I paraphrase]: "If your heaven is as glorious as the land of the musk ox in spring, when the young animals wobble through the bright flowers and the fledglings tumble across the wide, clean sky, I'd be happy to go. Otherwise, I'll stay here." Nonetheless, even today, to the Euro-Americans who follow Hearne the northern taiga and tundra remain the Barren Lands.

> **Divergence 1:** In the 1750s Thomas More coined the terms Utopia—no place, land of no where—and Eutopia, the place of ideal happiness and good order. The almost simultaneous appearance of these homophonic twins has nothing to do with sustaining Cartographies of Control, and everything to do with the techniques and strategies of psychotopography.

> Misinformation is inestimably valuable (as is regular-
> ly shown by both the news media and advert propa-
> gandists) because humans tend to form strong
> impressions of areas without visiting them. Confusion
> is best seeded by homophones which encode both a
> concept and its exact opposite.

> **Proposition 2:** Movements do not precede
> maps, maps always accompany movements. In
> fact, it is possible that motion always follows
> maps, and never the reverse. (Even information
> ordinarily only follows routes designed and made
> possible by maps: computerized telephone links,
> media waves, roads and postal networks, geodet-
> ic or intelligence satellites, etc.)

Despite his bleak designation for the north, Hearne's depiction of
it is rich and rather romantic. That depiction reflects his character. It
is his attitude, and his humility, that sets him apart from most other
Englishmen and Europeans of his day. He sets off on the strength of
an urge. He casts aside his assumptions and learns to travel as the
autochthonous peoples do; and, in the process, becomes devoted more
to aptitude than authority, committed more to curiosity, coexistence,
and survival than exploitation. Though he's an alien, he seeks and
earns the respect and friendship of an accomplished man within the
northern cultural milieu. He is a prototype, a forerunner for the kind
of eccentric hyperborean adventurer who will not appear for another
century.

The published account of Hearne's overland caper effects North
American subarctic travel more than any other single report. Later
travellers who adapt to the country and its people the way he does,
accomplish more and survive longer than those who flaunt their cul-
ture-bound beef. In his narrative, Hearne mentions some remarkable
animals, strange long-haired cold-resistant quadrupeds, which he
calls musk oxen. He reports herds of caribou as large as the herds of
buffalo that roam the central plains. And, toward the end of his memoir, he describes a band of people reputed to live at a woodland paradise deep in the treeless wilderness. The oasis abounds with game
and birds, and the waters surrounding it teem with fish. No other
part of the north, he says, "seems to possess half the advantages req-
uisite for a constant residence that are ascribed to this little spot."

These intriguing details—especially the musk oxen, and the strange wilderness oasis—will tantalize his spiritual heirs.

But Hearne had not headed off into the untracked wild. The first peoples had already supplied three maps that he could have consulted. Though the first (drawn in 1716) was rudimentary, it clearly featured the copper mines. Moses Norton solicited the second and third maps, which were drawn in 1760 and 1767 respectively, and they were conceived more exactingly. The latter one, based on the peregrinations of the great Matonabbee, is so accurate that the outline of Great Slave Lake is clearly discernable at the heart of it. The map Hearne drafted benefitted from its predecessors. (It is, however, valid to wonder whether Norton permitted Hearne the occasion to study the other maps *before* he set out.)

> **Proposition 3:** Maps are stratagems. They are tactical projections in space; manoeuvres to come. Cartographic topophilia isn't of the earth, or "reality" removed from desire. It is predetermined and imaginary. Maps reflect neither the absolute limits imposed by the earth, nor the serendipity of the eventual. They dispense determining grids, vanishing lines, escape machines, and beacons of fascination.

Norton died, and Hearne took over Prince of Wales Fort. He soon reconfirmed his remarkable attitude toward misplaced values, surrendering the indefensible fort to four hundred Frenchmen who attacked him and his thirty-nine subordinates in 1782. He willingly risked himself and the lives of those who voluntarily followed him in a subsequently successful bid for freedom—crossing the North Atlantic in a small boat—but he refused to *sacrifice* a single life. The one truly unfortunate victim of the surrender was someone Hearne least wanted to harm: by the time he returned to Hudson Bay from England to re-establish HB Company's presence, his despairing friend Matonabbee had hanged himself.

Matonabbee had staked all his prestige on his alliance with the English. During the fifty years that lapsed between Hearne's and the next Barren Ground forays, smallpox destroyed most of Matonabbee's tribe.

Hearne's instructions to Europeans who planned to enter the Barrens were straightforward: link closely with the first peoples, listen to their advice and follow it, and don't assume preeminence over them in matters of judgement. Had the men who followed him been sensible, and not Royal Navy men in futile pursuit of the Northwest Passage to India (chimeric Okeanos, the River Ocean), they might have found them valuable. But in the 1820s and 30s, John Franklin and George Back embodied imperialist British puissance. So they ignored the cowardly Hearne's advice, recognizing only the metaphor he had coined for the north country. And being truly masterful, they chose to charge headlong toward it. The Barrens were unimportant in themselves. Franklin and Back were outbound to the coast.

After a preliminary glance at Hearne's memoir, John Franklin led two different "exploration" parties north to practice starvation and cannibalism (incidentally mapping the arctic coast east and west of the mouth of the Coppermine River as they did so), then sailed off with the crews of the Erebus and Terror in a determined and successful effort to self destruct. His exit prompted a number of sea-borne hunts for him, but only two groups chased overland: a HB Company man named Anderson followed George Back's map north, and a US Army Lieutenant Schwatka journeyed northwest from Chesterfield Inlet. Neither of them found any sign of Franklin.

George Back—who accompanied Franklin on the two earlier overland trials—was more fortunate than his trainer, though not more sensible. His party, guided by chief Akaitcho, dragged a two-ton, thirty foot-long, clinker-built boat from Great Slave Lake down the Great Fish River to the Arctic Ocean. The eccentricity of the enterprise astounded Akaitcho's people. "The Indians were not more astonished at their own voluntary subjection to our service," Back said, "than at the sight of a [totally impractical] boat manned by Europeans and stored with provisions of the southern country." However, when Back arrogantly tried to push across the Arctic Ocean into the teeth of the approaching northern winter his own crew mutinied, forcing him to return south. On his return to England, Back was acknowledged a great explorer. Until 1948, his chart remained the only map of the narrow avenue he followed through the Barrens. But, though Anderson later used the chart to search for Franklin, Back's "success" did not prompt any emulators.

> **Divergence 2:** When notions of cognition and knowledge were replaced by the "ideal of causal laws" toward the end of the eighteenth century, it became extremely difficult to avoid seeing mapping as the mapping of progress. But once empires push outward

as far as they can, are they able to turn their progressive attentions inward?

Neither Back nor Franklin registered what they were seeing. They were bound to an expansionist imperial project, and were thus incapable of recognizing a localized place in space and time. The mindlessly frenetic reality of their situation escaped them. In the Barrens, where the summer sun never set, they barely looked around themselves. Their imaginations lay fixed beyond the frontier, past the nuisance of the prairies they were crossing.

European governments were not, of course, the only institutions that saw potential in the Barrens. The Roman Catholic Church wanted to shake its infernals at some new souls, and in the mid nineteenth century itinerant priests began a northwestern reconnaissance. Petitot appears in the written record as the first priest to visit the western Barrens—between 1862 and 1873 he systematically mapped both the topography and the local languages—but oral histories chart a different chain of contact.

In 1840, it is said, a priest named Gossot travelled with two Yellowknife (Copper) Indians from Great Slave Lake to the Barrens. It was winter. They started along a back trail from old Fort Rae, and two days from the fort they stopped at a small lake near the Yellowknife River. Yellow hills surrounded the place. When Gossot bent to drink from a nearby stream he noticed that its water was stained a deep greenish blue. His guides pointed out an enormous black boulder—which he found to be rich copper ore—and told him that before the traders came this was the place the Yellowknives had gotten metal for their knives. The priest never saw the place again, but he sketched a map to it.

While the priest's name may actually have been Grollier, and the proffered date of his trip is suspect, the subtext of this bit of apocrypha is clear. It suggests that the Catholics were motivated by more than merely the need to save souls. And, what seems even more telling, it suggests that for Europeans a proscriptive cartography was already in place. For these priests curiosity is not motive enough. Penetration of fabulous domains demands a sound rationale. The Catholics sought to turn such rationalizing to their own advantage. Mineral deposits concentrated favorable attention on the Barrens, which justified invading them. (Imposing the same sorts of intellectual praxis on the natives will constitute a Catholic step towards "civilizing" them.)

A Bit of Jesuitry: How can geographical orientation generate psychological drift?

For at least the past several hundred years, every human touched by "western civilization" has been held thrall by an empire of some kind. Imperialisms (aesthetic, economic, ideological, political, religious, sexist, etc.) persuade their subjects (who are never truly allowed to naturalize anywhere; even in the imperial heartland) to leave their homes, in order that the empire certify them as valuable. As with all attempts to fix or devalue personal referents, such coerced and humiliated colonials enter into a labyrinth of infinite regress. By accepting an otherness, through silent conjectures and proffered associations, their minds experiment with the extent of reality, groping always outwards, proliferating received images as the *only* possible order of perceptual space. Gradually, the spontaneously naive selves they were dissipate in concentric circles toward the interior. As systole and diastole they throb, inhaling geographies of Us and It. During imperialist expansionist phases even true-born heartlanders look consistently outward, and once colonials are revalued they return hesitantly to the outer rim, eternally primed to depart. Unable to recognize it, they have been certified to yearn for the home they had and the selves they once were.

Proposition 4: If topography is "the study of spatial description," then psychotopography is "the scrutiny of spatial ascriptions."

My colleague Hakim Bey suggests that by the end of the nineteenth century the entire globe suffered from a "closure of the map," a lack of *terra incognita*. However, by that time the Euro-American empires had not drafted their charts. They had merely sketched their frontiers. Children create carefully designed worlds in tiny spaces—a small room, a yard, a neighborhood. Empires impose their tiny designs on the greater world, hoping thereby to shrink it.

Whenever superficial maps "close," the external search for utopias mutates. It turns inward, scrutinizing the unexplored territory within the declared boundaries. It probes the niches and black holes, restricting event horizons to those entropic criteria that generate individual adventures. For it assumes— knowing that such assumptions are irrational—that the niches it finds will prove to be portals that open beyond all frontiers.

Hearne's "Barren Ground" is just one example of the mysterious lacunae that remained in the Euro-American imperialist map. By the end of the nineteenth century, *terra incognita* was within the pale, rather than beyond it.

> **Divergence 3:** It seems by no means coincidental that Sigmund Freud's book *The Interpretation of Dreams* appears in 1900, at approximately the same historical moment that the geographical maps "closed." Progress had stopped being imperial, and was transformed into an individual adventure. At the moment it was required, an instrument for internal exploration became generally available.

> **Axiom 2:** Psychotopographical inquiry is an antidote to geographies of Us and It. Psychotopographies suggest, gesture towards certain features; features (toponymical, social, imaginal, linguistic, etc.) that enjoy potential despite their positions on the overtly tactical cartographers' grids. Psychotopography is the art of dowsing for lacunae in the Cartographies of Control.

Geographical/topological maps are always territorially centered, but at their most useful they are also, to some degree, sympathetic and magical. For instance, though Matonabbee's map looks eastward from Great Slave Lake, outward from the Chipewyan heartland, it is clearly pragmatic. It conveys his profound desire to return safely to his tribal homeland. It is drawn for aliens sheltering in a fort, but gestures confidently—even proudly—toward a world which Matonabbee feels has much to offer. It gives concise directions to zones where he has roamed and endured. It is offered as a gift, in response to a direct request, and is motivated by a hope that the English traders will take upon themselves some of the tremendous effort required to obtain the things they profess to desire.

Hearne's narrative map is likewise sympathetically magical, recording his inquisitiveness, his struggles with alien physical and cultural environments, and his warm appreciation for the kindnesses extended to him. But, as imperial representations, the maps that Franklin and Back design are coldly factual. They have restricted the dimensional compass of their corridors. They glance back toward Europe and ahead toward the rich East. They exhibit only the arrogant advance of dominion, concentrating on what *must be* rather than on what is. They avoid the first peoples' vision.

> **Proposition 5:** Psychotopography concerns itself
> with the genius loci, the spirit of place. In the muddle
> of tongues, toponymic images unceasingly coalesce in
> the great desolate silent void lying just out of sight.

The curious headstrong wanderers, most like Hearne, didn't reach the Barrens until the last decade of the nineteenth century. By then the maps were "closed," and the empires in place, but imperialist interdictions called to them in the way a hole in a tooth draws a tongue. Though Hearne had employed the musk oxen rather than the more traditional dragons to mark them, like the best of the travellers who borrowed the charts of Anaximander, Marcus Agrippa, Cosmas the Alexandrian, and Jachim Boaz, these rovers moved unerringly toward the unexplored territories.

Two Englishman and an American were the first to enter the northern hinterzone. Warbutron Pike was by no means an eremite searching for an empty wasteland, though wild liberties held definite attractions for him. He set off for the supernal cold having recently published a translation of Dante. Hearne's semi-mythical musk ox was the bait that had hooked him. He was a gentleman trophy-seeker roaming the world (read: the British Empire), and had discovered that in the *terra incognita* of the Barrens a fantastical beast lived. He recorded his quest which helped prompt Frank Russell to trek north.

Within four years of Pike's trip, Russell rode an anthropological *schtick* to the Barrens. Like Pike, he was chiefly interested in the musk ox. The exhilarating expanses and freedoms of the country soon snared him, however, and his personal experience began overriding his "scientific" concerns. Soon D.T. Hanbury also arrived to chase the musk oxen, and stayed for several years. For the first time since Hearne, white men roamed loose on the arctic prairies.

But rumors of gold ultimately overthrew the barriers, obviating any need to rationalize a journey to the Barrens. By 1897 the lunatics were on the move. During the thirty years that followed so many of them drifted eastward from the Mackenzie River into the Barren Grounds that in this short essay it is possible to mention only a few of them. Some called themselves explorers; like Cosmo Melvill, the Douglas brothers, and Radford and Street—who were eventually slaughtered by traumatized Eskimos. There were priests, like Rouvier and LeRoux, whom the Eskimos also exterminated. And trappers and wolfers who went native, or "bushed": Bilida, Bode, Greathouse, Lorringer, Murphy, Olsen, Roberts et al. Blacky Lanner, the wolfer who built a still out on the Barrens, got so cocky that he insisted on living entirely off the land and starved to death.

Then there were the truly eccentric. C.J. "Buffalo" Jones went bust, taming and herding buffalo on the central plains. Later, when he heard about the musk oxen, he started north. "My mission," he wrote, "was to bring out from the Arctic regions musk oxen alive, if possible, also silver-grey fox, marten, and other valuable fur-bearing animals to propagate on an island in the Pacific Ocean." Though he didn't succeed in bringing out any musk ox calves, he was wise enough to stop at Edmonton to buy a rubber life preserver before taking to the northern rivers.

There were writers, too. G. Caspar Whitney, a *Harper's Magazine* reporter, so antagonized the northern natives that none would travel with him when he ran from Edmonton to the Barrens and back on snowshoes. Ernest Thompson Seton headed to the arctic prairies to meet the wild animals.

A few people made homes for themselves on the Barrens, or returned so frequently that they seemed permanently fixed there. Freedmen, like James Mackinlay and Joseph Hodgson the poet, left the Hudson's Bay Company to strike out on their own. Pete McCallum and the prospectors Jack Stark and Charlie Sloan lived out long lives in harmony with the Yellowknife and Bear Lake Indians.

Psychotopographics is by no means a purely cerebral and imaginary science. In fact, it is so powerfully active that it can be projected onto the physical world. Though he never settled there, the Barrens so intoxicated anthropologist V. Stefansson that he learned to read what he called "land sky." "When clouds of a uniform color hang low," he said, "there is reflected in them a map of the earth below them. Snow-free land and open water are shown in black on the clouds; the pure white sea ice appears in white, and the land covered with snow soiled by blown sand etc. is reflected darker than the sea but lighter than snowless land. This sky map is of the greatest use...[W]here the landmarks themselves are below the horizon their position is accurately indicated by their reflection in the clouds."

> **Proposition 6:** Since neither toponyms nor topographs embody "reality," disappearance need not always be a catastrophe; and invisibility ain't necessarily so.

John Hornby first reached the Barrens in 1908, in company with Cosmo Melvill. Melvill soon left, but Hornby stayed on. Small, tough, and eccentric, he thrived on the spirit of the Barrens. Until the beginning of the First World War he roamed ceaselessly over them, often living with an Indian woman named Arimo and creating idiosyncratic topographical maps sprinkled with names of his own choosing. Unfortunately, the European war unhinged him, and when he returned to the north he found a fellow named D'Arcy Arden married to Arimo.

Though Hornby had imbibed the best Barren Grounds nectar—its spring and summertime sweetness shared with the people who most appreciated it—he now consumed its stupefying dregs. His once joyous obsession with the Barrens transformed into the *gout du gouffre*, "taste for the abyss." A vision of Hearne's hidden paradise began drawing at him. He now knew that it was on the Thelon River, and was convinced that things would work out for him if he just managed to reach it.

In the 1920s Hornby convinced the Canadian government that he was qualified to report on the Barren Ground caribou. That gave him the licence of Power, but indicated how estranged he was from his prewar conception of the Barrens. Though he knew that when he had been most helpless his Indian friends had assisted him, he now insisted that he was more capable than them. Solipsism is one of the dangers of psychotopographic exploration. Hornby began playing chess on a little board with red and white men, obsessively trying to control human drifts by sympathetic magic.

Even men like D'Arcy Arden, whose life he had shared, couldn't disabuse Hornby of his fixation. "Why would a man like that write little notes like he did to me, to tell me about the crooked Indians?," D'Arcy Arden asked later. "The Indians never robbed him. He was a stubborn man. That's why he's dead. I said, 'You go where there are no Indians, Jack, and you'll die. Every time you've starved, Jack, an Indian has come to your assistance. You get away from those Indians and you'll die like a rat'." But Hornby was determined to reach the Thelon River paradise, and he wanted it to be *his* when he got there.

In May of 1926, Hornby set off with two inexperienced youngsters to winter at the Thelon River sanctuary. He was elated to finally be on his way. Throughout the long summer he lingered recklessly wherever fancy held him. But, though Hearne had insisted that the oasis abounded with game and birds, and the waters surrounding it teemed with fish, when Hornby got there the migrating caribou and game-birds had passed. Still, Hornby's death was only a catastrophe for the boys he had with him and their families. It firmly fixed him in the history of northern exploration; and assisted the government to deter others from wandering the Barrens.

Proposition 7: Psychotopographical integrity and the Cartographies of Control remain forever at odds.

As everyone with any sense knows, disinformation is pervasive in mediated environments. But even at the turn of the century, when personal interaction was the glue that gummed people together, there were encroachments on the truth. Power recognizes the extreme difficulty of policing neutral zones like the Barrens, and isn't above misrepresenting them in spectacular simulations of control.

The valley of the Nahanni River lies about six hundred miles due west of the western edge of the Barrens. Because of the hot springs there, early northern travellers called a section of the Nahanni the Tropical Valley. But in the first decade of the twentieth century part of the Nahanni was renamed The Headless Valley. Though not actually in the Barren Grounds, a salient instance of proscriptive toponymics centers in the Nahanni and concerns the men who policed the north, so it is germane to my purpose.

Local histories maintain that in 1904 William McLeod ventured up the Nahanni. He returned with several ounces of coarse gold. The following year he moved back there with his brother and another man, leaving a map to his claims behind with the local Catholic priest. The McLeod party vanished; but, say locals, the bodies that were found weren't headless because of a monster or psychopathic killer, as the general story has it. In fact, North West Mounted Police Sergeant Nitchie Thorne (Hollywood's Sergeant Thorne of the Mounted) went to the Nahanni to find the miners. When Thorne found the bodies it was winter. There wasn't room to carry them in his dog sled, so he lopped off their heads for identification. The desecration so affronted the Catholics that they insisted that the government suppress the true story.

For many years the monster story served the interests of both the police and the priests: it kept most wanderers from visiting a particularly remote area, and it lent an air of satanic mystery and horrible sanctity to the Nahanni River Valley. The men who eventually mined the deposit that McLeod had mapped did not find the gold they sought, but, as in the case of the Barrens, the monstrous toponym stuck.

CULMINATION

THIS ARTICLE IS, OF COURSE, A HEURISTIC EXERCISE. THE nature of psychotopography is slippery (and utopias are bivalently nebulous). To try to define things categorically is ridiculous. To suggest more than that ideas can recommend the real is presumptuous, and probably smacks of metaphysics.

One general benchmark for gauging the Barrens' enduring psychotopographical impact might be the effect the image of them had on Glen Gould. Arch eccentric, cerebral and emotional intuitivist, iconoclast, true libertarian—(free even of running dog constitutionalist pretensions), Gould manifested one of the most obvious recent mutations of Hearne's attitude toward that extraordinary hinterland. The naked potential he saw encoded in the barrenized north intrigued him. Since his was the melodic voice that Euro-Americanism fired off as its silver-bullet attempt to commune with life in the interplanetary barrens, Gould's meditation on metaphoric enormity deserves consideration.

"Admittedly," he writes, "it's a question of attitude, and I'm not at all sure that my own quasi-allegorical attitude to the north is the proper way to make use of [the idea of north], or even an accurate way in which to define it. Nevertheless, I'm by no means alone in this reaction to the North; there are very few people who make contact with it and emerge unscathed. Something really does happen to people who go into [or become obsessed with] the north—they become at least aware of the creative opportunity which the physical [enormity] of the country represents and, quite often I think, come to measure their own work and life against that rather staggering creative possibility— they become, in effect, philosophers."

Fortunately, the barrenness of the north has ultimately worked to preserve it and enhance its creative potential. Its actual rigors have combined with aspects of its myth to keep run-of-the-mill rapacious entrepreneurs at a distance. Though pseudoeconomics enslaved it— the Mackenzie Valley Pipeline chained it, the DEW Line protected and policed us all, and now a diamond rush drags in outside capital— its size and climate impose severe constraints on how easily it is exploited. And as the first peoples reawaken themselves, their voices are being heard returning the eutopian Barren Grounds to life. Recently the Canadian government began agreeing to return control of the arctic prairies to the people who originally inhabited them. *Nunavut* and *Denende* will soon be recognizably in place. Perhaps now a newly mutated metaphor for vastness will emerge.

> **Some Technique:** Tracing five component modules can help enhance psychotopographical cogencies:
>
> **1) Corridors** — avenues of frequent travel restrict environmental experience; ideological or emotional tendencies warp specific perceptions but can work to stitch some intuitive conceptions together.
>
> **2) Boundaries** — edges hint at the limits of an image, the extremities of particular visions; to some extent territorial parameters fix speculation.
>
> **3) Nodes** — at strategic junctions, corridors and environments intersect. Boundary-generated frustrations coalesce at particular interstices; also at sites where successive toponymies overlap.
>
> **4) Ranges** — small spheres of common identity, shared metaphors, and shared functional zones coordinate and interact. They suggest alternative visions.
>
> **5) Bench marks** — some reference points stand out distinctly and are explainable in non-intuitive language. These serve to concentrate attentions.

Can life-maps (psychotopographs) overthrow conventional Cartographies of Control? To answer that it helps to disregard whether or not you're oppressed by the view that the present running-dog empires are inexorable forces propelled toward universal and homogeneous tyranny. First, search for localized avenues of escape by laying down any conventional map of topographical features. Next, determine *de facto* centers of control; stretch out transparencies of ethical and moral inconsistencies and abuses; mark positions of minor insurrections and locations where eccentricities of any kind have manifested a presence (whether from transient or chthonic eccentrics is unimportant). Then, free your own capacities, sensitivities, and humors to range. Wherever nodes in the resultant grid shimmer to life you'll discover that there *are* currents flowing into and through what once seemed a kind of vacuum. These are *your* benchmarks. Now, post a *Gone to the Forbidden Zone* sign and start scrutinizing the boundaries.

REFERENCES

Bey, Hakim. "The Psychotopography of Everyday Life," in *T.A.Z.* New York: Autonomedia, 1991, pp. 102-108.

Foss, Paul. "Ozymandias," in *Oasis* (Semiotext(e), volume IV, Number 3, 1984), T. Simone, et al, eds. New York: Semiotext(e), 1984, pp. 63-65.

Franklin, John. *Narrative of a journey to the shores of the polar sea in the year 1811, 1812, 1813, and 1814.* London: 1824.

Hanbury, David. *Sport and Travel in the Northland of Canada.* New York: Macmillan Co., 1904.

Helm, J. "Matonabbee's Map," in *Artic Anthropology,* Vol. 26, No. 2, 1989, pp. 28-47.

Inman, H. *Buffalo Jones' Forty Years of Adventure.* Topeka, Kansas: Crane and Company, 1899.

Mowat, Farley (ed.) *Tundra.* Toronto: McClelland and Stewart Limited, 1973.

Payzant, Geoffrey. *Glen Gould, Music and Mind.* Toronto: Key Porter Books, 1978.

Pike, W. *The Barren Ground of Northern Canada.* London: MacMillan and Co., 1892.

Russell, F. *Explorations in the Far North.* Iowa City, Iowa: University of Iowa Press, 1898.

Seaton, E.T. *The Arctic Prairies.* New York: Charles Scribner's Sons, 1911.

Sussman, E. (ed.) *on the passage of a few people through a rather brief moment in time: The Situationist International, 1957-1972.* Cambridge, Mass.: The MIT Press, 1989.

Tyrrell, J.B. (ed.) *The Journals of Samuel Hearne and Philip Turnor.* Toronto: the Chaplain Society, 1934.

Whalley, George. *The Legend of John Hornby.* Toronto: Macmillan of Canada, 1962.

Whitney, J. Caspar, *On Snowshoes to the Barren Grounds.* New York: Harper and Brothers, 1896.

Wulf, Christof. "The Temporality of World-Views and Self-Images," in *Looking Back at the End of the World,* D. Kampter and C. Wulf eds. New York: Semiotext(e), 1989, pp. 49-63.

Zinovich, Jordan. "What Really Happened?" in *Up Here: Life in Canada's North,* January/February 1989, pp. 15-16, 41-45.

Zinovich, Jordan. *Battling the Bay.* Edmonton: Lone Pine Publishing, 1992.

Zinovich, Jordan, and E.H. Nagle. *The Prospector: North of Sixty.* Edmonton: Lone Pine Publishing, 1989.

III
Imagining Futures Past

TRICKSTER

Joy Harjo

Crow, in the new snow.
You caw, caw
like crazy.
Laugh.
Because you know I'm a fool
too, like you
skimming over the thin ice
to the war going on
all over the world.

348

1992
(Part 1)

Guillermo Gomez–Peña

"Columbus arrived in America without papers.
Don't we all secretly wish he had been deported right away?"

From a radio theatre piece entitled, "1992 (Part 1)."

Ishi

MANIFEST MANNERS
The Long Gaze of Christopher Columbus

Gerald Vizenor

CHRISTOPHER COLUMBUS WAS DENIED BEATIFICATION because of his avarice, baseness, and malevolent discoveries. He landed much lower in tribal stories and remembrance than he has in foundational histories and representations of colonialism; nonetheless, several centuries later his mistaken missions were uncovered anew and commemorated as entitlements in a constitutional democracy.

Columbus has been envied in a chemical civilization that remembers him more than the names of the old monarchs and presidents. The dubious nerve of his adventures would be heard more than the ecstasies of the shamans, or even the stories of the saints; alas, he has been honored over the tribal cultures that were enslaved and terminated in his name.

The 1893 Columbian Exposition in Chicago, for instance, celebrated his discoveries as an enviable beat in the heart of the nation. Antonin Dvorak composed his occasional symphony *From the New World*. Frederick Jackson Turner presented his epoch thesis, "The Significance of the Frontier in American History," that same summer to his colleagues at the American Historical Association. At the same time the federal government issued a memorial coin on the quadricentennial with an incuse of Columbus on one side and "the *Santa Maria* on the reverse." A similar commemorative coin was struck for the quincentenary, and a "certificate of authenticity" was issued with the purchase of each coin.

President Ronald Reagan announced that Christopher Columbus was a "dreamer, a man of vision and courage, a man filled with hope for the future." In other words, the adventurer must be the simulation of manifest manners, the countenance of neocolonial racialism. "Put it all together and you might say that Columbus was the inventor of the American Dream."

Columbus wrote at the very end of his first journal, "I hope to Our Lord that it will be the greatest honor for Christianity, although it has been accomplished with such ease." He has become the invariable conservative candidate in the constitutional democracy that has honored his names with such ease.

"The Spaniards were unable to exterminate the Indian race by those unparalleled atrocities which brand them with indelible shame, nor did they even succeed in wholly depriving it of its rights," wrote Alexis de Tocqueville in *Democracy in America*, "but the Americans of the United States have accomplished this twofold purpose with singular felicity; tranquilly, legally, philanthropically, without shedding blood, and without violating a single great principle of morality in the eyes of the world. It is impossible to destroy men with more respect for the laws of humanity."

ISHI AND LITERAL BANISHMENT

THE OUTSET OF MANIFEST MANNERS, THAT FELICITOUS vernacular of political names and sentimental neocolonial destinies, was the certain denial of tragic wisdom and transvaluation of tribal consciousness; the tribal stories that were once heard and envisioned were abused, revised, dickered for a mere sign of discoveries, and then the stories were construed as mere catecheses.

Tribal nicknames were translated as surnames, and without their stories, a literal banishment; the ironies and natural metaphors of bent and chance were burdened with denatured reason, romantic nominations, and incumbent names.

The metaphors turned over here are about the representations of a consumer culture and the political power of common names in histories; the images, names, and gazes that would represent historical significance. Tribal nicknames, in this and other senses, were seldom heard in the vernacular of manifest manners. Consider the communal humor of nicknames, the clever humor that honors the contradictions and preeminent experiences heard in tribal stories, the natural and uncertain shimmer of metonymies that would overturn the "long gaze" of neocolonial assurance.

Ishi, for instance, was a new nickname, a tribal word that means "one of the people" in the language of Yana, but that was not the name he heard in his own tribal stories. Alfred Kroeber, the anthropologist, decided that would be his name at the museum. Ishi was esteemed by those who discovered him as the last of his tribe, an awesome representation of survivance in a new nickname; this natural mountain man had evaded the barbarians and then endured with humor the museums of a lonesome civilization.

"Long gaze" Columbus, on the other hand, could become one of the most common surnames discovered and discounted in this quincentenary; indeed, "long gaze" could become an ironic nickname for those who recount manifest manners and the mistaken colonial discoveries.

Christopher Columbus is an untrue concoction, the ruse of his own representation. He is the overstated adventurer, to be sure, and the lead signalment of colonial discoveries on this continent; at the same time, he is the master cause of neocolonial celebrations in a constitutional democracy. The obverse of his dubious missions is manifest manners and the reverse is censure.

Columbus must be the slaver, the one who sailed on the inquisitions and landed on a commemorative coin at a national exposition, and heard a new symphony in his name. The "long gaze" of his names has reached from colonial monarchies to the *Santa Maria* and on to the White House in Washington.

"Representation is miraculous because it deceives us into thinking it is realistic," wrote David Freedberg in *The Power of Images,* "but it is only miraculous because it is something other than what it represents."

Columbus is the "miraculous" representation of the long colonial gaze, that striven mannish stare with no salvation. Indeed, the quincentenary is a double entendre, the "long gaze" celebration of colonial civilization in his names, and the discoveries of his name in a constitutional democracy. The want of humor must cause a vague nostalgia for lost monarchies, and must simulate once more the grievous tragic ironies of colonialism.

The Dominican Republic, for instance, commissioned an enormous and expensive quincentenary monument to celebrate the "long gaze" of Columbus. The *El Faro a Colón* "is equipped with lights that can project the shape of a cross high into the clouds" over the slums of Santa Domingo, reported the *Sunday Times* of London.

"Despite criticism that such extravagance is incompatible with the country's grim economic predicament," the blind, octogenarian president Joanquin Balaguer said, "the people need shoes but they also need a tie." Columbus is a commemorative curse not a communal tie; his names are the same as disease and death in the memories of the tribes on the island.

The Spaniards first landed on Hispaniola, wrote Bartolomé de Las Casas in *The Devastation of the Indies.* "Here those Christians perpetrated their first ravages and oppressions against the native peoples. This was the first land in the New World to be destroyed and depopulated by the Christians, and here they began their subjection of the women and children, taking them away from the Indians to use them and ill use them, eating the food they provided with their sweat and toil." The long colonial gaze is now a cross in the clouds, a remembrancer of cruelties and abandoned death.

The Government of the Bahamas has issued a one dollar note that commemorates the unmeant ironies of colonial cruelties in the name of Christopher Columbus. The narrow gaze simulation of the adventurer on the souvenir note is based on a portrait by the Florentine painter Ridolfo Ghirlandaio.

"The long gaze fetishizes," continued David Freedberg, "and so too, unequivocally, does the handling of the object that signifies. All lingering over what is not the body itself, or plain understanding, is the attempt to eroticize that which is not replete with meaning."

Columbus is the national fetish of discoveries.

Ishi is the representation of survivance.

Tribal nicknames are metonymies, neither surname simulations nor a mannish western gaze; tribal nicknames bear a personal remembrance in communal stories, and are not mere veneration, cultural separations, or the long gaze fetishism of discoveries in a lonesome civilization.

Professor Alfred Kroeber, for instance, an eminent academic humanist, is seldom remembered for his nicknames. Mister Ishi, on the other hand, remembered the anthropologist as his "Big Chiep," which was his common pronunciation of "chief." Ishi used the tribal word *saltu,* or white man, a word that could be used as a nominal nickname commensurate with his own: Mister Ishi and Mister Saltu.

Now, consider my proposal to change the name Kroeber Hall at the University of California, Berkeley, to Big Chiep Hall to celebrate a nickname, rather than the reverence of a surname, and to honor the stories of his close association with a noble tribal survivor. Anthropology would be located in Big Chiep Hall. Ishi Hall and Big

Chiep Hall, or even Saltu Hall, would be located on the same campus; the stories of two men and their nicknames, and the nature of an honorable encounter with an erotic shimmer of trickster humor.

Ishi told a tribal interpreter, "I will live like the white people from now on." The Bureau of Indian Affairs had promised him protection but he would remain with his new friends in a public institution. "I want to stay where I am, I will grow old here, and die in this house." Tuberculosis ended his life five years later.

Kroeber wrote that "he never swerved from his declaration." Ishi lived and worked in the museum at the University of California in San Francisco. "His one great dread, which he overcame but slowly, was of crowds." Ishi said *hansi saltu* when he was taken to the ocean and saw the crowded beach for the first time. The words were translated as "many white people."

Ishi is the representation of tribal survivance; nevertheless his name and stories must be rescued from manifest manners. He told stories that were to be heard, and he told his stories with a natural humor, a sense of presence that was communal and unnerved the want of salvation. His tribal touch has been revised and simulated, but his humor must never end in a museum.

NICKNAMES IN THE QUINCENTENARY

NATIVE AMERICAN STUDIES IS LOCATED IN DWINELLE HALL, near Sproul Plaza, at the University of California, Berkeley. In the past two decades this new course of undergraduate studies has grown stronger in tribal histories, literatures, and film studies, and now includes a doctorate program in the Ethnic Studies Department.

"Gerald Vizenor, a visiting professor in the Ethnic Studies Department, has made an official proposal," reported *The Daily Californian* on October 15, 1985, "to rename the north part of Dwinelle Hall as Ishi Hall." The student senate unanimously supported the name change.

My first proposal landed in a common space committee, and there a faculty member, concerned with manifest manners, said the name could be misunderstood as a slang variation of the word "icky." The proposed naming ceremony to be held on May 16, 1986, seventy years after the death of Ishi, never recovered from literal banishment in a committee dominated by manifest manners and the "long gaze" of Christopher Columbus.

Chancellor Chang-Lin Tien received my second proposal six years later "to change the north part of Dwinelle Hall to Ishi Hall in honor of the first Native American Indian who served with distinction the University of California."

Christopher Columbus and the quincentenary of his dubious missions should not overshadow the recognition and survivance of Native American Indians. The chancellor must have read that this would be an unmistakable moment for historical emendation, and the precedence of a tribal name on a campus building would be sincere and honorable.

My proposal is both moral and practical at the same time because nothing would be taken from the honor of the existing name, and a new tribal name for the north section of the building would resolve a serious problem of identification between the two wings.

Dwinelle and Ishi would name sections of the same structure; their names would reverse the racial surnames and entitlements in a state that once hounded the tribes to death and, at the same time, honored those who stole the land and resources and wrote the histories of institutions. One of the most eminent universities in the world was founded on the receipt of stolen land.

John Whipple Dwinelle was born September 7, 1816 in Cazenovia, New York. He studied the origin of words and practiced law when he moved to San Francisco in 1849. Dwinelle was elected to the state legislature and wrote the charter that established the University of California. The bill was passed on March 21, 1868, about six years after the estimated birth of Ishi in the mountains of Northern California.

Dwinelle served as a member of the first Board of Regents. He died on January 28, 1881. *The Daily Californian* reported that "he fell into the Straits of Carquinez from a transfer ferry and was drowned." Dwinelle Hall was dedicated in his honor on September 1952.

"The process of naming, or renaming, a campus building involves review at several levels on the campus and at the Office of the President," wrote Chancellor Tien. "Your proposal must" pass through the Dwinelle Hall Space Subcommittee, "the Provost of the College of Letters and Science, the Naming of Buildings Subcommittee, and the Space Assignments and Capital Improvements Committee. Following positive review of these parties, if I concur, I would forward the proposal to the President for consideration and final approval by the Regents."

The Dwinelle Hall Space Subcommittee twice denied the proposal to honor the name of Ishi. The historians resisted the name, as if the ironies of institutional histories would sour with new communal narratives. Dwinelle was circumstantiated at the university. Ishi and other tribal names have been renounced in the histories of the state.

Ishi lived five years in the museum; his name endures with honor but he would never survive the denatured reason of modern governance, the bureaucratic evasions, and the incredulous responses of the university administration. Once more my proposal has been terminated in a common space committee, as were tribal nicknames and histories in the past; the other reviews are the neocolonial sanctions of manifest manners.

The sheriff secured a "pathetic figure crouched upon the floor," the *Oroville Register* reported on August 29, 1911, thirty years after the death of Dwinelle. "The canvas from which his outer shirt was made had been roughly sewed together. His undershirt had evidently been stolen in a raid upon some cabin. His feet were almost as wide as they were long, showing plainly that he had never worn either moccasins or shoes. In his ears were rings made of buckskin thongs."

Alfred Kroeber confirmed the newspaper report and contacted the sheriff who "had put the Indian in jail not knowing what else to do with him since no one around town could understand his speech or he theirs," wrote Theodora Kroeber in *Alfred Kroeber: A Personal Configuration*. "Within a few days the Department of Indian Affairs authorized the sheriff to release the wild man to the custody of Kroeber and the museum staff...." Ishi was housed in rooms furnished by Phoebe Apperson Hearst. She had created the Department and Museum of Anthropology at the University of California.

Ishi served with distinction the cultural and academic interests of the University of California. Alfred Kroeber, who has been honored by a building in his name, dedicated in March 1960, pointed out that Ishi "has perceptive powers far keener than those of highly educated white men. He reasons well, grasps an idea quickly, has a keen sense of humor, is gentle, thoughtful, and courteous and has a higher type of mentality than most Indians."

Saxton Pope, a surgeon at the medical school near the museum, said he took Ishi to Buffalo Bill's Wild West Show. "He always enjoyed the circus, horseback feats, clowns, and similar performances," he wrote in "The Medical History of Ishi." A "warrior, bedecked in all his paint and feathers, approached us. The two Indians looked at each other in absolute silence for several minutes. The Sioux then spoke in perfect English, saying: 'What tribe of Indian is this?' I answered, 'Yana, from Northern California.'

"The Sioux then gently picked up a bit of Ishi's hair, rolled it between his fingers, looked critically into his face, and said, 'He is a very high grade of Indian.' As we left, I asked Ishi what he thought of the Sioux. Ishi said, 'Him's big chiep....' "

Thomas Waterman, the linguist at the museum, administered various psychological tests at the time and concluded in a newspaper interview that "this wild man has a better head on him than a good many college men."

Some of these college men, however, had unearthed a tribal survivor and then invented an outsider, a wild man as the "other," the last one to hear the stories of his mountain tribe, with their considerable academic power and institutional influence over language, manners, and names. These were not cruelties or insensitivities at the time, but these scholars and museum men, to be sure, would contribute to the cold and measured simulations of savagism and civilization. That tribal survivance would become a mere simulation in a museum, and three generations later an observance in a common academic space committee, is both miraculous and absurd in the best postcolonial histories. Miraculous, because the name is neither the representation nor simulation of the real, and absurd because the felicities of manifest manners are so common in academic discourse and governance.

Ishi is one of the most discoverable tribal names in the world; even so, he has seldom been heard as a real person. The quincentenary of colonial discoveries and manifest manners is not too late to honor this tribal man with a building in his name, a nickname bestowed with admiration by Alfred Kroeber.

Ishi "looked upon us as sophisticated children," wrote Saxton Pope. "We knew many things, and much that is false. He knew nature, which is always true....His soul was that of a child, his mind that of a philosopher."

Theodora Kroeber wrote that "Ishi was living for the summer with the Waterman family where Edward Sapir, the linguist, would be coming in a few weeks to work with him, recording Ishi's Yahi dialect of the Yana language....They noticed that he was eating very little and appeared listless and tired. Interrupting the work with Sapir, they brought Ishi to the hospital where Pope found what he and Kroeber had most dreaded, a rampant tuberculosis."

Ishi died at noon on March 25, 1916. Kroeber was in New York at the time and wrote in a letter, "As to disposal of the body, I must ask you as my personal representative to yield nothing at all under any circumstances. If there is any talk about the interests of science, say for me that science can go to hell. We propose to stand by our friends....We have hundreds of Indian skeletons that nobody ever comes near to study. The prime interest in this case would be of a morbid romantic nature."

Four days later the San Mateo *Labor Index* reported that the "body of Ishi, last of the Yano tribe of Indians, was cremated Monday at Mount Olivet cemetery. It was according to the custom of his tribe and there was no ceremony." Saxton Pope created a death mask, "a very beautiful one." The pottery jar that held the ashes of Ishi was placed in a rock cairn.

THE DERANGED HUMORS OF CIVILIZATION

PRESIDENT RONALD REAGAN TOLD STUDENTS IN MOSCOW, "Maybe we made a mistake in trying to maintain Indian cultures. Maybe we should not have humored them in wanting to stay in that kind of primitive lifestyle."

Reagan is a master of felicities and manifest manners but he must have been talking about simulated Indians in the movies. Many of his friends from the movies played Indians on screen. Maybe he made a mistake in trying to maintain the movies as a real culture; he should not have humored so many of his friends to play Indian in western films. Reagan embodies the simulacra of the mannish western movies.

"Long gaze" Reagan might have been thinking about his many *sooner* friends at the University of Oklahoma. He honored the mannish manifest manners of the frontier more than he would even remember the beleaguered tribes that lost their land to thousands of neocolonial *sooners*.

H. L. Mencken wrote in *The American Language* that the sooners were those "people who insist upon crossing bridges before they come to them." The people who "sneaked across the border before the land was thrown open to white settlement." These were the "long gaze" *sooners* who stole tribal land in the name of manifest manners.

President Richard Van Horn, University of Oklahoma at Norman, was concerned about a "better learning environment" and asked students to be more friendly toward minorities, according to a letter and a report in the *Daily Oklahoman.* "Saying hello to minority students on campus...will help to create a better living and learning environment for all."

Van Horn's manner is simple enough, his statements are generous over brunch, even romantic overseas, but he does not seem to understand the nature of institutional racism. Such academic salutations, the measures of manifest manners, would burden minority students with even more blithe, simpering, and ironic atonements; the *sooners* maintain their "long gaze" of racialism and neocolonial domination. How would students be taught to recognize the minorities on campus so that they might please the president by saying hello? Would recognition be made by color, by class, by manners, humor, gestures, the *sooner* "long gaze," or by being the obvious "other," the outsider?

"Long gaze" Columbus says "hello" to Ishi.

"Hello, hello, hello at last," said an eager white fraternity student to a crossblood Native American Indian. That casual interjection is not an invitation to a discourse on tribal histories, miseries, or even the weather on campus; the gesture is a trivial cue to turn the other cheek to a western gaze and manifest manners. Moreover, racial salutations and other public relations snobberies serve those who dominate minority students rather than those who liberate the human spirit from institutional racism.

"Go out on the campus and say hello to our tribal neighbors," sounds too much like the basic instructions given to missionaries. Never mind, it would seem to the president, that treaties were violated, tribal lands were stolen, and that the crimes continue to be celebrated in state histories as a beat in *sooner* civilization.

The University of Oklahoma and other state institutions were founded on stolen tribal land; such moral crimes are not revised with salutations and manifest manners. The University of California was founded on the receipt of stolen tribal land.

Native American Indian scholars hired to teach in various academic departments on the campus would create a better "learning environment" than a new order of pale sycophants saying hello to minorities. "Long gaze" Reagan and Van Horn must have learned their manifest manners with other presidents at the western movies.

Rennard Strickland, the lawyer and historian, wrote in *The Indians in Oklahoma* that the "process by which the Indian became landless is part of the dark chapter in white Oklahoma's relations with its Indian citizens. Millions of acres and other accumulated resources were wrested from the Indians. Of the thirty million allotted acres more than twenty-seven million passed from Indians to whites" by fraudulent deeds, embezzlement, and murder. "The Oklahoma Indian was asked to sacrifice many of the best parts of his culture for most of the worst parts of the white culture."

Chitto Harjo, the traditional tribal leader who resisted the allotment of tribal land at the turn of the last century, said that "when we had these troubles it was to take my country away from me. I had no other troubles. I could live in peace with all else, but they wanted my country and I was in trouble defending it."

"Long gaze" Van Horn would be better heard and remembered if he learned how to say the words "tribal reparations" more often than common interjections. Reparations are wiser invitations to an education on campus than mere racial salutations and manifest manners.

"Yet, despite all the sorrows and emotion-laden events in the Indian's history in Oklahoma," wrote H. Wayne and Anne Morgan in *Oklahoma,* a standard history of the state, "he gave the new state a unique heritage. Many of his attitudes persisted amid the burgeoning white civilization. His image and customs were more than quaint, as much a heritage of America's frontier civilization as those of the whites who displaced him....Oklahoma's past remains vivid, exciting, and unique. She will not abandon it lightly, nor should she. The question is, can she learn from it?" Such rhetorical poses are misrepresentations that bear no historical burdens for the sins of the *sooner* state.

"Say Hello, OU President Urges," was the headline on the front page of the *Daily Oklahoman* in Oklahoma City. Once more, manifest manners seemed to be one of the most important stories of the day. The same conservative newspaper published an unsigned editorial the following day: "Some have chuckled at OU President Richard Van Horn's modest suggestion for students to 'Say hello to minority students' on campus. That's a gesture, but he's on track. Respect. Diversity. Dialogue. These create an environment in which learning can occur. The words describe values which are not black, white, Hispanic, or Asian, but American." One blithe gesture in the *sooner* "long gaze" begets another, but the unnamed editorial writer never mentioned Native American Indians.

The Oklahoma Tourism and Recreation Department, on the other hand, has published a folded calendar map that celebrates the "Year of the Indian." Thirty-seven tribes, forty-three galleries and gift shops, and thirty bingo halls are named on a state map. "Oklahoma is Indian country," the calendar announces. "A place where time-honored American Indian traditions, cultural experiences and artistic expression are components of everyday life. Oklahoma currently leads the nation in total Indian population and offers a wealth of Indian-related museums, art galleries, festivals and powwows."

President Van Horn, in the "Year of the Indian," must create at least fifty new faculty positions in the next decade for Native American Indians. The presence of tribal scholars in various departments, and their new courses on tribal histories, literatures, economics, legal studies, comparative cultures and religion, would be more than manifest manners. Real reparations would overturn the mannish western gaze at the campus movies; reparations for colonial domination, institutional racism, and manifest manners are measures of how a state and a civilization would endure in popular tribal memories.

The University of Oklahoma and the University of California owe more to tribal cultures than any other universities in the nation and must learn how to practice reparations for the moral and civil crimes that have been perpetrated against tribal cultures. At least a hundred or more new and permanent faculty positions for Native American Indians at these universities in the next decade would be an honorable gesture of reparations for stolen land, the fetish misrepresentations of tribal cultures, and the cold mannish gaze of manifest manners.

" 'Long gaze' Presidents Say 'Hello' to Ishi."

"Now that's a real *sooner* headline," said Griever de Hocus, the novelist and crossblood chair of postmodern manifest manners. "Columbus and Reagan said the same thing, you know, but even so none of them could ever be more than a Little Chiep."

The University of California and the University of Oklahoma have natural reasons and moral warrants to lead the nation in Native American Indian scholarship, and these universities must demonstrate to the world that the tribes are neither the eternal victims of racial simulations nor the fetish cultures of the "long gaze" of Christopher Columbus.

President Van Horn could encourage the students to say "no, no, no to hello, no more western gaze, no long gaze, overturn manifest manners, and sustain tribal reparations." Chancellor Tien must do more than hold a pose over the remains of tribal cultures and the receipts of stolen land.

Ishi said "everybody hoppy" in Little Chiep Hall.

Columbus, Reagan, Tien, Van Horn, and other mannish adventurers, presidents, chancellors, saints, curators, and discoverers, tried to be heard over the trickster stories on campus, but no one listened to them that year in Little Chiep Hall.

Pierre Clastres wrote in *Society Against the State* that a tribal chief must "prove his command over words. Speech is an imperative obligation for the chief." The leader "must submit to the obligation to speak, the people he addresses, on the other hand, are obligated only to appear not to hear him."

Tricksters are heard as traces in tribal stories; the erotic shimmer and beat on a bear walk, the beat that liberates the mind with no separations as cruel as a chemical civilization. There are no last words in tribal stories, no terminal creeds, no closures. Tricksters are nicknames near an end that is never heard. Ishi heard trickster stories; he was not a chief, and he never set his new watch to western time.

Christopher Columbus and the other discoverable men of manifest manners are the "long gaze" chiefs on a tribal coin struck to commemorate the lonesome heroes in a chemical civilization; with each coin the tribe will issue a certificate of authenticity.

THE DREAM OF INJUN JOE
A Page From the Alcatraz Seminars

Jack D. Forbes

DEAR READER: I WAS INDEED FORTUNATE TO BE ALIVE in 1969-1970 and to be able to join the throngs of Native Americans visiting or living on Alcatraz Island in those exciting days. For those too young to remember, I will provide only this background: for several years that sad rock in the Bay of San Francisco, long the locale of a notorious prison, was liberated from its forlorn destiny by Indians from many tribes. For a brief time, then, the Isla de los Alcatraces knew a different existence, one filled with the sounds of drumming, singing, laughter, and angry but proud speeches.

I remember very distinctly my impressions: the blueness of the bay dotted with little boats of every description making their way to the miniature island, the happy faces of the Native People, long black hair tied back with red head-bands; the put-put-ing of ancient motors in old boats whose sea worthiness was open to doubt; and the fog banks courteously holding themselves out to sea, allowing the sun to have a few hours of dominion.

One thing that especially struck me was how the United States government had spent great sums of money to build and maintain a massive prison on the island, only to be ultimately—and inevitably—defeated by the intrepid and natural liberators of salt and water, fog, and wind.

I thought to myself: "Thus it will be! All the might and wealth of empires cannot prevent their ultimate decay." It seemed like natural law had led the Indians to Alcatraz, to begin a process of rebirth amid the visible signs of rusting cell doors and decaying barred windows.

"We must become like the salt and the waters of the earth. We must slowly, but certainly, rust away this prison erected all around us."

Enough of my personal feelings! What I want to recount, dear reader, is a little about the nature of the intellectual life which developed on the island in those days and, more especially, I wish to convey as faithfully as I can from my notes, some of the contents of the now legendary Alcatraz seminars. Needless to say, I personally do not endorse all of the ideas presented.

The colloquium commenced when a Cherokee scholar named Marshall (I can't recall whether this was his first or last name) asked and then answered a rhetorical question: "How can we describe the character of the whites who came over here from Europe, especially the negative traits that cause so much trouble?

"What is it that dominates their character?

"It isn't just materialism nor is it just greed—what makes many white people so strange and so dangerous is a restless dissatisfaction which is constant—never satisfied—they are crazy for wealth, voracious, they will go to any lengths, go to any place, use any means, to get what they want.

"In less than a century they have consumed most of the United States' oil and gas reserves, reserves which took millions of years to accumulate.

"They have wiped out forests, destroyed grasslands, turned deserts into dust-bowls, and seriously diminished almost every other natural resource. What are their characteristics? *Igana-noks-salgi.* Those who are greedy for land, the old Creek Indians called them. They are always gobbling up land, taking it from Indians, Mexicans, or less successful white people.

"They are always looking for gold, for uranium, for oil, for more profits, for new real estate deals, for better-paying jobs, for a new place to live.

"In truth, it is not wealth that they want. It is always *more* wealth, or *new* wealth.

"It is not so much *having* something, but *getting* something, which drives them. If they already have, they want to get more—always more." He paused for a moment, staring up at the high prison ceiling with its bare patches where plaster and paint had fallen away.

"They are crazy—driven, restless, dissatisfied—but it is *to get* that they are crazy. Of course, many are crazy to spend, to display, to show-off, but this need for consumption only serves to make the *getting* all the more important.

"They are crazy with the *getting* of wealth, the *getting* of land, the *getting* of gold, the *getting* of a new car, the *getting* of a chance to spend the way the Hollywood stars spend, or the way the oil-rich Texas millionaires spend.

"Since they are Getting-Crazy People they seldom enjoy merely *having*. This is the root of their restless character. This is why they plunder Lake Tahoe, the Sierra Nevada foothills, the Arizona desert, the Colorado Rockies, and so on. They want *to get* a place at the beach, or on the lake, or in the desert. They don't care that one of the consequences of their getting such a place will be the destruction of that very place.

"It is not the *having*, but the *getting*! After the place bores them, or is destroyed, they can *get* some other place. So what else is new?

"Maybe this is also why some of them chase after religious cults in such a relentless, frenetic, 'capitalistic' way. They have a need not to *have* a spiritual life but to *get* some kind of experience. Many will try dozens of techniques, cults, and formulas, different brands to be consumed and tossed aside."

He paused and someone asked him: "What do we do with them?" Many people smiled or laughed to themselves.

"What do you do with them? For one thing, it's no good to set up a communist society. The Getting-Crazy People will shrewdly figure out that they can still wheel and deal. Sure, they will join the party! They will work their way up to leadership positions and become a new ruling class, getting new cars, new apartments, country estates, privileges of all kinds, just as in Russia. Some will become scientists or technicians and join the technical bureaucratic new rich.

"What can you do with them? They create a world of pornography, dancing naked girls, selling sex as a commodity, motels with piped-in X-rated movies, waterbeds and vibrators, prostitution, Las Vegas, Reno, Tijuana, Gay Paree. Get some sex! Buy it! Sell it! Soon every house (maybe offices too, and subway stations) will have robot crawl-in sex machines right next to the washer and dryer or the soft-drink dispensers. The psychologists will endorse the machines because they will solve the rape problem and diminish sexual aggression!"

Discussion then ensued on this point for a while, but soon shifted back to an anthropology of white people. Marshall had a great many stimulating thoughts, not surprising for an Indian who had studied at the Sorbonne and had written plays in Cherokee.

"Right now the Alcatraz Nation is negotiating with white bureaucrats and a political appointee of the vice president. What do you know about any of them? What do I know? What kind of people are they? It is highly likely that they are a part of, or at least work for, the Getting-Crazy culture I spoke of before.

"Yet that isn't enough. That's too general. Ultimately we, of all people, have to understand what makes specific kinds of white people tick. When the bureaucrats and engineers planned Kinzua Dam, which broke a treaty and flooded a reservation, what motivated them? How could they just sit down at their drawing boards and wipe out a people? What kind of principles of loyalty, of obedience to directions, were they following? Are they the same kind of faceless ones who can work for a Hitler, or a Stalin, or some other dictator? Are they Royal Prussian clerks or do they do it on their own, but if so, or in either case, what happens to the supposed white values of democracy, law and order, sanctity of contract, constitutional protection, etcetera? A treaty is a contract, but one was broken at Kinzua.

"And then what about a president like Kennedy who refused to stop the dam. What were his values? What made him tick?

"I'm not just talking about studying gun-carrying KKK'ers, or Nazis, or white vigilante groups. I'm not just talking about studying Holy-Rollers or Rattlesnake-Handlers. I'm talking about studying the Kissengers, Bundys, Rostows, Nixons, Erlichmans, and Johnsons, in short, the ruling class of leadership in this society."

That particular gathering also included an Iroquois young man who, although completely traditional in appearance, had traveled widely and was always setting forth deep thoughts. He rose and began speaking:

"Let's get back to the question of what can be done with white people. We may not have the power to *do* anything, but I have learned a lot about studying Europeans by just dealing with the question.

"I'll tell you what. Let me describe an Indian and his ideas, or maybe I should say dream. Since my name is Joe, I'll call him Injun Joe. They could be my own day-dreams but I'll just say that they belong to Injun Joe since I know they are shared by other dreamers among us.

"Now this Injun Joe often day-dreamed. Sometimes he would go back in time, in the spaceship of his mind, to the days of Osceola when the Seminoles and their Black allies were fighting for the simple right to have a homeland. That was back in the 1830's and 1840's. The Seminoles, Miccosukees, and their colored allies were great fighters but Joe knew that there were too few Indians to defeat the whites in Florida. The available manpower could never be sufficient to wage both offensive warfare and at the same time defend liberated zones. Joe's strategy was, therefore, to organize a large assault force which would trap and cut to pieces the major enemy units without, however, holding any territory. It would remain a mobile force, striking at will, disarming whites everywhere, but not setting up any garrisons. Its major purpose, after eliminating U.S. units in Florida, was to strike deep into Georgia, towards the Guale coast, in order to free and arm thousands of slaves.

"Joe was able to recruit several thousand Creeks, mixed-bloods, and freed slaves to join his main force. Rapidly this unit was supplemented by armed slave armies organized in Georgia. In this manner the white settlers in Florida, cut off on the north and mostly disarmed, were forced to flee to fortified positions. It was now they who were on the defensive while the liberation armies were free to probe into Alabama and central Georgia.

"The U.S. government was caught off guard by the loss of its invading units in Florida and this provided the liberation forces with the chance to move tens of thousands of freed slaves into the area.

"Gradually, armed liberation units, using captured artillery pieces, were able to capture all of the invader's positions in Florida (which was now called the Republic of Bimini). To the north, meanwhile, the slave population was rebelling throughout Georgia and Alabama, with guerrilla units spreading also into South Carolina.

"In the meantime, the Freedom-Fighters had set up an effective system of sending news bulletins to newspapers in Boston, New York, and Philadelphia. By this means it became clearly established in people's minds that the war was nothing more nor less than a struggle between slave-owner imperialism on the one hand and freedom and justice on the other. Would New England and the North support a war to crush the Indians and colored people in order to advance the interests of the slave-owning classes?

"Joe knew that it didn't matter. The freedom-fighters could get some help from New England but the problem still remained that the slavocracy ran the federal government and that tens of thousands of whites from Kentucky, Tennessee, North Carolina and so on would enroll in the militia in order to crush the hated red and brown and black niggers, and in order to get a reward of so-called bounty land, that is to say, Indian land.

"The Bimini strategy was to remove all Indian and colored women and children from South Carolina, northern Georgia, and Alabama and to send them either to Bimini itself or to safe regions in Guale and along the Appalachee River. Northern Georgia and Alabama was to serve as a No-man's land buffer zone where whites were disarmed but otherwise left alone and where slavery ceased to exist.

"Another element in the Bimini strategy was to send out spies to locate places where the white governments were assembling militia units or stockpiling arms. These areas were then hit by mobile assault forces before the state troops were prepared or organized. A similar strategy was followed as regards the organizing of U.S. regular forces.

"The Bimini intelligence system was quite good. It had to be, since the freedom forces were the weaker party and their success hinged entirely upon preventing any large army from being fully organized.

"Gradually, as the ex-slaves and free Indians became more experienced and confident, and as thousands were armed with liberated weapons, it became possible to launch major rapid assaults into the tidewater of southside Virginia, North Carolina, and into other areas where the slaves numbered more than half of the population. Guerrilla units were organized in many areas, as the war zone expanded.

"Anyway, this was one of Joe's dreams. This one, like most of them, came up against some hard realities. *What do you do with white people if you defeat them militarily?* Joe was not about to adopt the white value system of enslavement and genocide. Still, many of the whites would be just as aggressive and villainous after conquest as before. They would scheme, and plot, and try to find ways to recover their lost empire. They were experienced at politics and knew how to organize. Few could be trusted to have any sympathy with non-whites.

"Joe hit on one plan. That was to divide up the rich planter's estates among poor and landless whites as well as among the ex-slaves. But would that really work? Would the poor whites appreciate having small farms of their own, or would they listen to the slave-owner's propaganda of white racial superiority and unity?

"Of course, another problem was this: would the U.S. government *ever* agree to allow Indians and coloreds to be free and independent? Could the U.S.A. ever tolerate a brown victory or would it keep recruiting new white armies, one after another, to try to crush the injuns and niggers, even if it meant a war of genocidal intensity and ever-expanding character?

"Joe realized that by the 1830's and 1840's it was too late for a real Indian victory. The whites were just too numerous. White families had 10 or 12 children every generation, the women being little more than walking (working) incubators. Indian families usually had only three or four children and many died because of always being pressed to the wall by constant white aggression. The slave birth-rate was higher than the Indian, but it too was being overwhelmed by the constant flood of European immigrants. In any case, the slaves were usually terrorized systematically and prevented from learning about things essential for effective rebellions.

"Joe also had other fantasies, some focused on earlier times, before the U.S. war for independence for example, or the locale was shifted to Mexico. Sometimes Joe's great Indian alliance system was able to defeat the white colonial settlers, free the slaves, and establish a benign federal democracy (patterned after the Iroquois league). But the problem still remained, *what to do with white people?*

"If you had 500,000, or a million, or 2 million whites under your control how could you change their culture so that they would stop trying to get more wealth all of the time? They reproduced so fast that if you didn't watch out they would be flooding into Indian regions by sheer numbers.

"Indian people traditionally are brought up to live in a democracy. They don't need big government, prisons, police, zoning commissions, investigative bodies, or things like that. They have small families, raise their children to be polite and observant, worship the Creator, and respect each other. So you could have a very loose confederacy, insofar as Indians are concerned.

"What can you do with a million or more restless, aggressive, materialistic, scheming, proliferating white people who like to break laws, don't respect other people, and consider themselves to be the New Israelites, God's chosen people, destined to get whatever they want?

"That's a real dilemma isn't it? Now, old Injun Joe realized that was why the U.S.A. was not, and probably could never be, a democracy. Indians can live in freedom. Whites have to be controlled or they will even exploit each other. So every white state has to have a big government. If it doesn't the factory-owners will enslave their workers, manufacturers will cheat (or poison) their customers, land speculators will get control of all of the good land, railroads will charge whatever the traffic will bear, and the earth, water, and air will be raped, scraped, looted, and polluted.

"Of course, white people also have had big governments to help control slaves and to support with laws and physical force the idea that free Indians and Africans can be captured or bought and kept in chains forever from that day forth.

"So, what do you do with them? Nobody knows, that's what the problem with U.S. politics is today, right now. The president doesn't know, he's one of them!

"So anyway what is Injun Joe going to do with white people in his dreams, in his fantasies? He's got them defeated, let's say, but how can he change them enough so that they can live in a democracy? Joe toyed with the idea of establishing Indian garrisons to control the whites, and a totally Indian-run colonial administration to supervise them. That bothered him because that's just what whites do to Indians.

"The bad thing about it, Joe thought, is that if Native People had to have standing armies, police, and colonial officials to control the whites they would have to change their own way of life to do it. What happened to the Mongols, the Manchus, the Turks, the Arabs, the Macedonians, the Greeks, the Romans? Injun Joe had studied history enough to know that ultimately empires enslave the victors as much as the defeated. He could not imagine a Black Elk, or a Tecumseh, or a Sitting Bull, or a Geronimo sitting around giving orders to white people, watching them, becoming fat and lazy off of other people's work. Indians were free because they let others be free. Many white people were slaves to their own systems of exploitation. Sure, he thought, the rulers can have all of the luxuries they want, but that only whets their appetites. They can have any slave woman they want, but that only corrupts their own natural sexuality, makes it into some kind of rape, the birth of sex as pornography.

"No, Indians must win, *but they cannot rule,* because to rule is to become a slave to the evil passions that come with secular power. The white people must be free, but how?

"Injun Joe's dreams led him to the conclusion that the only means available was to divide up the land in the liberated areas in such a way that every rural family, white, mixed, and black, had at least a forty acre farm. These farms would be given out in such a manner that most areas would have blacks and browns mixed in with the whites. Of course, the whites would outnumber the coloreds about three to one over-all, but during a transition period the former slave-owners and other exploitative classes would be prohibited from holding office. Schools and colleges would favor non-white enrollment and no whites could bear arms.

"Joe fantasized that immigration from Haiti, Mexico, and other non-white areas might gradually help to increase the brownness of the population while race mixture and cultural borrowing might blunt the hard edges of the European character. The result might be something like a Brazil or a Puerto Rico, a land full of mixed people, but, and this was the big one, without the political oppression resulting from the uninterrupted economic and political power of white elites and the uninterrupted poverty and ignorance of the brown masses.

"Utopia you say? A land of mixed-bloods in North America, guided towards democracy by wise Native guardians, could it ever be? Could it ever have been?

"But Joe's dreams were not too far-fetched. Back in Oklahoma, before 1890, it was happening in the Muscogee Creek Republic, and in the Seminole Republic as well. Indians, Blacks, whites, Red-Blacks, mulattoes, half-breeds, you name it, living together, intermarrying, sharing life, getting along, until the sacred treaties were broken and the white ruling class decided that brown people had no right to self-government anywhere in the territory of Yankee-Dixi-Doo. Paradise was plundered and terror replaced tolerance.

"What do you do with the Getting-Crazy People? If only they would leave you alone, or maybe they could find another planet (with lots of gold) and go there.

"Now, I want to emphasize that in Joe's dreams there was always a place for good people of all races. He realized, in fantasy as in real life, that the majority of white people were not bad, that they were also victims. He tried, in his dreams, to fantasize ways that Indians could somehow communicate with these silent white people.

"He never found a way."

For a long time there was nothing but silence in the seminar. All of the people just sat there looking inward, vibrations of Injun Joe filling the room.

Marshall broke the silence: "Do Indians have dreams? You bet we do! How else could we have survived all these years?

"The white people have never known of our dreams, our fantasies. They think Indians just sit, staring into space, from the top of a mesa somewhere.

"Our dreams belong to us. Now the time has come to share them with each other and to see what we can do with them."

THE DOWNFALL OF DISEASE-GIVER

Carlos Cortez

Long ago before the god of the Blue Eyes
Was known by the Tribe,
The Tribe knew many Gods and Spirits:
Earth Spirit, Water Spirit, Sky Spirit, Corn Spirit,
Buffalo Spirit, Fish Spirit, Moon Princess, and many others
Who were believed in and loved by the Tribe.
Only one Spirit was feared, and that was Disease-Giver,
Who terrorized everyone.
Everyone but one crazy young man named Tall Coyote.
Tall Coyote laughed at Disease-Giver.
And said he did not believe in him.
So why should he be afraid of him?
The rest of the Tribe shook their heads sadly, for they knew
For such defiance, Disease-Giver would punish
Poor crazy Tall Coyote.
Sure enough, one day Disease-Giver accosted Tall Coyote
In front of all the Tribe, and said to him:
"Tall Coyote, I have come to kill you!"
That crazy Tall Coyote, he just laughed and said:
"Disease-Giver, I don't believe in you; you cannot hurt me!"
Disease-Giver, he got red in the face and told him to die.
But Tall Coyote kept on laughing.
Again Disease-Giver told him to die;
But Tall Coyote kept on laughing.
After long hours Tall Coyote still laughed;
And Disease-Giver said: "Tall Coyote, please die!"
But Tall Coyote kept on laughing.
Disease-Giver said: "Please, Tall Coyote,

At least have a headache! You are making me lose face!"
But Tall Coyote laughed harder than ever.
It was then Disease-Giver decided
To leave the village of the Tribe
With his tail between his legs,
And was never seen again.
The mind can be a jail, but it can also be a mountain.
Ey—Yaa!

About the Contributors

ARLOA (Cherokee/Dakota), a freelance artist, enjoys working in black and white. One goal she has with her work is to remind everyone that the indigenous people of the Americas are still here, in spite of the atrocities of the last five hundred years.

RACHEL BUFF is a cultural historian living in Minneapolis, Minnesota. She is a graduate student in the Program in American Studies at the University of Minnesota. Her main interests concern the cultural politics of diasporas. Currently, she is researching Pan-Indian movements of the nineteenth century, the "invention" of Mexican food in the U.S. in the twentieth century, and the history of steel drumming in Brooklyn. With Rich Kees, she collaborates on many projects concerning culture, politics, alienation, and dislocation.

AMY CORDOVA is a painter whose archetypal imagery and use of brilliant, saturated colors express the strong emotional content of her work. Her images take on symbolic significance to convey both the conceptual and narrative messages in her work.

CARLOS CORTEZ is the son of a Chicano Wobbly father and a German socialist pacifist mother. He grew up in Milwaukee and later moved to Chicago; spent two years in the federal pen for draft resistance during World War II; wrote the satirical "Left Side" column for the IWW's *Industrial Worker* for many years, and is an acclaimed woodblock print artist, muralist and cartoonist.

WILLIAM CROOK, JR. is a visionary in the Vachel Lindsay mold (with Springfield, Illinois being the hometown of both). He is a shameless romantic in love with the subtle charms of the Midwestern landscape. Through his drawings he acts as an environmental interpreter for the bioregion, and, as a deep ecology activist, he seeks to protect the local flora and fauna from human and institutional predators. A self-taught artist, his drawing style was greatly influenced by R. Crumb, and he has done illustrations in conjunction with the work of such underground comics luminaries as Harvey Pekar and Tucker Petertil. Most recently, he has edited a book entitled *Fresh Brewed* which is a compilation of comics by inmates of the Jacksonville Correctional Center in central Illinois. He is presently working on a voluminous series of Sangamon River drawings.

JACK D. FORBES is of Powhatan-Renápe, Delaware-Lenápe, and other ancestry. He is the director of Native American Studies at the University of California, Davis. He is the author of *Columbus and Other Cannibals,* (Autonomedia, 1992); *Africans and Native Americans* (Blackwell, 1988; to be issued in a revised edition by University of Illinois Press); *Native Americans of California and Nevada* (Naturegraph, 1982); *Tribes and Masses* (D-Q University Press, 1978); *Apache, Navaho and Spaniard* (Greenwood, 1980); and other books, monographs, and articles. He is also a published poet and short story writer, and has almost finished a novel, *Red Blood.* He was born in Suanga (Long Beach) and grew up along the Río Pubuna and Río Azusa at Bahia de los Alamitos and El Monte and along the hills in Eagle Rock, all in California.

GUILLERMO GOMEZ-PEÑA es un escritor, artista de performance, y activista Mexicano que ha vivido en los estados unidos desde 1978.

JOY HARJO was born in Tulsa, Oklahoma in 1951 and is an enrolled member of the Creek Tribe. She graduated in 1968 from the Institute of American Indian Arts and from the University of New Mexico in 1976. She received her M.F.A. in Creative Writing from the Iowa Writer's Workshop at the University of Iowa in 1978. She also attended the Anthropology Film Center in Santa Fe and as a dramatic screenwriter has produced many works including *Apache Mountain Spirits* for Silvercloud Video Productions. She has published four books of poetry, including *She Had Some Horses* (Thunder's Mouth Press) and her most recent *In Mad Love and War* (Wesleyan University Press, 1990). She also has collaborated with photographer/astronomer Stephen Strom to produce *Secrets From the Center of the World* (University of Arizona Press). Currently she is a professor in the creative writing program at the University of New Mexico. She is on the Steering Committee of the En'owkin Centre International School of Writing (for Native American writers) and travels extensively around the country giving readings and workshops, when not playing saxophone with her band Poetic Justice.

NEAL KEATING, omnigyne and vagabond, currently lives in New York where he is studying entropology and working odd jobs. His applied interests revolve around the collapse of complex societies and the demystification of cultural hegemonies.

RICHARD J. KEES was born somewhat northwest of Tahlequah, Oklahoma, but lived most of his childhood in the Chicago area. He moved to his present home in Minnesota when he was 21 years of age. His family and many close friends over the years have provided the inspiration to continue his research and writing on Métis history; despite the rigors of working as a wage slave. He collaborates with Rachel Buff on projects concerning culture, politics, alienation, and dislocation.

JOHN KNOEPFLE has been interested in the spoken language and the folk history of the Midwest since he began his writing career in the early 1950s. He has authored many books of poetry, including *Rivers into Islands* (University of Chicago, 1965) and *poems from the sangamon* (University of Illinois, 1985); most recently he has published the prose *Dim Tales.* He has also tape recorded the recollections of fifty steamboat men of the inland rivers, transcriptions of which are in the Public Library of Cincinnati and Hamilton County, Ohio. He translated, with Robert Bly and James Wright, *Twenty Poems of Cesar Vallejo;* and with

Wang Shouyi, Heilongjiang University scholar, *T'ang Dynasty Poems* and *Song Dynasty Poems* (both from Spoon River Poetry Press, 1985).

JAMES KOEHNLINE is a freelance iconographer to the member churches of the World Congress of Weird Religions, who is also working for the reestablishment of ancient Hebrew Jubilee Legislation (with ten years of zero-work revels, 1993-2002, to kick it off). Formerly of Chicago, he now resides in Seattle, where he continues to believe that it is the straying that finds the path.

HUGO PROSPER LEAMING was born in 1924 in Providence, Rhode Island. After getting his B.A. at the University of Richmond, Virginia in 1943, he taught history in the American South and the Middle East. From 1948-1953 he was Religious Education Director of the Free Religious Fellowship in Chicago, then the only Unitarian Church that admitted "Negroes". He went on to hold ministerial positions in the Unitarian Church congregations of Miami, Florida; Trenton, New Jersey; and Fort Wayne, Indiana. From 1963-1968 he was the pastor of the All Souls First Universalist Society in Chicago, during which time he was arrested in a "sit-in" against racial discrimination in housing held at the University of Chicago. Subsequently, he was again arrested in Albany, Georgia in a civil rights protest led by Martin Luther King. He received his Ph.D. from the University of Illinois in 1979. His doctoral dissertation is entitled, "Hidden Americans: The Maroons of North Carolina and Virginia." He presently resides in Olympia Fields, Illinois.

RICARDO LEVINS-MORALES is a Puerto Rican immigrant/artist/printmaker/speaker/writer/organizer. He is founder of the Northland Poster Collective, and the editor of *huracàn* (a counter-Quincentennial publication of the Alliance for Cultural Democracy). As he puts it, "My work is that of a storyteller — helping to keep alive our collective memory."

MERIDEL LESUEUR was born in Murray, Iowa in 1900. The daughter of radical educator Marian Wharton and stepdaughter of radical lawyer Arthur LeSueur, she divided her childhood between various socialist communities and People's College in Fort Scott, Kansas and St. Paul, Minnesota. As a teenage girl she lived briefly in Emma Goldman's commune in Greenwich Village, then worked as a movie double and in grassroots theater in California. During her life, she has published many stories, with her most famous novel being *The Girl*. Her most recent novel, *The Dread Road*, published when she was 91 years old, is by design radical in both form and content.

PETER LINEBAUGH has authored the book *The London Hanged* and edited *Albion's Fatal Tree*, as well as writing such seminal articles as "Jubilating" and "All the Mountains Shook." He is presently a lecturer in History and Literature at Harvard University.

THOM METZGER has written books that include *Big Gurl, Shock Totem* and *Drowning in Fire* (Penguin/NAL) and *This is Your Final Warning* (Autonomedia). He was a contributor to *Semiotexte USA* and *Semiotexte SF*. He is the prime mover behind Ziggurat, publisher of tracts, testaments, prophesies, and other fugitive texts. He can be reached at Box 25193, Rochester, New York, 14625.

TIMOTHY MILLER is a member of the faculty in the Department of Religious Studies at the University of Kansas. He specializes in the study of new and alternative religions, and has long had an interest in the history of the communitarian tradition in the United States. He is currently writing a history of American communes and cooperative settlements in the twentieth century.

DAVID PORTER edited *Vision on Fire: Emma Goldman on the Spanish Revolution* and has written various articles on Goldman, Spanish anarchism and the anarchist movement generally. He is currently doing research on the themes of this essay. He teaches social sciences and history at Empire State College.

MARCUS REDIKER teaches history at Georgetown University. He is author of *Between the Devil and the Deep Blue Sea: Merchant Seamen, Pirates, and the Anglo-American Maritime World, 1700-1750* (1987) and is a contributing author of volume I of *Who Built America? Working People and the Nation's Economy, Politics, Culture, and Society* (1989).

RON SAKOLSKY is a cultural activist, a writer for indie music publications, an occasional dancehall disc jockey, an intrepid mail art networker, and the holder of a Wobbly red card. He does "pirate" radio workshops in such diverse places as New York City (for Media Network) and West Lima, Wisconsin (for Dreamtime Village), and is a co-conspirator at Black Liberation Radio in Springfield, Illinois. He has taught at The Evergreen State College, and is currently an educator in the field of cultural studies and social change at Sangamon State University. He is a national board member of the Alliance for Cultural Democracy (ACD), and is the former editor of their national magazine, *Cultural Democracy.*. He has had recent articles published in such magazines as *Social Anarchism* and *Our Generation,* and in such books as *Within the Shell of the Old* (Charles Kerr), *A Passion for Radio* (Black Rose) and (under the pseudonym of Karen Eliot) in *Cassette Mythos* (Autonomedia).

PAUL Z. SIMONS is a fire-breathing anarchist agitator who has been associated with the Anarchist Switchboard and the journal *Black Eye*. His extremist rants have been reprinted all over the North American anarchist press.

TOMAS SISNEROS is a striving freelance comic artist and graphics illustrator currently residing in Seattle, Washington. He is a graduate of the Kubert School of Cartoon and Graphic Art. In 1989, he received honorable mention as a National Hispanic Scholar. He has also worked as an editorial cartoonist, has self-published three comic books and his illustrations have been displayed at the International Comic Convention in Angouleme, France.

DOUG SIVAD has studied at St. Edwards University, School of Fine Arts, and Huston-Tillotson College of Austin, Texas. He is the author of *The Black Seminole Indians of Texas,* first published by American Press, Boston, Massachusetts (1984). The second edition was co-sponsored by the Texas Association for the Study of Afro-American Life and History, Inc. (1986). The book is in its third reprint, now called *The African Seminole Indians.* He has had articles printed in *The Griot,* a periodical, (Los Angeles, California), the *NOKOA Newspaper,* (Austin, Texas,) and several are scheduled for release in the *Handbook of Texas,* by the Texas State Historical Association, University of Texas at Austin, in 1993. He has written (and performs) the one man play, "Juan Nickla — Seminole Indian Chief." He is vice-chair/historian on the Executive Board of the Texas Association for the Study of Afro-American Life and History, Inc, and a board member of the Carver Museum and Cultural Center, Austin, Texas.

SANDY SPEILER was a teenager in Washington, D.C. during the tumultuous sixties, and moved to Minneapolis in 1973, where she is currently the Artistic Director of In the Heart of the Beast Puppet and Mask Theatre. She has been a puppeteer and graphic artist for many years. She credits her two pre-schoolers, Micah and Rose, for teaching her humility and patience and inspiring her daily in the fight against the "conquistador energy which surrounds us with all its subtle ugliness." She wishes to express her gratitude to the community of husband, grandparents, friends and co-workers who nourish and support her in the "difficult balancing act of being a mother and a theatre artist."

GAIL TREMBLAY is of Onondaga /Micmac and French Canadian ancestry. Her most recent book of poetry is entitled *Indian Singing in Twentieth Century America,* Calyx Press, 1990). As a visual artist, she was a contibutor to the recent touring *Submuloc Show / Columbus Wohs.* Most recently she has herself curated three exhibits on contemporary Native American art: "Decolonizing the Mind: End of a 500-Year Era"; "Spirits Keep Whistling Us Home: Contemporary Art by Native American Women from the Basin Plateau Region"; and "Defining Ourselves: Contemporary Native American Women Photographers." She is on the board of the Women's Caucus for the Arts, and is a faculty member at the Evergreen State College.

GERALD VIZENOR teaches Native American Indian literature at the University of California, Berkeley. He is a member of the Minnesota Chippewa Tribe. His most recent books are *The Heirs of Columbus,* a novel, and *Landfill Meditation,* a collection of stories. *Griever: An American Monkey King in China* won the Fiction Collective Prize and the American Book Award. *Dead Voices: Natural Agonies in the New World,* his fifth novel, was published last year.

SALLY ROESCH WAGNER is a Research Affiliate of the Women's Resources and Research Center at the University of California, Davis, and a nationally-recognized lecturer, historical performer and author on the subject of 19th century women's history. She was a founder of one of the earliest Women's Studies programs in the country, at California State University, Secramento, and received one of the first doctorates awarded in the country for work in Women's Studies.

DARREN WERSHLER-HENRY is a doctoral student in English at York University in Canada. His work has appeared in both academic and subcultural journals, including *Open Letter, RD,* and *Virus 23.* He is currently writing on images of the armoured, accelerated, and abandoned male body—and the textual strategies that support them—in contemporary culture.

ROBERT WALDMIRE is an itinerant artist who drew his first poster in 1969 (of his hometown Springfield, Illinois), and has been on the road drawing and peddling his posters ever since. Describing himself as "a self-appointed spokesman for the earth and all her beings," Waldmire specializes in animal portraits and "biore-gionally-flavored" bird's-eye-view posters. Having completed posters of 34 towns, he proceeded to do bird's-eye-view posters for five states (Illinois, Arizona, New Mexico, California, and Missouri). No more state posters are planned because, as he puts it, "I don't want to reinforce peoples' concepts of `places' defined by politi-cal boundaries." Forthcoming posters will show whole bioregions.

PETER LAMBORN WILSON divides time/space amongst: The Ramapo Bioregion (Moorish Orthodox Ashram), Manhattan/Brooklyn (Autonomedia/WBAI-Pacifica), Boulder, Colorado (Naropa/Jack Kerouac School of Disembodied Poetics), West Lima, Wisconsin (Dreamtime Village), and other temporary or not-so-temporary autonomous or semi-autonomous zones. As an editor of Semiotext(e)/ Autonomedia he works on the "New Autonomy" Series, and helps edit the maga-zine *Wild Children* (writing and art by and for kids age 0 through 18). He collabo-rates with various anarchoid groups, e.g., Libertarian Book Club, John Henry Mackay Society, the North American Phalanx, and Universal Pantarchy (New York and New Jersey), the Bender Hollow Phalanx and "G" School Association (Wisconsin), the Moorish Orthodox Church of America, etc. His research into the "lost history" of the Moorish Science Temple appears in *Scandal: Essays in Islamic Heresy* (New York: Autonomedia, 1988) and in *Sacred Drift: Essays On The Margins Of Islam* (San Francisco: City Lights, 1993).

JORDAN ZINOVICH has lived as an exile in the evil empire for the past twelve years. He has written two books (published by Lone Pine Publishing) and some short fictional pieces about exploration in the Canadian north. At the moment he is struggling with a novel about sheep stealing in the Cretan mountains. He is a member of the Autonomedia Collective, and General Project Editor for *Semiotext(e) CANADAs*.

MORE AUTONOMEDIA / SEMIOTEXT(E) TITLES

TAZ
Hakim Bey $6

THIS IS YOUR FINAL WARNING!
Thom Metzger $6

CASSETTE MYTHOS
Robin James, ed. $12

FRIENDLY FIRE
Bob Black $6

THE DAUGHTER
Roberta Allen $8

THE LIZARD CLUB
Steve Abbott $6

MAGPIE REVERIES
James Koehnline $10

FIRST & LAST EMPERORS
Kenneth Dean & Brian Massumi $6

INVISIBLE GOVERNANCE
David Hecht & Maliqalim Simone $6

ON ANARCHY & SCHIZOANALYSIS
Rolando Perez $10

GOD & PLASTIC SURGERY
Jeremy Barris $10

MARX BEYOND MARX
Antonio Negri $10

THE NARRATIVE BODY
Eldon Garnet $10

MODEL CHILDREN
Paul Thorez $10

ABOUT FACE
Timothy Maliqalim Simone $10

RETHINKING MARXISM
Steve Resnick & Rick Wolff, eds. $13

SCANDAL
Peter Lamborn Wilson $10

CLIPPED COINS
Constantine George Caffentzis $10

HORSEXE
Catherine Millot $10

THE TOUCH
Michael Brownstein $6

THE ARCANE OF REPRODUCTION
Leopoldina Fortunati $10

TROTSKYISM AND MAOISM
A. Belden Fields $10

FILM & POLITICS IN THIRD WORLD
John Downing, ed. $10

COLUMBUS & OTHER CANNIBALS
Jack Forbes $10

ENRAGÉS & SITUATIONISTS
René Viénet $10

POPULAR REALITY
Irreverend David Crowbar, ed. $10

XEROX PIRATES
Autonomedia Collective, ed. $12

ZEROWORK
Bob Black & Tad Kepley, eds. $10

MIDNIGHT OIL
Midnight Notes Collective, $10

A DAY IN THE LIFE
Alan Moore & Josh Gosniak, eds. $8

SEMIOTEXT(E) ARCHITECTURE
Hraztan Zeitlian, ed. $15

SEMIOTEXT(E) USA
Jim Fleming & P. L. Wilson, eds. $12